CW00656252

THE JAGUAR FILE

AN ERIC DYMOCK MOTOR BOOK

THE JAGUAR FILE

ALL MODELS SINCE 1922

AN ERIC DYMOCK MOTOR BOOK

First published in Great Britain in 1998 by
DOVE PUBLISHING
Old Chapel House, Sutton Veny, Wiltshire BA12 7AY
and
G. T. Foulis & Company, an imprint of Haynes Publishing,
Sparkford, nr. Yeovil, Somerset, BA22 7JJ.

Text copyright © Eric Dymock 1998

Designed by Ruth Dymock
Jacket design Andrew Barron

All rights reserved. No part of this publication may be reproduced, stored in a retrieval system,
or transmitted in any form or by any means, electronic, mechanical, photocopying, recording or otherwise, without the prior
permission of the copyright holder

British Library Cataloguing-in-Publication Data A catalogue record
for this book is available from the British Library

ISBN 0 85429 983 1

Library of Congress catalog card no 97-61072

Colour separation by
Fotographics Ltd, London and Hong Kong

Printed in Slovenia by Printing House Mladinska knjiga by arrangement with Korotan Ljubljana

Foreword

Style, performance, and value for money. Seventy-five years ago, these were the qualities William Lyons believed would transform his tiny Blackpool sidecar company into a world class luxury car manufacturer. Great victories at Le Mans underscored his cars' high performance credentials and a long line of export-boosting luxury saloons helped define Jaguar's image as the creator of some of the world's most refined luxury cars. William Lyons' unique eye for style, together with his team of extraordinarily talented engineers, designed and built some of the world's most sought-after cars – all of which have been painstakingly catalogued by Eric Dymock in this totally comprehensive book of reference. It is the complete product heritage of Jaguar – from the earliest handbuilt cars to come from Blackpool to today's luxurious, high performance saloons and sports cars.

Nick Scheele
Chairman and Chief Executive, Jaguar Cars Ltd

Grace, Pace and Space

Jaguar's influence on British social history was profound, although just how deeply it had penetrated the national psyche only became apparent when its reputation faltered in the 1970s. Under the ill-starred British Leyland Motor Corporation Jaguar fell from grace, and far from being the icon of affluence and personal prosperity that it had been in the 1960s, it became a symbol of the motor industry's distress. Ravaged by labour disputes, the mood was sombre, management had squandered control, and unwieldy conglomorates seemed to thrive.

Facing page: Chief executives. Sir William Lyons on the right Jaguar's founder, with Sir John Egan who turned the company round before it was bought by Ford, at Wappenbury Hall, Sir William's home from 1937 until his death in 1985.

Great names that had been part of the historical fabric of motoring in Britain were discredited; some were lost. The Jaguar factory at Browns Lane Coventry was almost renamed Leyland Large Car Assembly Plant, its dignity, quality and morale collapsed, and with them went Jaguar's traditional rich middle-class market.

It was a temporary aberration. The firm's commercial heritage was rich, it recovered, and by the 1990s Jaguar was brimming with confidence and on the threshold of the most promising model programme in its history.

The watershed was 1945. To the post-war generation a Jaguar was a sign of good taste and elegant design. It was what marketing people called "aspirational", something to long for, save for, earn even. In the Home Counties' amorphous stockbroker country, the "Gin and Jag belt" was a jokey tribute to a sure sign of accomplishment. A Jaguar parked in the drive was a signal of success. Two Jaguars were better than one Rolls-Royce, because they implied cash to spare for living it up in the Swinging Sixties.

Grace, Pace and Space

Jaguar was reaching its prime. The lingering pre-watershed doubts about whether they were cars fit for gentlemen were dispelled. But things had not always been easy for the great marque created by Sir William Lyons, and in the 1930s SS Jaguars, as they were known, had been widely regarded as more suitable for *nouveau riches* than Old Money. The disdain of dyed-in-the-wool sports car enthusiasts persisted well into the post-war years, and it was not until the dazzling brilliance of the XK120 in 1948 and victory in Britain's favourite motor race, the 24 Hours of Le Mans in 1951, that Jaguar was able to live down its slightly ambivalent reputation.

When it did, Jaguar gained respect and SS Jaguars made in the 1930s became truly prized alongside the great Edwardian, vintage, and classic makes. Jaguars had been looked upon as rather "flashy", not quite a match for the thoroughbred Bentley or Aston Martin, or even the Rovers favoured by the well-bred middle-class. The *Daily Express* summed up the SS as "The car with the £1,000 look", when it sold for £310. It was intended as a compliment, for the car was good value at £310. But could William Lyons create a car that would satisfy the *cognoscenti*?

Left: Sir William Lyons understood the upper middle class that became Jaguar's market-place. He identified it precisely and made the cars he knew it would like. *Right:* Young man in a hurry. Lyons raced this Harley-Davidson on Blackpool sands. *Far right:* Second factory, Cocker Street, Blackpool.

Grace, Pace and Space

Jaguar began in 1922. Blackpool, on the eastern seaboard of industrial Lancashire, seemed an unpromising launch platform for a car that became as aspirational in Hollywood or Hong Kong as it was in Buenos Aires or Beijing.

In the years following the end of the first world war, Sir William – then plain Bill – Lyons appeared to be a pushy young motorcycle sidecar manufacturer with delusions of grandeur. Ambitious to move up to cars, in 1927 he used his Swallow Sidecars workers' coachbuilding skills to make bodies for Austin Sevens, giving them a status they scarcely deserved. They were sold by his chums, the motor trade entrepreneurs Bertie Henly and Frank Hough, from classy new premises at 91 Great Portland Street, London. Henly boldly ordered five hundred cars. To the Bright Young Things in the West End they were Just the Job, gleaming with bright colours and flashing with chrome when other cars were plain green or staid black.

But to the posh Brooklands crowd, even after the factory moved to Britain's motor city Coventry, the Swallows and their successors the SS1 and SS2 were a bit *infra dig*. They were derided for having a long bonnet but a feeble engine. Most of their components were made by volume manufacturers such as Standard, and enthusiasts who may not have known any better refused to be taken in by cosmetic tricks such as two-tone paint or a low roofline.

They believed it was impossible to build a good car cheaply, unaware that Lyons achieved it by keeping a tight control on unnecessary expenditure rather than skimping on production or materials. As well as having a gift for how a car should look, Lyons drove a hard bargain with suppliers. Costs were ruthlessly held down.

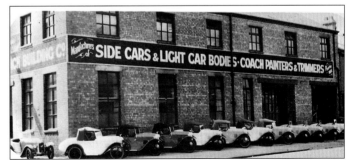

Grace, Pace and Space

Above: Steel rails
embedded in the wooden
floor were relics of
Coventry's first world
war role in munition
production. Body-shop
scene as Swallow bodies
await mounting on
their chassis.

It was the 1960s before more than a handful of staff at Jaguar Cars actually had a Jaguar with the job. Lyons regarded that as a privilege earned only by the most senior executives in his own firm or anywhere else. It was a culture that applied throughout the company. Jaguar apprentices were an elite band who paid a premium to work there. They received such a sound training that the British motor trade and industry became littered with former Jaguar apprentices in high executive positions.

Lyons' choice of SS as the name of his cars was something of a mystery. He said SS was not a contraction of Standard Swallow (the SS1 was effectively a re-bodied Standard Sixteen) or Standard Special. George Brough, who made the Brough Superior and SS90 motorcycles, believed Lyons got the idea from him, but perhaps it was just a catchy symbol of speed and celebrity culled from liners whose names were traditionally prefixed SS.

Nothing caught the mood of the moment so well. Ocean steamships were trend-setters, cosseting the globe-trotting jet-setters of their day in sumptuous furnishings of splendid art-deco. SS still carried no sinister ring, and Lyons began looking through lists of birds and animals before deciding on the fastest creature with a name that could be applied to a car. He chose Jaguar, and once permission had been granted by Armstrong-Siddeley (it had been used on an aero engine), the name was introduced for new models in September 1935, and until 1940 they were known as SS Jaguars omitting even the full-points from 1936, "as the letters no longer stand for anything," rather like MG.

SS gradually gave way to SS Jaguar and the SS motif on the chrome radiator shell was discreetly modified. Lyons asked publicity chief E W Rankin for a symbolic leaping jaguar mascot, after an accessory company produced one he disliked. "It looked like a cat shot off a fence," said Rankin.

Left: Whether SS ever meant Standard Swallow was immaterial. The entwined insignia was not to last, soon replaced by the stylised SS in its hexagon. *Above:* Coventry factory.
In November 1928 Swallow moved to four blocks of the old shell-filling factory buildings at the top of the picture. War-time expansion brought the new factory at the bottom, intended for production of the Avro Manchester bomber, where Jaguar production re-started after the war.

Grace, Pace and Space

Above: Name the price.
The famous Mayfair
Hotel trade lunch
where the guests
guessed the price
of the 1935 SS Jaguar.

Frederick Gordon Crosby, an artist whose work appeared in *The Autocar*, was invited to provide one. Alas the symbolic jaguar which adorned Jaguar cars from 1935 on may not have been a jaguar at all. It first appeared at the Olympia motor show in 1930 on an MG as a tiger. It closely resembled one designed in the 1920s by a French sculptor Casimir Brau (a panther according to his catalogue), and it was certainly a close relation of the one Crosby produced for his friend Cecil Kimber, founder of MG. Crosby made mascots for the MG 18/100 Mark III, a 2.5-litre 6-cylinder car known as a Tiger or Tigress.

One of the original mascots stood on Cecil Kimber's desk in the MG factory at Abingdon-on-Thames, where a 1933 photograph, taken two years before Jaguar adopted it, shows the sculpture acting as a paperweight. The Jaguar jaguar is identical in almost every respect, save for its rear paws tucked up behind; MG's had them extended. Whether Lyons and Rankin knew about the mascot on the MG is immaterial and Jaguar Cars was unabashed about the revision to its company history. "It was an anatomically correct jaguar," its spokesman the late David Boole told the author.

So up to 1939, even if a Jaguar was not looked upon as exactly counterfeit, it was definitely not completely *bona fide*. And when the make was revived after the war it had as much to live down as live up to. Some substance had to be found behind the glitter, and as soon as a buyer's market returned, the competition recommenced. Many cars of 1945 were carry-overs from the 1930s, some were newer, younger, and more stylish, and among the good names with which SS Jaguar contended were AC, Alvis, Armstrong-Siddeley, Bentley, Bristol, Daimler, Humber, Jensen, Lagonda, Lanchester, Lea-Francis, Riley, Rolls-Royce, Rover, and Wolseley. Each may not have been as dynamic as they had been in the 1930s, they all decreed that the best car was a hand-built car, and nothing made in large numbers on a production line with no hand-finished panels, hand-sewn upholstery, or hand-made furniture and hand-assembled engines could hope to keep up.

If Sir William Lyons can take credit for anything, he can take credit for demonstrating that it was possible

Below: Armstrong-Whitworth Whitley with SS Jaguar under its wing. Repair and refurbishment of the world war 2 bomber was Jaguar's responsibility, together with the manufacture of parts for Short Stirling, De Havilland Mosquito, Avro Lancaster, and Spitfire aircraft. During the war Jaguar made 10,000 sidecars and 50,000 trailers.

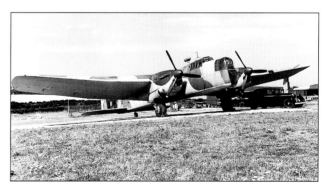

Above: Generations apart, but a family resemblance survives. Jaguar is in the genes of both the 1937 2½-litre that belonged to Lady Lyons and the 1986 Sovereign V12.

to match the bespoke coachbuilt individually-made car to one on a production line, and at half the price. He did it so well that within a decade only Rolls-Royce and Bentley were still making luxury cars in the old craft tradition. In 1945 SS, which by then had the implication of *Schutzstaffel*, the notorious Nazi police, was officially dropped from Jaguar's title.

Rover disappeared into the maw of British Leyland and took many years to re-emerge in anything like its old form. Bristol, created in 1945 to make BMW clones, was reduced to devising American-engined anachronisms in small numbers. Daimler was acquired by Jaguar. The others simply disappeared, overwhelmed.

Once Jaguar offered something much better at a lower price, these rivals not only lost their market, they lost their point. Until the recovery of the German industry in the 1970s, and the Japanese assault on the luxury market in the 1980s, the Jaguar had no equivalent. It was a phenomenon whose influence may have been difficult to comprehend in the 1990s following the remarkable improvement in the style,

Grace, Pace and Space

Above : Ron Flockhart
in the Ecurie
Ecosse D-type
on its way to victory
at Le Mans, 1957.

Above: New unfinished
Forth Road Bridge forms
backdrop to publicity
department picture of
early E-type. TES 1 was
demonstration car of
Rossleigh, then Jaguar's
main Edinburgh dealer.

status, and quality of middle-class volume-produced
cars such as upper-range Ford Mondeos. Jaguar reigned
supreme. It carved its own niche in what had been the
upper-premium segment and the opposition was all but
annihilated.

If the key event that led to Jaguar's recognition
in 1951 was winning Le Mans (an achievement repeated
five times in all up to 1957 when Jaguar finished 1st,
2nd and 3rd, and twice more in 1988 and 1990), the key
technical ingredient was the XK engine. In the closing
years of the war it seemed to Lyons and his engineers
Claude Baily, Walter Hassan, and William Heynes that
a new technically-educated generation would demand
something better than a pushrod engine. Post-war
Jaguar engines would have to emulate the racing engines
of pre-war, and must look the part. Twin overhead
camshafts, and polished cam covers, would be needed
for efficiency and under-bonnet elegance.

Lyons did not set out to make a sports car.
His intention was to make the sort of touring cars
and luxury saloons that a later generation would call
executive-class. He knew that the best means of

publicizing his new engine would be to create a short production run of 200 dramatic-looking sports cars. They could be raced a few times, gain a bit of a reputation, and be put away again. Lyons had a flair for publicity as well as keen business acumen, an aptitude for engineering and a genius for car styling. He was one of a rare breed of multi-discipline managing directors that was all but swept away in the accountancy culture of the 1970s.

After Baily, Hassan, and Heynes had designed and built engines designated X (for eXperimental), variants I and J, they reached the 6-cylinder X variant K. A "limited edition" batch of engines became the powerhouse of the great XK120 two-seater, (120mph was the projected top speed) which turned out as much of a fashion statement as it was a sports car. The XK120 owed something to the 1940 Mille Miglia BMW 328, although sleeker and better proportioned.

When the first aluminium-bodied XK120 appeared at the Earls Court Motor Show in October 1948, the response was so enthusiastic there was nothing for it but to get it into production. This meant a steel body, and it was made alongside the Mark VII saloon, for which the engine had been intended in the first place.

After proving it could do 130 mph without the aerodynamic drawback of a windscreen, the XK was entered for racing. It suffered from overheating brakes, a result of the immense performance, and the shrouding effect of the bodywork and disc wheels. Yet it acquitted itself well as a sports car in the best sense of the term, namely taking part in sport, showing that it was more than just something to catch the eye on the promenade.

Yet it was not until the advent of the XK 120C (for Competition) version that the racing world took the car and Jaguar to heart. The classic-status sports car makes remained in contention; AC, Allard, Alvis, Aston Martin, Bristol, Frazer Nash, HRG, Healey, Jowett Jupiter, Lea-Francis, MG, Riley, Triumph, and Morgan. There was also a trickle of imports from Porsche, Alfa Romeo, Mercedes-Benz and Ferrari, but Jaguar occupied a niche of its own with a car whose appearance on a street could halt traffic. One by one the British classics died; all save Aston Martin, Morgan and MG.

Grace, Pace and Space

Jaguar nomenclature in the 1960s came from the engineering, not the marketing department. The racing XK120 known as the XK120C, quickly became the C-type and was followed logically enough by the D-type.

The XK 120 became the 140, then the 150 with largely cosmetic changes, the numbers now outstripping top speeds by a substantial margin. They were cars in which the occupants sat atop a deep box-section frame, orthodox when the car was rushed into production in 1949, and by 1959 scarcely worthy of the advanced XK engine. The monocoque XKSS that was developed from the D-type would have gone into small-scale production but for a disastrous fire in 1957, which destroyed much of a new million square feet factory.

Far from being a small series produced for publicity, more than 12,000 XK 120s, 9,000 XK 140s, and 9,400 XK 150s were sold, so Jaguar sports cars paid their way. The range included open two seaters, coupes, and two-plus-twos, a euphemism for cars with back seats described as "occasional", when what was meant was "small".

By 1960 the XK was no match for modern, low-built, space-framed sports cars with less body roll, less weight, and a lower centre of gravity. Tall and narrow with big wheels and heavy gearshifts, they were dignified tourers, rather than the avant garde sports machines they had been in 1949.

Yet if the XKSS represented Jaguar sports cars' lost generation, when the E-type came in 1961 it was a striking descendant. It became the yardstick by which almost every other road-going sports car was judged. It was breathtakingly beautiful and its road manners were near faultless. It rode bumps like a limousine and handled with an exquisite precision. Performance was unparalleled; its steering and cornering were matchless. And it was about one-third the price of a Ferrari.

If Jaguars had a fault it lay in their longevity. Restoration of veteran E-types can involve campaigns against rust. But for sheer value they were scarcely matched, and when the V-12 versions appeared in 1971, just in time to suffer from the effects of the first world oil crisis with a fuel consumption of around 15-17 mpg, they were just as competitively priced.

Grace, Pace and Space

The succeeding XJS in 1975, although less of a sports car than the E-type, was a resounding success, surviving more than 20 years with V12 and 6-cylinder engines, open and closed bodies, despite styling which compromised both the intuitive Sir William Lyons and the clever aerodynamicist Malcolm Sayer.

A sprinkling of XJS character and even one or two of its components were carried over to the XK8 of 1996, which quickly took Jaguar to new sales records. Its first quarter 1997 sports car sales were the best in the company's history.

In some technical aspects, notably the E-type's independent rear suspension, the XK engine and its successors, Jaguar was sophisticated. In others, such as 1950s gear-boxes and auxiliary equipment, it remained in the automotive dark ages. By the 1980s its Whitley Engineering Centre was in the forefront of world-class

automotive technology, developing successors to the saloon cars that had their origins in the SS series pre-war. Jaguar saloons had progressed through the warmed-over post-war series to the Mk V and then the Mk VII, that not only made its mark in the executive car park, but turned out to be an unlikely winner of the 1956 Monte Carlo Rally.

Right: Return to round. The XJ Sport of 1995 featured "windswept" fairings on the headlights.

Grace, Pace and Space

This was the year before Jaguar moved into monocoque structures with the 2.4 saloon. This abandoned the chassis structure of the Mark VII and its successors, and laid the foundations for a series of mid-range saloons that lasted almost until 1970. From there the XJ series took over as the main production saloon range until the threshold of the 21st century.

Jaguar acquired Daimler in 1960 and by the time Sir William Lyons died at the age of 83 in February 1985, the group also included Coventry-Climax Engines, Guy Motors, and Henry Meadows the engine makers. In 1966 Lyons had to accept a proposal from Sir George Harriman for a merger with the British Motor Corporation after Pressed Steel, Jaguar's source of bodies, became part of BMC.

The combined company, British Motor Holdings, was absorbed into British Leyland two years later despite misgivings about its structure, which its subsequent nationalisation more than justified. Sir William retired in 1972, but lived to see the revival under Sir John Egan which led Jaguar back into private ownership in 1984.

The Egan regime restored Jaguar's self-confidence but failed to staunch the losses that followed a downturn in the American market. Jaguar had been starved of investment under Leyland, and no longer generated the cash to finance its own new model programme. It needed a partner, and at first it looked like just what General Motors might want, a swanky European up-market marque to which buyers of its mass-produced cars could aspire.

But Ford wanted Jaguar too. GM was ready to take a 30 per cent share. It already owned Lotus and had been talking to Vickers about taking 40 per cent of Rolls-Royce in 1991 in an effort to pre-empt BMW.

Ford owned 75 per cent of Aston Martin but wanted something a little more worldly, and in the end paid £1.6 billion ($2.5 billion) for Jaguar, quickly learning the extent to which its new purchase was burdened with high costs and out-of-date plant. The first Ford-appointed chief executive, William Hayden, famously remarked that his new factory was superior only to those in the Soviet Union. It looked as though

Grace, Pace and Space

Ford had bought a splendid image and not much else.

Ford was taking a long view. Hayden also pointed out to his colleagues that Ford bought Lincoln in 1923 and only started to make a return on it in the 1980s. It was not quite like that, but he made his point.

This book is a car-by-car account of what it took to make Jaguar's reputation. It entered the century-old motor industry at barely one-third of its span, and with graceful styling, superior ride and handling, high performance, and world-class sporting fame became one of Britain's cherished symbols. The XK8, the car that marked the second watershed in Jaguar history some 50 years after the first, was emblematic of the new perspective at Jaguar. This was the recognition that it could not survive without the backing of Ford, and that the way forward was to take all that was good about Jaguars in the past and recreate its reputation with all that was best from Ford in the present.

Right: Jazz age to space age. A 1920s Swallow sidecar poses at Browns Lane with a 1992 XJ220.

Sidecars 1922-1939

William Walmsley, who partnered Lyons in the new Blackpool company, built the so-called Stockport Zeppelin with an octagonal-section aluminium-panelled body before Swallow Sidecars officially named it Model No 1. It sold for £28 and was still listed although perhaps no longer made in 1927. Model 1 was more correctly the 1922 Model 1 Swallow sidecar Coupe Sports de Luxe, and Model 2 in 1924 the Swallow sidecar Light Weight de Luxe. It was 70in (177.8cm) long and was lighter than the Model 1, weighing about 100lb (45.36kg) including the twin axle chassis. It was also easier to make and stripped for racing it weighed only 80lb (35.28kg).

There was a Model 3, but not many seem to have been made and it was in most respects a stronger 2 for more powerful motorcycles. Model 4 was the most popular. It was much like a Model 2 but showed Lyons's styling flair for the first time, being stretched to 85in (215.9cm) with a long pointed tail. It was only £1 dearer than a Model 2 unless the customer specified a soft coupe top at an extra £3.

Model 5 was a Sports Model which went back to polished octagonal aluminium panelling and a curved windscreen in strong celluloid. It cost £23.10s (£23.50) or £25 with the two-axle chassis. It does not seem to have been made in large numbers.

Lightweight racing sidecars were rare but one was the Model 6 which cost £15 in 1927 and acted as a prototype for the Model 7 known as the Semi Sports which also featured an upswept nose and one-piece side panels. In 1928 the Model 7 was advertised as the cheapest Swallow sidecar at £12.12s (£12.60) and in due course it was relegated to the description 'utility' and the covering was fabric rather than stylish aluminium.

Right: Early advertisement. Lyons's style was restrained, dignified, elevated the product to a prestige class.

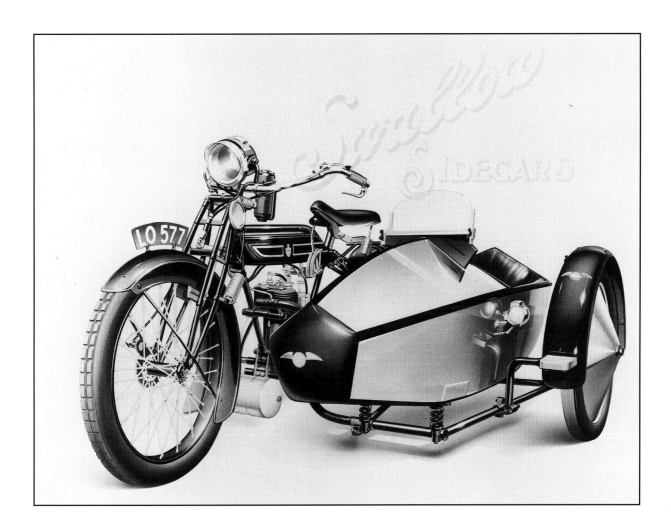

The sidecar business went with Lyons to Coventry in the autumn of 1928, becoming a department in the new Swallow Coachbuilding Company of 1931, and SS Cars Ltd in 1934.

New variants of Swallow sidecars were made up to a Model 15 including the Model 8, a touring design which developed into the two-seat 8A Hurlingham, and the 10 and 11 with their curious marine features of pointed bow, mahogany deck, and even chrome miniature handrails.

The liner analogy which perhaps led to the adoption of SS, took many forms. Mutations throughout the 1930s brought in hinged bootlids, proper weather equipment, dickey seats, and sporty models with cutaway sides.

In 1935 it was known as the Donington, after the racing circuit where the British Grand Prix was run, but by 1939 was more staid, known as the Shelsley and not recommended for racing.

The department was given over to war production in 1939, building over 9,000 sidecars for the military, before the business was sold.

Ranelagh Saloon

An extremely elegant, luxurious coachbuilt saloon, which has been evolved as a direct result of our desire to provide the discriminating motor cyclist with a de luxe sidecar which shall be a fit companion to the most expensive motor cycles produced. It is mounted on the new type "Swallow" chassis suitable for machines of unlimited capacity, and has car type ½" elliptic springing front and rear, thus adding enormously to the comfort of the passenger throughout the longest of journeys. The exquisite design, superb finish, and first-class workmanship to be found in this model is such that we think we can confidently claim we have produced the finest sidecar obtainable.

2 5

Austin-Swallow 2-seater 1927-1932

Herbert Austin planned his Seven as an alternative to the motorcycle and sidecar of the sort that Lyons was making in Blackpool. Style and aerodynamics were not on his mind when he set aside the billiard room of his home for a young draughtsman to draw up a simple car in secret that would revolutionise the industry. Despite a derisive reception by the press, the Baby Austin scored an immediate success when it was announced in 1922. It was conceived as a car in miniature, and although it had the features of its full-sized contemporaries, it was plain.

Lyons gave it a long tail, domed front wings, a splendid chromed rounded radiator in place of the ordinary flat one (the standard starting handle had to be sawn through and an extension welded on), with the headlamps on either side of it and not on the scuttle. There was a mahogany instrument panel, the upholstery was leather, and the hard-top of the first two-seater was lined in Bedford Cord. The Swallow Sidecar and Coachbuilding company mounted the body on an Austin chassis in a mirror image of the bespoke, upper-crust coachbuilding industry of the most luxurious cars in Britain.

BODY
Saloon; 2-doors; 2-seats; weight 355.6kg-508kg (784lb-1120lb).

ENGINE
4-cylinders, in line; front; 56 x 75.2mm; 747.5cc; RAC hp 7.8; 7.8kW (10.5bhp) @ 2400rpm; 10.4kW/L (14bhp/L).

ENGINE STRUCTURE
Side valve; side camshaft; cast iron cylinder head and block; 2-bearing crankshaft; lubrication by pump; Magneto ignition; water cooled by thermosyphon, fan optional.

TRANSMISSION
Rear wheel drive; single dry plate clutch; 3-speed gearbox; semi-floating rear axle with torque-tube; helical bevel final drive, ratio 4.9:1.

CHASSIS DETAILS
A-frame chassis, inverted U-section; semi-elliptic transverse front spring, quarter-elliptic rear; brakes on all four wheels (hand-brake front, foot-brake rear); worm & sector steering; 18.2L (4 Imp gal) (4.8US gal) fuel tank; 3-stud wire wheels 26in non-skid tyres, 3in rim width.

DIMENSIONS
Wheelbase 190.5cm (75in); track 101.6cm (40in); length 269.2cm (106in); width 116.8cm (46in).

PERFORMANCE
Max speed 56.2kph (35mph); 51.3kg/kW (38kg/bhp).

26

Austin-Swallow saloon 1927-1930

As soon as the first 2-seater reached production, a Swallow saloon was announced with split windscreen, sliding windows, and bigger doors. It also had a subtle feature which the 1927 prototype did not have.

The A-shaped Austin Seven chassis terminated behind the radiator, unlike most full-sized cars which had the side-members projecting forwards as anchors for the half-elliptic front springs. The Seven had a transverse spring, so the wily Lyons shaped his new front wings to look like projecting chassis 'dumb-irons' and lend an air of sophistication.

In 1930, like sidecars with spoof decking and chrome guard-rails, the Swallow saloon gained a couple of ship-style forward-facing ventilator cowls on the scuttle, ahead of the windscreen. A feature of the interior was a Houbigant Ladies' Companion Set in the passenger's glove compartment. Swallow was quick to impose a policy of continuous development, or planned obsolescence, and the little Austin had no fewer than five radiator surrounds in its five years' production. Wilmot Breeden bumpers were 60 shillings (£3.00) a pair, and a chrome bar introduced on the radiator.

BODY
Saloon; 2-doors; 2-seats; weight 355.6kg-508kg (784lb-1120lb).

ENGINE
4-cylinders, in line; front; 56 x 75.2mm; 747.5cc; RAC hp 7.8; 7.8kW (10.5bhp) @ 2400rpm; 10.4kw/L (14bhp/L).

ENGINE STRUCTURE
Side valve; side camshaft; cast iron cylinder head and block; 2-bearing crankshaft; lubrication by pump; Magneto ignition; water cooled by thermosyphon, fan optional.

TRANSMISSION
Rear wheel drive; single dry plate clutch; 3-speed gearbox; semi-floating rear axle with torque-tube; helical bevel final drive, ratio 4.9:1.

CHASSIS DETAILS
A-frame chassis, inverted U-section; semi-elliptic transverse front spring, quarter-elliptic rear; brakes on all four wheels (hand-brake front, foot-brake rear); worm & sector steering; 18.2L (4 Imp gal) (4.8US gal) fuel tank; 3-stud wire wheels 26in non-skid tyres, 3in rim width.

DIMENSIONS
Wheelbase 190.5cm (75in); track 101.6cm (40in); length 269.2cm (106in); width 116.8cm (46in).

PERFORMANCE
Maximum speed 56.2kph (35mph); 51.3kg/kW (38kg/bhp).

Morris Cowley-Swallow 1928

Some of Cecil Kimber's rationale for MG found an echo in William Lyons's recipe for a stylish two-seater based on the Morris Cowley. The Cowley body with flat radiator was shapely on its own and with special paintwork, Ace polished aluminium wheel discs, a few cosmetic touches and some astute modifications to make it look lower than it really was, it quickly became the Morris-Swallow.

A sloping vee windscreen and changes to the seating position, which included lowering the steering wheel by six inches, produced a car of which only a handful was ever made. Henlys advertised it at £220 with a cape-hood, a flimsier affair than the proper saloon-coupe at £230. Yet the Morris Cowley-Swallow was not as quick as the contemporary and more expensive Morris Oxford-based MG. The two-colour paint, matching leather upholstery, and polished wood were all very well, but keen drivers preferred the more overtly sporting MG. Lyons and Walmsley quickly acknowledged that it was not going to be a success and it was omitted from the range when the time came to move the factory to Coventry.

BODY
Cape-hood or saloon coupe; 2-doors; 2-seats.

ENGINE
4-cylinders, in line; front; 75 x 102mm; 1802cc; 26.1kW (35bhp); 14.5kW/L (19.4bhp/L).

ENGINE STRUCTURE
Side valve; 2-valves per cylinder; pushrod/ohc; side camshaft; cast iron cylinder head and block; water cooled.

TRANSMISSION
Rear wheel drive; wet cork clutch; 3-speed gearbox.

CHASSIS DETAILS
Half-elliptic front suspension; three-quarter elliptic shackled rear suspension; 12in drum brakes with servo assistance; bolt-on wire wheels.

DIMENSIONS
Wheelbase 261.6 or 274.3cm (103 or 108in); track 121.9cm (48in).

Right: Famously reluctant to pay modelling fees, William Lyons used office girl Alice Fenton to pose in publicity picture of Morris Swallow at Stanley Park gates in Blackpool. Together with a number of long-term employees, Miss Fenton rose to a senior management position, becoming director of home sales in the 1950s.

Alvis-Swallow 12/50 1928

Evolved from the side-valve 10/30, the 12/50 was the first Alvis with overhead valves, and one of the classic sports cars of the vintage era. In the fashion of the time, it had open and closed bodies by Alvis, but some went to outside coachbuilders for a variety of other styles, notably the handsome polished aluminium "duck's back" 2-seater Super Sports with a tiny dickey seat in the boat tail and a strikingly straight outside exhaust system.

The 12/50 was a car with a great sporting pedigree which began with its victory in the 1923 Brooklands 200 miles race, and the ambitious Lyons and Walmsley were anxious to add it to their repertoire. They had already rebodied a Clyno but it was not a success, so the Alvis was bought in as a chassis from Henlys, not from the Alvis works which disapproved. A saloon body was made for it by Cyril Holland, the coachbuilder responsible for sidecar construction from the beginning, with Swallow's distinctive pen-nib two-colour bonnet, but it was a one-off exercise which was not repeated.

BODY
Sports; 2-doors; 2-seats.

ENGINE
4-cylinders, in line; front; 1496cc; 69 x 110mm, 1645cc; 37.3kW (50bhp) @ 4000rpm; 24.9kW/L (33.3bhp/L).

ENGINE STRUCTURE
Pushrod ohv; cast iron cylinder head and cylinder block; 3-bearing crankshaft; single carburettor; water cooling by thermosyphon.

TRANSMISSION
Rear wheel drive; Alvis single plate clutch; 4-speed gearbox.

CHASSIS DETAILS
Channel-section steel chassis; suspension semi-elliptic springs front & rear, 4.77:1 axle underslung at rear, friction dampers; 4-wheel drum brakes; Marles steering; 45.5L (10 Imp gal) (12 US gal) fuel tank.

DIMENSIONS
Wheelbase 286cm (112.5in); track 127cm (50in); length 388.6cm (153in), width 151.1cm (59.5in).

PERFORMANCE
Maximum speed 112.4kph (70mph).

Right: The Alvis-Swallow coachwork followed the lines of the 1931 seen here except for the pen-knife lines on the bonnet and small rounded Alvis radiator. Photographs of the solitary Alvis-Swallow model are rare.

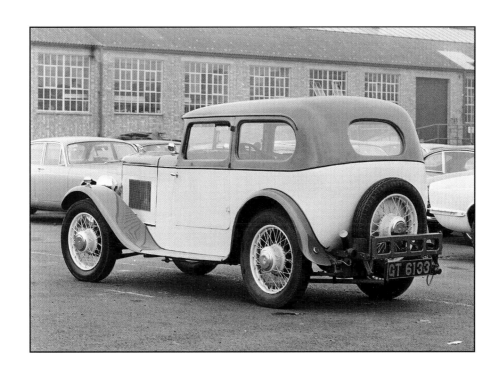

Fiat-Swallow 1929

The first large version of the Swallow shape with characteristic vee windscreen and overhanging roof, two-colour paint, and rounded rump, was the sole 12/50 Alvis made in the Blackpool factory. The first of the big-bodied cars to reach the market came after the firm moved to Coventry, and Swallow's Glasgow dealer James Ritchie sold it a number of obsolescent Fiat 509A chassis. The model had been introduced in 1925 with a clever overhead camshaft 9hp engine and the standard Fiat Weymann bodies sold in Britain were resonating upright affairs. It had a robust chassis however, and one version, the 509SM (Spinto Monza) was sold as a sports car with a 30bhp (22.37kw) engine and a dashing lightweight wooden body.

The Swallow production run was probably no more than one batch of 50 or 100 chassis left over after the car had been superseded by the Fiat 514. All were made in 1929, following the move to Coventry and an old factory up an unmade lane, soon to be famous as Swallow Road.

BODY
Saloon; 2-doors; 4-seats; weight 795kg (1752lb).

ENGINE
4-cylinders, in line; front; 57 x 97mm; 990cc; compr. 5.35:1; 16.4kW (22bhp)@ 3400rpm; 16.4kW/L (22bhp/L).

ENGINE STRUCTURE
Overhead camshaft; gravity fuel feed 1 carburettor; hi tension Magneto ignition; water cooling by thermosyphon.

TRANSMISSION
Rear wheel drive; single dry plate torque-tube clutch; 3-speed; helical spur final drive, 6.1:1.

CHASSIS DETAILS
Steel chassis; suspension semi-elliptic springs front & rear; mechanical 4-wheel drum brakes; worm & helical steering; 24.5L (5.3 Imp gal) (6.4 US gal) fuel tank; 715 tyres, 15in rims (4.75 tyres, 15in rims).

DIMENSIONS
Wheelbase 255cm (100.39in) track 120cm (47.25in); ground clearance 17.5cm (6.75in); turning circle 950cm (31ft); length 370cm (145.67in); width 142cm (55.90in).

PERFORMANCE
Max speed 78kph (48mph); 48.5kg/kW (36.1kg/bhp); average fuel consumption 9L/100km (18.4mpg).

Nine colour schemes were available for the 1930 model year including cherry red/maroon, cream/violet, and intriguingly sky blue/Danish blue. Like the entire range of cars, the Fiats were offered with a Swallow mascot, at £260 against the standard saloon's £225.

Swift-Swallow 1929-1931

One of Coventry's pioneer bicycle manufacturers, Swift produced high quality, low powered, premium priced family cars from the turn of the century. It was not a good combination, bringing it into direct competition with cheaper mass-produced makes. The firm was reorganised in 1919 under Bean which collapsed a year later, leaving Swift with a range of 10, 12, and 14hp cars and the Cadet of 1930 produced just before the firm finally went to the wall in 1931.

The 10hp car was the basis for the Swift-Swallow of which some 150 were made in 1929-1930. Introduced in 1923, the Swift Ten changed from quarter-elliptic to half-elliptic springs at the front in 1926, and the rear in 1930. Working practices for Swallow bodies changed, although the same ash frame and aluminium skin principles remained. The move to larger premises in Coventry meant that the wooden parts had to be cut to shape and pre-assembled with glue and screws instead of the coachbuilder cutting, shaping, and assembling the entire frame *in situ*. The workforce demurred, but Lyons had his sights on 50 bodies a week and carried the changes through.

BODY
Saloon; 2-doors; 4-seats; weight 812.8kg (1792lb).

ENGINE
4-cylinders, in line; front; 62.5 x 97mm; 1190cc; 16.4kW (22bhp) @ 3000rpm; 13.7kW/L (18.3bhp/L).

ENGINE STRUCTURE
Side valve; 3-bearing crankshaft; 6 volt electrical system; Auto-vac fuel system; water cooled.

TRANSMISSION
Rear wheel drive; fabric faced single plate clutch; 4-speed gearbox right-hand change or 3-speed gearbox; final drive 5.4:1.

CHASSIS DETAILS
Suspension semi-elliptic springs *(see text)*, rear dampers; axle ratio 5:1; rod-operated 4-wheel brakes; 27 tyres, 4.4in rims.

DIMENSIONS
Wheelbase 251.5cm (99in) or 259.1cm (102in); ground clearance 17.5cm (6.8in); turning circle 950cm (31ft); length 370cm (145.7in); width 142cm (55.9in).

PERFORMANCE
Max speed 85.1kph (53mph); 49.7kg/kW (37kg/bhp); average fuel consumption 5.7-6.3L/ 100km (45-50mpg).

Austin-Swallow 'Mark 2' saloon 1930-1932

The Austin was Swallow's mainstay from its inception in 1927 to 1932, and underwent two price reductions, the later one in the final autumn to sell off remaining stock. The open sports came down from £170.10s (£170.50) to £150, the coupe with detachable hard-top from £180.10s (£180.50) to £160, and the saloon from £187.10s (£187.50) to £165. Some 2,500 Austin-Swallows were made of which 800 were 2-seaters, and although the design remained broadly the same throughout, changes kept abreast of fashion.

The radiator cowl altered slightly in shape every year, the fifth being introduced in the car's last-but-one season, at the 1930 motor show. It was broader than the earlier model, with a bar down the centre and 'Austin Swallow' offset. Among the other modifications was a louvred apron ahead of the spoof dumb-irons. The radiator cowl of the final models was chromed instead of polished aluminium; cellulose paint was used instead of coach enamel and varnish, and the extraordinary scuttle ship-style ventilators became standard fittings. The wood and leather theme was maintained inside, with individual bucket seats replacing the split-bench.

BODY
Saloon; 2-doors; 4-seats; weight 355.6kg-508kg (784lb-1120lb).

ENGINE
4-cylinders, in line; front; 56 x 75.2mm; 747.5cc; RAC hp 7.8; 8.9kW (12bhp) @ 2400rpm; 12kW/L (16.1bhp/L).

ENGINE STRUCTURE
Side valve; 2-bearing crankshaft; lubrication by pump; side camshaft; Magneto ignition; cast iron cylinder head / block; water cooling by thermosyphon cooling, fan optional.

TRANSMISSION
Rear wheel drive; single dry plate clutch; 3-speed gearbox; semi-floating rear axle with torque-tube; helical bevel final drive, ratio 5.25:1.

CHASSIS DETAILS
A-frame chassis, inverted U-section; semi-elliptic transverse front spring, quarter-elliptic rear; brakes on all four wheels; worm & sector steering; 18.2L (4 Imp gal) (4.8US gal) fuel tank; 3-stud wire wheels 26in non-skid tyres, 3in rims.

DIMENSIONS
Wheelbase 205.7cm (81in); front track 101.6cm (40in), rear track 109cm (43in); turning circle 10.1m (33ft); length 269.2cm (106in); width 116.8cm (46in).

PERFORMANCE
Max speed 72.2kph (45mph); acceleration 0-64kph (40mph) 37sec; 40kg/kW (29.6kg/bhp).

Right: Scuttle-mounted ventilators and different radiator cowl distinguished Mark 2 Austin Swallow.

Standard-Swallow 9 1930-1933

The significance of the Standard-Swallow, produced from 1930 to 1932, lay less in its shape and style than in the link that it created between Swallow and the Standard Motor Company. Although it was essentially a companion to the Austin, Swift, and Fiat-Swallows, it represented an important step to the sidecar manufacturer towards becoming a car manufacturer. The principle of buying-in components had been well-established by William Morris for car assembly at Cowley. Morris made hardly anything of its own, but this could be a high-risk strategy for a small manufacturer. Dedication to making its own nuts and bolts had brought down Swift.

Swallow, for the time being at any rate, bought-in what it needed, and made no secret of its obligations to Austin, Fiat, Swift or Wolseley. In acknowledging the chassis and engine maker by name, Swallow still seemed content to describe itself solely as a coachbuilder.

BODY
Saloon; 2-doors; 4-seats.

ENGINE
4-cylinders, in line; front; 1287cc; 6.7kW (9bhp); 5.2kW/L (6.9bhp/L).

ENGINE STRUCTURE
Side valve; coil ignition; 2-valves per cylinder; side camshaft; coil ignition; water cooled.

TRANSMISSION
Rear wheel drive; 3-speed gearbox.

CHASSIS DETAILS
Steel chassis; front suspension, semi-elliptic springs; rear suspension, worm axle, semi-elliptic springs; Marles & Weller steering.

DIMENSIONS
Wheelbase 100.5in (255.27cm).

PERFORMANCE
Maximum speed 72.2kph (45mph); average fuel consumption 7.1-7.4L/100km (38-40mpg).

Right:
The Standard-Swallow marked a shift in emphasis. As *The Autocar* put it, "The Standard Nine chassis is s pecially prepared by the Standard Motor Co Ltd for the Swallow Company..."; There was a hint here of the Standard-Swallow being something more than simply bespoke coachwork, or an alternative version of another make of car.

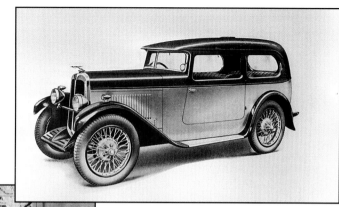

Morris Minor-Swallow 1930

A solitary Morris Minor Swallow was produced for display in Henlys Euston Road branch in 1930. Lower and better-proportioned than the Austin Seven-Swallow, which it closely resembled in shape and size, its square radiator shape gave it a slightly severe appearance.

Many of the later Austin-Swallows had what has come to be known as 'pen-nib' bonnets, in which the two-colour paint line converged towards the radiator in curving lines resembling the writing point of an old-style fountain-pen. The upright Morris front did not encourage this treatment and the waistline division made the car look longer.

The Morris Minor initiative did not survive. MG exploited it with success in the later Midgets, but for Lyons another model beckoned. Ever ambitious, he hankered after a new car that was due from Morris's burgeoning Nuffield empire; effectively a Morris Minor with two extra cylinders, the Wolseley Hornet was in the offing.

BODY
Saloon; 2-doors; 4-seats.

ENGINE
4-cylinder; 57 x 83mm; 847cc; 8.05RAC hp; 20bhp @ 4000rpm;

ENGINE STRUCTURE
Single gear driven overhead camshaft; ohv; 3 ring aluminium pistons; cast iron cylinder block and head; SU carburettor;

TRANSMISSION
Morris single dry plate clutch; 3-speed gearbox; final drive ratio 8:43; 5.37:1.

CHASSIS DETAILS
Shackled half elliptic springs front & rear; scuttle mounted petrol tank; cable foot brakes and transmission hand brake; wire wheels 19 x 3; Dunlop Cord 27 x 400 tyres;

DIMENSIONS
Track 106.7cm (42in); wheelbase 218.4cm (86in).

Right: the one-off Morris Minor-Swallow's square radiator suited the lines familiar on the rounded-front Austins, but the bonnet top was not decorated in the customary pen-nib fashion.
Far right: At the rear it was identical to this Austin-Swallow.

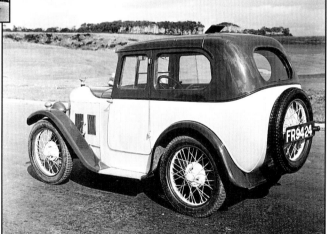

Standard-Swallow 16 1931

By 1931 Swallow was making 100 bodies a week, offering serious business for a collaborative car manufacturer. Standard under John Black saw the opportunity to make a useful number of sales, albeit at trade price and without bodies. An extra 4,000 to 5,000 chassis and engines a year would improve the company's economies of scale.

Swallow took the Ensign 16, with its smooth-running side-valve 6-cylinder engine and 7-bearing crankshaft, and announced in May 1931 the biggest Swallow-made car yet and the first in a long line of Standard 6-cylinders. In June 1931 the advertising gushed: "Nothing so magnificent, so marvellous, or offering such astonishing value for money has ever been placed before the car-buying public. Here is surely another 'dream' car – a car with a £1,000 appearance, with a performance equalled by no other £16 tax car in the world." The £16 Road Fund licence was based on the engine's horsepower rating calculated on the cylinder bore.

BODY
Saloon; 2-doors; 4-seats.
ENGINE
6-cylinders, in line; front; 2054cc.
ENGINE STRUCTURE
Side valve; 2-valves per cylinder; side camshaft; cast iron cylinder head and block; 7-bearing crankshaft; water cooled.
TRANSMISSION
Rear wheel drive; X-speed gearbox; spiral bevel final drive.
CHASSIS DETAILS
Steel chassis; semi-elliptic springs front and rear; drum brakes mechanical front and rear; Marles-Weller steering.

Right: The Standard Swallow might have made a reputation for itself, but it turned out only to be a stage in the development of Jaguar. By 1931 the real significance of the agreement with Standard was about to be revealed.

WAIT!

THE "*SS*" IS COMING

2 New Coupés of Surpassing Beauty

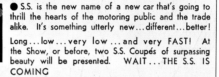

● S.S. is the new name of a new car that's going to thrill the hearts of the motoring public and the trade alike. It's something utterly new...different...better!

Long...low...very low...and very FAST! At the Show, or before, two S.S. Coupés of surpassing beauty will be presented.   WAIT...THE S.S. IS COMING

AND THE EXTREMELY SUCCESSFUL STANDARD SWALLOW 4-SEATER SALOONS TO BE CONTINUED

BIG NINE FULL 4-STR. SALOON, £250.   15 h.p. 6-cyl. full 4-seater Saloon, £275.

EXCLUSIVE COACHWORK

SWALLOW COACHBUILDING COMPANY, FOLESHILL, COVENTRY.   Telephone : Coventry 8027.
London Showrooms : Henly House, Euston Road, N.W.1.   Agents throughout the country.

Wolseley Hornet-Swallow 2-seater 1931-1933

Under its new Nuffield regime, the old-established Wolseley company introduced overhead camshaft engineering to popular cars, and in 1930 brought the first small six cylinder engine to the British market. The 1.3-litre Wolseley Hornet was not in the first rank of sports cars, but it had the makings of one and its rather weak chassis attracted a number of coachbuilders so that by 1931 there was a score of bespoke body styles.

Notwithstanding its flimsy frame, in reality a Morris Minor chassis lengthened by 12½in (31.75cm), the Hornet engine became the basis for all the MG sixes commencing with the F-type Magna, and was immediately spotted by Lyons as the basis for a shapely 2-seater. Close-fitting wings and a pointed tail gave hints of Aston Martins and Bugattis; the heavily louvred bonnet intimated an engine of great power.

Wolseley was one of the first manufacturers to equip its cars with hydraulic brakes and its top-gear flexibility was impressive. Testers found that it could set off from rest in top and accelerate to 60mph through the gears in around half a minute. Top speed in first was 15mph, second 43mph, and top over 60mph.

BODY
Open 2-seater; 2-door; 2-seats; chassis weight 597kg (1316lb).

ENGINE
6-cylinders, in line; front; 57 x 83mm; 1271cc; RAC 12hp; 23.9kW (32bhp) @ 4300rpm; 18.8kW/L (25bhp/L).

ENGINE STRUCTURE
Ohv; shaft driven overhead camshaft; cast iron cylinder head and block; 4-bearing crankshaft; one SU carburettor; water cooled.

TRANSMISSION
Rear wheel drive; single dry plate clutch; 3-speed gearbox; spiral bevel final drive, 4.77:1.

CHASSIS DETAILS
Steel chassis; semi-elliptic springs front & rear, hydraulic dampers; Lockheed hydraulic drum brakes on all four wheels, 12in drums; worm & wheel steering; 18.2L (4 Imp gal) (4.8 US gal) fuel tank; bolt-on wire wheels; 27in tyres, 4.40in rims.

DIMENSIONS
Wheelbase 230cm (90.5in); track 106.7cm (42in); ground clearance 15.9cm (6.25in); turning circle 11.9m (39ft); length 307.3cm (121in); width 129.5cm (51in).

PERFORMANCE
Maximum speed 104kph (65mph); acceleration 0-96kph (60mph) 30sec; 25kg/kW (18.7kg/bhp); average fuel consumption 8.6L/100km (33mpg).

Right: An eloping English couple in 1931 might be married at the anvil of the blacksmith's shop in Gretna Green, first stop over the Scottish border. Wolseley Hornet-Swallow would have required a good start to outpace pursuing relatives.

SS1 F H Coupe 'series 1' 2054cc 6-cylinder 16hp 1931-1932

The Standard Motor Company chairman John Black's assertion, that the chassis supplied to Swallow was something special, was no accident. His letter to William Lyons said: "The chassis referred to ... will be reserved exclusively for you." For the first time the chassis of a production Swallow was to be unique, and that justified a change of name, a change of course for what would in due time be the SS Jaguar.

William Walmsley, Lyons's partner from the early Swallow sidecar days, disagreed with the styling for the SS1, prepared in something of a rush in the best tradition of the motor industry for the 1931 motor show. It was stretched the following year and the chassis underslung at the back to give the low build so close to Lyons's heart. Yet there was no doubt about the thrust of the style; it was a long bonnet and a low roofline, a small well-furnished interior, and a distinctive recognisable "face". It had character, it had style, it set fashion more than it followed it, and captured with astonishing precision the idiom of the sports racer, the rally car, the vogue-ish look for which Lyons had a supreme aptitude.

BODY
Coupe; 2-doors; 2-seats; weight 1080kg (2381lb).

ENGINE
6-cylinders, in line; front; 65.5 x 102mm; 2054cc; compr 5.8:1 approx; 33.6kW (45bhp) @ 3800rpm; 16.8kW/L(22.5bhp/L).

ENGINE STRUCTURE
Side valves; duralumin connecting rods; cast iron cylinder head and block; 7-bearing crankshaft; RAG carburettor; Lucas coil ignition; water cooling by thermosyphon, assisted by an impeller.

TRANSMISSION
Rear wheel drive; single-plate clutch; 4-speed manual gearbox; spiral bevel final drive, ratio 4.66:1.

CHASSIS DETAILS
Steel with coachbuilt body; beam axle, semi-elliptic leaf springs front & rear; cable-operated Bendix duo servo shoes in drum brakes front & rear; steering Marles-Weller cam & lever; 54.6L (12 Imp gal) (14.4 US gal) fuel tank; 5.5 tyres, 18in rims.

DIMENSIONS
Wheelbase 284cm (112in); front track 124cm (49in); rear track 124cm (49in); turning circle 12m (39.5ft); length 442cm (174in); width 152cm (60in); height 137cm (54in).

PERFORMANCE
Maximum speed 113kph (70mph); acceleration 0-96kph (60mph) 31sec; 33.1kg/kW (24kg/bhp); average fuel consumption 15.3-14.1L/100km (18.5-20mpg).

Far right: Subtle change in a later car, with tapered radiator and smoothed wing lines.

SS1 F H Coupe 'series 1' 2552cc 6-cylinder 20hp 1931-1932

The 20hp SS1 was promoted less vigorously at only £10 more than the 16. Sycamore for the facia, beautiful cabinet work with centre panels in the fillets, and door cappings in "fiddle black", pleated Vaumol furniture hide for the seats and door casings, a luggage trunk blended into the tail, no running boards or steps, and voluptuous wings hugging the wheels made the SS1 look stunning. It had huge Lucas P170 headlights, louvred bonnet, chrome radiator, metal apron between the dumb-irons, Pytchley sliding roof, Wilmot-Breeden bumpers, a leather-grained roof and dummy hood irons.

The Motor was ecstatic. (There was a) "...sensation of tautness and correctness about the whole build... one is reminded of a racing car, for the long and shapely bonnet suggests immense power and the lowness of build ... gives an instinctive feeling of security ... immediately after taking over the SS1 we were taking corners at quite 30 per cent greater speed than usual."

How well the tactics worked. "Reminded" of a racing car ... "suggests" immense power, phrases that would be repeated many times throughout the history of Jaguar.

BODY
Saloon; 2-doors; 4-seats; weight 1321kg (2912lb).

ENGINE
6-cylinders, in line; front; 73 x 101.6mm; 2552cc; RAC 20hp; compr 5.8:1; 41kW (55bhp) @ 3800rpm; 16.1kW/L (21.6 bhp/L).

ENGINE STRUCTURE
Side valves; duralumin connecting rods; cast iron cyl head and block; 7-bearing crankshaft; RAG carburettor; Lucas coil ignition; water cooling by thermosyphon.

TRANSMISSION
Rear-wheel drive; single plate clutch; 4-speed manual gearbox; spiral bevel final drive, 4.66:1.

CHASSIS DETAILS
Steel, coachbuilt body; beam axle, semi-elliptic leaf springs; cable-operated drum brakes front & rear; Marles-Weller cam & lever steering; 54.6L (12 Imp gal) (14.4 US gal) fuel tank; 5.50 tyres, 18in rims.

DIMENSIONS
Wheelbase 284.5cm (112in); 'series 2': wheelbase 302cm (119in); front and rear track 129.5cm (51in); turning circle 11.9m (39ft); length 472cm (186in); width 161cm (63.5in); height 139.7cm (55in).

PERFORMANCE
Max speed 115.6kph (72mph); 28.4kph (17.7mph) @ 1000rpm; accel 0-96kph (60mph) 30sec; 32.2kg/kW (24kg/bhp); average fuel consumption 14.1-15.7L/100km (18-20mpg).

Right: The low build gave the car good handling, each engine furnishing a lively turn of speed. Like Corsica-bodied Daimler Double-Six, it was all wheels and bonnet, small cockpit, the very essence of a sports car.

William Lyons had an artist's eye for proportion. Traffic in the 1930s was still sparse, and it was only when it was alongside an SS1 that anybody was likely to notice the 4-cylinder 9hp SS2 had a shorter bonnet, smaller headlamps, and an altogether daintier appearance than its 6-cylinder counterparts. It still had a low roof; it still had the fine appointments; it still had the raciness of the 6-cylinders, but on a Standard Nine chassis it was small.

SS2 did not denote a successor to SS1. It appeared at the 1931 London motor show at Olympia alongside the SS1, and its close-fitting "helmet" wings outlived those on the SS1 until the last one was delivered to a customer in Bury St Edmunds in September 1933. It gained a four speed gearbox in its second year of production and acquired the later long stroke engine.

The original 60.25mm x 88mm 1006 cc SS2 lasted two full model years, made only as a fixed-head coupe priced at £210. A total of 274 were produced in 1932, and 275 in 1933, before the larger engine variants were introduced for 1934.

BODY
Coupe; 2-doors; 2-seats; weight 788kg (1737lb).

ENGINE
4-cylinders, in line; front; 60.25 x 88mm; 1003.6cc; compr 6:1 approx; 20.9kW (27bhp) @ 4000rpm; 20.8kW/L (26.9bhp/L).

ENGINE STRUCTURE
Side valves; 2-valves per cylinder; side camshaft; cast iron cylinder head and block; 2-bearing crankshaft; Stromberg carburettor; coil ignition; water cooled.

TRANSMISSION
Rear wheel drive; single dry plate clutch; 3-speed manual gearbox (4-speed from 1932), spiral bevel final drive, 5.25:1.

CHASSIS DETAILS
Steel X-braced chassis with coachbuilt body; front suspension beam axle, semi-elliptic leaf spring; rear live axle, semi-elliptic leaf spring; cable-operated drum brakes front & rear; Burman worm & nut steering; 40.9L (9 Imp gal) (10.8 US gal) fuel tank; centre lock wire wheels; 4.75 tyres, 18in rims.

DIMENSIONS
Wheelbase 227cm (89.5in); front and rear track 112cm (44.25in); length 366cm (144in); width 152cm (60in); height 137cm (55in).

PERFORMANCE
Maximum speed 96.6kph (60mph); acceleration 0-80kph (50mph) 26.6sec; 37.7kg/kW (28.1kg/bhp); average fuel consumption 9.1L/100km (31mpg).

Right: Restrained lines of SS2 kept Coupe shape and offered rear window too.

Wolseley Hornet-Swallow Special 4-seater 1932-1933

Nothing made a car look sporting so much as making it look low, yet there was not much Lyons could do about the height of the Wolseley Hornet's bonnet. The overhead camshaft engine, with its vertical shaft which also drove the armature-shaft for the dynamo, was tall. It had to be disguised by an appliqué strip which doubled cleverly by the scuttle and continued round the top of the doors to lower the waistline from stem to stern.

The first Hornet-Swallows had a single SU carburettor engine and in April 1932 Wolseley offered the twin carburettor Hornet Special in chassis form for £175. A four speed gearbox was among the improvements.

The shapely little car was effectively the last of Swallow's coachbuilt specials on proprietary chassis. Abbey Panels, Kevill-Davis & March, Maltby, Patrick, Jensen, and Eustace Watkins continued, but Lyons had outgrown the species. Henceforward the Coventry factory would make cars of its own brand.

BODY
Open 4-seater; 2-doors; chassis weight 600kg (1323lb).

ENGINE
6-cylinders, in line; front; 57 x 83mm, 1271cc; 12 RAC hp; 32.1kW (43bhp) @ 4500rpm; 25.2kW/L (33.8bhp/L).

ENGINE STRUCTURE
Ohv; 2-valves per cylinder; single chain-driven overhead camshaft; Duplex valve springs; aluminium pistons, centrifugal cast iron liners; cast iron cylinder head and block; 4-bearing crankshaft; twin SU carburettors; water cooled.

TRANSMISSION
Rear wheel drive; 4-speed gearbox; spiral bevel final drive, 4.89:1.

CHASSIS DETAILS
Steel chassis; semi-elliptic springs front and rear, hydraulic dampers; Lockheed hydraulic brakes on all 4 wheels, 12in drums; worm & wheel steering; 22.7L (5 Imp gal) (6 US gal) fuel tank; centre-lock wire wheels, 27in tyres, 4.75in rim width.

DIMENSIONS
Wheelbase 230cm (90.5in); track 99.1cm (39in); ground clearance 15.9cm (6.25in); turning circle 11.9m (39ft); length 307.3cm (121in); width 129.5cm (51in).

PERFORMANCE
Maximum speed 110kph (70mph); average fuel consumption 8.6-9.4L/100km (30-33mpg).

Right: Shape of things to come. Hornet Special had hints of later Jaguars in its elegant tail.

SS1 'series 2' 2054cc 6-cylinder 16hp 1933-1935

Taciturn and dignified, William Lyons must nevertheless have been well pleased with the reception his SS cars had in 1933. The organisers of the 1931 Olympia motor show had assigned Swallow to the coachbuilding sector, but now the firm was gaining recognition as a fully fledged manufacturer. *The Motor* wrote reassuringly: "These SS cars are not just built round a certain popular chassis. The design is original and distinctive. The chassis is manufactured in cooperation with the Standard Motor Co in a special section of the works of that famous concern, to an individual design available only in the SS range and developed specially therefore."

True enough. It was not quite the same as the Standard chassis. The chassis for 1933 was underslung, with the rear axle above the frame contributing to the low build and providing extra room in the close-fitting rear seats. There was close attention to detail. Most manufacturers considered four coats of cellulose paint sufficient. SS, to the delight of the Zofelac Paint Co, used eight. The timber used in framing the body was carefully seasoned. Swallow's suppliers Gliksten had one of the largest seasoning yards in the country.

BODY
Coupe; 2-doors; 4-seats; weight 1295kg (2855lb).

ENGINE
6-cylinders, in line; front; compr 6:1; 65.5 x 101.6; 2054cc; 16hp; 35.8kW (48bhp) @ 3600rpm; 17.4kW/L (23.4bhp/L).

ENGINE STRUCTURE
Side valves; 2-valves per cylinder; side camshaft; aluminium cylinder head; cast iron block; 7-bearing crankshaft; coil ignition; one RAG M-Type carburettor; water cooled.

TRANSMISSION
Rear wheel drive; single dry plate clutch; 4-speed manual gearbox; spiral bevel final drive, 4.66:1.

CHASSIS DETAILS
Steel with coachbuilt body; semi-elliptic leaf springs front & rear; cable-operated duo servo drum brakes front & rear; 40.9L (9.0 Imp gal) (10.8 US gal) fuel tank; 5.50 tyres, 18in rims.

DIMENSIONS
Wheelbase 302cm (119in); front track 130cm (51in); rear track 130cm (51in); turning circle 12m (39.5ft); length 472cm (186in); width 161cm (63.5in); height 137cm (54in).

PERFORMANCE
Maximum speed 120.8kph (75mph); acceleration 0-96kph (0-60mph) 28sec; 36.2kg/kW (27kg/bhp); average fuel consumption 15.3L/100km (18.5mpg).

CONVERTIBLE:
Weight
1320.9kg (2912lb).
Performance
Maximum speed 122kph (76mph); 36.9kg/kW (27.5kg/bhp).

SS1 'series 2' 2552cc 6-cylinder 20hp 1933-1935

The low build of the SS1 was a triumph of packaging. It was perfectly possible for a moderately tall adult to rest an elbow on the roof only 4ft 7in (139.7cm) from the ground. Yet although getting in and out required a certain agility, even a 6-foot tall driver had adequate legroom behind the near-vertical steering wheel, with the short remote-control gear lever close by. The back seat was less generously proportioned, with armrests both sides and in the middle. The absence of rear side windows and the small back window might seem claustrophobic to later generations accustomed to airy and light interiors, but the style of the time was for privacy. Besides, there was no interior heater, so the car's smallness may not have been wholly regarded as a disadvantage.

The wide range of colours that had been a feature of Swallow cars from the beginning continued with the SS series. Body and wheels were available in Nile Blue, Apple Green, Carnation Red, Buff, Birch Grey or Primrose, with the head and luggage box trimmed in black with a choice of green, Lake, or Chocolate.

BODY
Coupe; 2-doors; 4-seats; weight 1295kg (2855lb).

ENGINE
6-cylinders, in line; front; 73 x 101.6mm; 2552cc; compr 6:1; 46.2kW (62bhp) @ 3600rpm; 18kW/l (24.3bhp/l).

ENGINE STRUCTURE
Side valves; 2-valves per cylinder; side camshaft; aluminium cylinder head; cast iron block; 7-bearing crankshaft; RAG M-Type carburettor; water cooled.

TRANSMISSION
Rear wheel drive; single dry plate clutch; 4-speed manual gearbox; spiral bevel final drive, 4.66:1.

CHASSIS DETAILS
Steel with coachbuilt body; front suspension beam axle, semi-elliptic leaf springs; rear suspension live axle, semi-elliptic leaf springs; Bendix duo-servo cable operated drum brakes front & rear; Marles-Weller cam & lever steering; 40.9L (9 Imp gal) (10.8 US gal) fuel tank; 5.50 tyres, 18in rims.

DIMENSIONS
Wheelbase 302cm (119in); front track 130cm (51in); rear track 130cm (51in); turning circle 11.9m (39ft); length 472cm (186in); width 161cm (63.5in); height (hood up)137cm (54in).

PERFORMANCE
Maximum speed 131.3kph (81.8mph); acceleration 0-96kph (60mph) 21.4sec; 28kg/kW (20.9kg/bhp); average fuel consumption 14-15.7L/100km (18-20mpg).

CONVERTIBLE:
Weight
1320.1kg (2912lb).
Maximum speed
135kph (84mph, screen flat); 28.6kW/L (21.3bhp/L).

SS2 'series 2' 10hp 1343cc; 12hp 1608cc 1933-1934

By the autumn of 1933 SS2 grew up, forsaking Standard Little Nine for new versions of the Standard 10hp (1343cc) and 12hp (1608cc). These stretched the wheelbase from 91in (231.14cm) of series 1 to 104in (264.16cm), so that by the Olympia motor show it was something nearer a full four seater. "Close-coupled" was never better applied than to the first SS2.

There was a Coupe and a new Saloon, really a Coupe with a window instead of the dummy hood-irons and fabric-covered rear quarters. The luggage trunk was more smoothly integrated with the body, and the spare wheel now had a smart metal cover with a chrome band round the circumference.

Although based on a lowly Standard, the SS2 chassis resembled the bigger SS1 with the underslung rear axle which was a feature of the Standard Ten. The rubber-mounted engine was described as "buoyant power", the different sizes achieved by enlarging the cylinder bores from 63.5mm to 69.5mm. The combustion chambers in the aluminium cylinder head were fully machined instead of having rough-cast finish.

[12hp in brackets.]

BODY
Saloon/coupe; 2-doors; 2+2 seats; weight 1016kg (2240lb).

ENGINE
4-cylinders, in line; front; 63.5 x 106mm [69.5 x 106mm]; 1343cc [1608cc]; 10hp [12hp]; compr 6:1; 23.9kW (32bhp) @ 4000rpm; [28.3kW (38bhp) @ 4000rpm]; 17.8kW/L (23.8bhp/L) [17.6kW/L (23.6bhp/L)].

ENGINE STRUCTURE
Side valve with machined combustion chambers; 2-valves per cylinder; one side camshaft; aluminium cylinder head, cast iron block; 4-bearing crankshaft; Lucas distributor; RAG T-Type carburettor; water cooled.

TRANSMISSION
Rear wheel drive; single dry plate clutch; 4-speed manual gearbox; spiral bevel fd 5.43:1 (5.5:1) (5.29:1 from 1935 for both).

CHASSIS DETAILS
Steel with coachbuilt body; front beam axle, semi-elliptic leaf springs; rear live axle, semi-elliptic leaf springs; Bendix duo-servo cable-operated drum brakes front & rear; Marles-Weller cam & lever steering; 54.6L (12 Imp gal) (14.4 US gal) fuel tank; centre-lock wire wheels; 4.75 tyres, 18in rims.

DIMENSIONS
Wheelbase 264cm (104in); front and rear track 112cm (44.5in); turning circle 11m (36ft); length 416cm (164in); width 142cm (56in); height 137cm (54in).

PERFORMANCE
Maximum speed 98.2kph (61.2mph)[103kph (64mph)]; standing km (quarter mile) 27.4sec; 57.1kg/kW (42.7kg/bhp) [57.7kg/kW (43.1kg/bhp)]; average fuel consumption 10.5L/100km (27mpg).

SS1 open 4-seater 16hp 2143cc and 20hp 2663cc 1933-1936

The languorous appearance of the SS1 open tourer suggested it was built more for comfort than speed, a view that gained weight when Sydney Light and Charles Needham won the Concours de Confort in the 1934 Monte Carlo Rally, and the Hon Brian Lewis and Reuben Harveyson did so again the following year.

Yet SS1s distinguished themselves in the more arduous Alpine Rally. In 1933 they were fortunate to finish 6th, 8th, and 11th after overheating. Five started again in 1934 with Charles Needham partnered by Harry Gill from the SS assembly line. Despite difficulties climbing the Stelvio Pass, they came third for the team prize, second in their class, and won Alpine plaques. A Zoller-supercharged SS1 for high-altitude driving did not get past the development stage once Lyons appointed W M Heynes to take charge of the new engineering department. A G Douglas Clease of *The Autocar* concluded after the tough Alpine passes: "These were not supercharged cars; they were standard models with full four-seater bodies, not narrow light bodies with small close-fitting wings as so many of the German cars were."

BODY
Sports tourer; 2-doors; 4-seats; weight 1346kg (2968lb).

ENGINE
6-cylinders, in line; front; 65.5 x 106mm [73 x 106mm]; 2143cc [2663cc]; compr 6.2:1; 16hp [20hp]; 39.5kW (53bhp) [50kW (68bhp)] @ 3600rpm; 18.4kW/L(24.7bhp/L) [18.9kW/L (25.5bhp/L)].

ENGINE STRUCTURE
Side valves; 2-valves per cylinder; side camshaft; aluminium cylinder head; cast iron block; 7-bearing crankshaft; coil ignition; RAG M-Ttype carburettor; water cooled.

TRANSMISSION
Rear wheel drive; single dry plate clutch; 4-speed manual gearbox, synchromesh on 2, 3, 4; spiral bevel final drive,4.71:1 (from 1935 4.5 for 16hp, 4.25 for 20hp).

CHASSIS DETAILS
Steel cruciform construction; front beam axle, semi-elliptic leaf springs; rear live axle, semi-elliptic leaf springs; Bendix duo-servo cable operated brakes; Marles Weller cam & lever steering; 40.9L (9 Imp gal) (10.8 US gal) fuel tank; 5.5 tyres, 18in rim width.

DIMENSIONS
Wheelbase 302cm (119in); front track 137cm (53.75in); rear track 137cm (53.75in); turning circle 12.2m (40ft); length 457.2cm (186in); width 166.4cm (65.5in); height (hood up) 139.7cm (55in).

PERFORMANCE
Maximum speed 130.8kph (81.5mph); acceleration 0-96kph (0-60mph) 24sec; 90.3kg/kW (67.3kg/bhp); average fuel consumption 14.1-15.7L/100km (18-20mpg).

SS2 Open 4-seater 10hp 1343cc; 12hp 1608cc 1934-1935

The first open SS2, announced in March 1934 for the 1934 model year on the 8ft 8in chassis, was a striking-looking 4-seater. There was a sporting quality about the twin cowls on the scuttle, just like those of Brooklands racers with small aero-screens. The windscreen folded flat, and the polished walnut facia array included a speedometer directly ahead of the driver, calibrated extravagantly with speeds in gears. Even the clock on the passenger's side had an inner 24 hour dial to enhance the effect of technical efficiency.

The smooth wing line and visual harmony of the radiator and headlamps that came to symbolise later Jaguars was starting to emerge. The hood folded away neatly and there was a special pocket for the detachable side-screens. The bonnet was heavily-louvred, like those on Bentleys, from whose large engines large amounts of heat had to be dispersed. The new SS had centre-lock wire wheels, cutaway doors, a big sprung-spoke steering wheel, short stubby gearshift, fly-off handbrake, pleated leather seats, and three hinges to fortify the doors against sagging, a not-infrequent affliction of open cars of the time.

BODY
Coupe; 2-doors; 4-seats; weight 1008kg (2224lb).

ENGINE
4-cylinders, in line; front; 63.5 x 106mm [69.5 x 106mm]; 1343cc [1608cc]; 10hp [12hp]; compr 6:1; 23.9kW (32bhp) [28.3kW (38bhp)] @ 4000rpm; 17.8kW/L (23.8bhp/L) [17.6kW/L (23.6bhp/L)].

ENGINE STRUCTURE
Side valve, machined combustion chambers; 2-valves per cyl; side cam; aluminium cylinder head, cast iron block; 4-bearing crankshaft; Lucas distributor; RAG T-Type carb; water cooled.

TRANSMISSION
Rear wheel drive; sdp clutch; 4-speed manual gearbox; spiral bevel fd 5.43:1 (5.5:1) (5.29:1 from 1935 for both).

CHASSIS DETAILS
Steel with coachbuilt body; front beam axle, semi-elliptic leaf springs; rear live axle, semi-elliptic leaf springs; Bendix duo-servo cable-operated drum brakes front & rear; Marles-Weller cam & lever steering; 54.6L (12 Imp gal) (14.4 US gal) fuel tank; centre-lock wire wheels; 4.75 tyres, 18in rims.

DIMENSIONS
Wheelbase 264cm (104in); front and rear track 112cm (44.5in); ground clearance 17.8cm (7in); turning circle 11m (36ft); length 416cm (164in); width 142cm (56in); height 137cm (54in).

PERFORMANCE
Max speed 103kph (64mph); accel 0-80kph (50mph) 22sec; standing quarter mile 27.4sec; 39.7kg/kW (29.6kg/bhp); average fuel consumption 9.4-10.5L/100km (27 30mpg).

Ingredients for one of the world's great classic sports cars were falling into place.

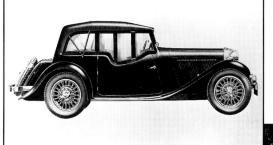

SS1 4-light saloon 16hp 2143cc 1934-1936

Although the picturesquely-named four-light saloon was really only the old Coupe with windows, it did give subtle hints of the Jaguar line to come. The proportions of the windows, the balance between bonnet and boot, the fine chrome trim on the body exterior, and the careful attention to detailing, such as door handles, were all hallmarks of Lyons's sure touch. He knew his middle-class owner-driver well, and cosseted him with a neat toolbox on the scuttle or in the lid of the luggage compartment, sunray pleats in the leather of the door casings, and the so-called no-draught glass louvres atop the side windows. These were premium features ordinary cars did not have.

In 1934 a 16hp SS1 sold for £340, the 20hp astonishingly only £5 more – good value against a contemporary but rather staid Rover Fourteen at £288. The rare and sporty Rover Speed 20 Hastings Coupe (whose lines resembled the SS closely) was £495, a Railton Eight Sandown saloon £498. In contrast a Ford Model Y came down to £100 a year later and a Rolls-Royce Phantom II was £2450.

BODY
Saloon; 2-doors; 4-seats; weight 1028.8kg (2268lb).

ENGINE
6-cylinders, in line; front; 65.6 x 106.6mm; compr 6.2:1; 2143cc; 39.5kW (53bhp) @ 3600rpm; 18.5kW/L (24.8bhp/L).

ENGINE STRUCTURE
Side valves with compression heads; 2-valves per cylinder; side camshaft; aluminium cylinder head, cast iron block; 7-bearing crankshaft; RAG M-Type carburettor; water cooled.

TRANSMISSION
Rear wheel drive; single dry plate clutch; 4-speed manual gearbox; spiral bevel fd, 4.75:1.

CHASSIS DETAILS
Steel with coachbuilt body; front and rear suspension semi-elliptic leaf springs; cable-operated drum brakes front & rear; 54.6L (12 Imp gal) (14.4 US gal) fuel tank; 5.50 tyres, 18in rims.

DIMENSIONS
Wheelbase 302.3cm (119in); front track 134.6cm (53in); rear track 135.9cm (53.5in); ground clearance 20.3cm (8in); turning circle 11.9m (39ft); length 472.4cm (186in); width 166.4cm (65.6in); height 139.7cm (55in).

PERFORMANCE
Maximum speed 117kph (75mph); acceleration 0-96kph (60mph) 28.4sec; 2.6kg/kW (19.4kg/bhp); average fuel consumption 14.5L/100km (19.5mpg).

Right: Wilmot-Breeden stabiliser bumpers, with counterweights on each end of the bumper blade, were fitted to help keep the front end of all SS models steady at speed on bumpy roads.

SS1 Saloon 20hp 2664cc 1934-1936

The Standard Motor Company's monopoly of SS engine production was by no means unchallenged. Soon after SS Cars Ltd was officially set up (as a subsidiary of Swallow) on 23 October 1933, Henlys, having acquired the British concession for Studebaker, brought one for SS to look at and appraise its straight-8 engine. It came to nothing, but Lyons was already conscious of the need for more reliable and powerful engines, paricularly in view of the cars' indifferent performance in the 1933 Alpine Trial.

In the course of developing the aluminium cylinder heads for the 1934 model year with the Coventry Motor Cylinder Company, Lyons came to know Harry Weslake, an independent consultant whose speciality was the design of engines and in particular cylinder heads.

Meanwhile the 20hp side-valve SS1 was revised with a new camshaft, high compression ratio, and the fitting of two RAG carburettors which were advertised as "fully synchronised". The capacity of the oil pump was enlarged and so was the ribbed aluminium sump.

BODY
Saloon; 2-doors; 4-seats; weight 1028.8kg (2268lb).

ENGINE
6-cylinders, in line; front; 73 x 106mm; compr 6.2:1; 2663.7cc; 50.7kW (68bhp) @ 3600rpm; 19kW/L (25.5bhp/L).

ENGINE STRUCTURE
Side valves with compression heads; 2-valves per cylinder; side camshaft; aluminium cylinder head, cast iron block; 7-bearing crankshaft; RAG M-Type carburettor; water cooled.

TRANSMISSION
Rear wheel drive; single dry plate clutch; 4-speed manual gearbox; spiral bevel fd, 4.75:1.

CHASSIS DETAILS
Steel with coachbuilt body; front and rear suspension semi-elliptic leaf springs; cable-operated drum brakes front & rear; 54.6L (12 Imp gal) (14.4 US gal) fuel tank; 5.50 tyres, 18in rims.

DIMENSIONS
Wheelbase 302.3cm (119in); front track 134.6cm (53in); rear track 135.9cm (53.5in); turning circle 11.9m (39ft); length 472.4cm (186in); width 166.4cm (65.6in); height 139.7cm (55in).

PERFORMANCE
Maximum speed 123.6kph (77mph) [130.8kph (81.5mph) 1935 2-carb 4.25 axle]; acceleration 0-96kph (60mph) 20.4sec; 20.3kg/kW (15.1kg/bhp); average fuel consumption 14.5L/100km (19.5mpg).

Right: Among the changes to the SS was a reversal of the members of the chassis cross-bracing, to stiffen it up and create a box-section where it joined the main frames.

SS1 Airline saloon 16hp 2143cc; 20hp 2663cc 1935-1936

The British motoring public was not yet ready for the rounded fronts of the Chrysler Airflow or small German "streamlined" cars, so SS kept flowing wings and free-standing headlamps for its new modern-styled Airline saloon with the tail smoothed-off in the style that came to be known as Fastback. The windows were extended rearwards, the main door pillar was attenuated at the waistline, and the rounded rump enclosed a small luggage boot. Two spare wheels were relocated to front wing side-mounts.

Lyons never liked it. He was right, as he usually was, to regard it as a flight of fashion which was soon to pass, as the Singer Airstream and the Chrysler itself would show. Still the Airline did have extra legroom in the back and the integral luggage boot indicated the shape of things to come.

The Airline was the last model made under the partnership of Lyons and William Walmsley, who had set up in business in 1922. In January 1935 SS Cars Ltd, founded as a subsidiary the previous year, was floated as a public company. Lyons became the major shareholder and Walmsley retired, wealthy, in his early forties.

BODY
Saloon; 2-doors; 4-seats; weight 1384kg (3051lb).

ENGINE
6-cylinders, in line; front; 65.5 x 106mm [73 x 106mm]; 2143cc [2663cc]; 16hp [20hp]; compr 7.0:1; 46.2kW (62bhp)[52.2kW (70bhp)] @ 4000rpm; 21.6kW/L (28.9bhp/L) [24.3kW/L (32.7bhp/L).

ENGINE STRUCTURE
Side valves; 2-valves per cylinder; side camshaft; aluminium cylinder head; cast iron block; 7-bearing crankshaft; 2 RAG (single optional) carburettors; coil ignition; water cooled.

TRANSMISSION
Rear wheel drive; single dry plate clutch; 4-speed manual gearbox; spiral bevel fd, ratio 4.25:1.

CHASSIS DETAILS
Steel with coachbuilt body; semi-elliptic leaf springs front & rear, transverse double Andre dampers; cable-operated drum brakes front & rear; Marles Weller cam & lever steering; 5.50 tyres, 18in rims.

DIMENSIONS
Wheelbase 302cm (119in); front track 134.6cm (53in); rear track 135.8cm (53.5in); ground clearance 17cm (6.75in); turning circle 12.2m (40ft); length 467cm (184in); width 161cm (63.5in); height 143.5cm (56.5in).

PERFORMANCE
Maximum speed 128.4kph (80mph); acceleration 0-96kph (62mph) 26.6sec; standing quarter mile 22.4sec; 30kg/kW (22.3kg/bhp) [26.5kg/kW (19.8kg/bhp)]; average fuel consumption 14.9-15.7L/100km (18-19mpg).

SS1 D H Coupe 16hp; 20hp 1935

The final SS1 was a supremely elegant drophead coupe with a hood that folded into the rear trunk, providing a flat, even waistline but not much in the way of luggage room. Long-distance motorists were perhaps not going to drive far with the hood down, so a conflict of interest was unlikely. Detachable sidescreens were inappropriate for a D H Coupe of quality, so Triplex glass windows fitted snugly against the fixed windscreen pillars and wound down into the doors. There were metal frames which clipped firmly to the top windscreen rail and could be stowed away when not required. The chromed hood irons, cantrails and pillars could all be packed into the panelled and cellulose-finished trunk.

The hood was made in light coloured fabric, lined to match the upholstery and provide an insulating layer for winter. Inside, accommodation was the same as the saloon, and headroom was sufficient for a tall man to sit upright in the rear without his hat touching the roof. It seemed important in 1935.

The 16hp Coupe cost £380, the 20hp £385. The last SS1 showed perfectly how SS Cars was aiming for the luxury market at astonishingly low prices.

BODY
Coupe; 2-doors; 4-seats; weight 1383.9kg (3051lb).

ENGINE
6-cylinders, in line; front; 65.5 x 101.6mm [73 x 101.6mm]; 2143cc [2663.7cc]; 16hp [20hp]; compr 7.0:1; 35.8kW (48bhp), [46.2kW (62bhp)] @ 3600rpm; 16.7kW/L (22.4bhp/L)[17.4kW/L (23.3bhp/L].

ENGINE STRUCTURE
Side valves; 2-valves per cylinder; pushrod; chain-driven camshaft; aluminium cylinder head; cast iron block; 7-bearing crankshaft; 2 RAG (single optional) carburettors; water cooled.

TRANSMISSION
Rear wheel drive; clutch single dry plate; 4-speed manual gearbox; spiral bevel final drive.

CHASSIS DETAILS
Steel with coachbuilt body; suspension semi-elliptic leaf springs front & rear; cable-operated drum brakes front & rear; 54.5L(12 Imp gal) (14.4 US gal) fuel tank; 5.50 tyres, 18 rims.

DIMENSIONS
Wheelbase 302cm (119in); front track 137cm (53.75in); rear track 137cm (53.75in); turning circle 11.9m (39ft); length 470cm (185in); width 161cm (63.5in); height 137cm (54in).

PERFORMANCE
Maximum speed 120.75kph (75mph) [20hp 129kph (80mph); 38.7kg/kW (28.8kg/bhp)[30kg/kW (22.5kg/bhp)]; average fuel consumption 15.7L/100km (18mpg).

Right: **Following the SS1's introduction in 1933 power was increased to 53bhp [68bhp]in 1934 and 62bhp [70bhp] in 1935.**

SS90 2663cc 6-cylinder 1935

Before William Walmsley left the company, he had two short-chassis SS1 sports cars made which may have served as prototypes of the SS90, itself something of a prototype for the ensuing classic, the SS100. Only 23 SS90s were made, including the prototype, by cutting 15in (38.1cm) out of an SS1 chassis to make an arresting open two seater effectively with an SS1 track of 54in (137.16cm) and an SS2 wheelbase of 104in (264.16cm). The cross-member was abbreviated and the frame underslung at the back. The broad half-elliptic springs had Silentbloc bushes for the shackles, and Andre Telecontrol shock absorbers altered the damper settings from the cockpit from hard to extremely hard, but it was used on Bentleys so it was deemed suitable.

The venerable old side-valve engine did not have a lot of power even for such a relatively light car, but from the low-set radiator to the flush-mounted spare wheel of the prototype, there was no mistaking the SS90 as anything less than a true sports car. It may not have had breeding in the sense that the Brooklands crowd granted, but it had style and it had presence, and it cost only £395.

BODY
Sports; open 2-seats; 2-door; weight 1142.6kg (2519lb).

ENGINE
6-cylinders, in line; front; 73 x 106mm; 2663cc; compr 7:1; 52.2kW (70bhp) @ 4000rpm.

ENGINE STRUCTURE
Side valves; 2-valves per cylinder; pushrod; chain-driven camshaft; aluminium cylinder head; cast iron block; 7-bearing crankshaft; 2 RAG (single optional) carburettors; water cooled.

TRANSMISSION
Rear wheel drive; single dry plate clutch; 4-speed manual gearbox, synchromesh on 2,3,4; spiral bevel final drive, 4.25:1 (3.75:1 for speed trials).

CHASSIS DETAILS
Steel, coachbuilt body; front susp beam axle, flat semi-elliptic springs, Andre Telecontrol dampers; rear live axle, flat semi-elliptic springs, Andre Telecontrol dampers; Bendix duo-servo cable operated drum brakes front & rear; 81.8L (18 Imp gal) (21.6 US gal) fuel tank; 5.50 tyres, 18in rims.

DIMENSIONS
Wheelbase 264cm (104in); front track 137cm (54in); rear track 137cm (54in); turning circle 10.8m (35.5ft); length 381cm (150in); width 160cm (63in); height 137cm (54in).

PERFORMANCE
Max speed 145kph (90mph); accel 0-96kph (60mph) 17.5sec; standing quarter mile 20.5sec; 21.9kg/kW (16.3kg/bhp); average fuel consumption 14.9L/100km (19mpg).

Right: Prototype SS90 with the Hon Brian Lewis (Lord Essendon) at the wheel. The car's rounded tail and flush spare wheel were soon to change.

SS Jaguar 100 2½-litre 1936-1941

The evolution of the SS90 into the SS100 took place after A G Douglas Clease of *The Autocar* scored second in class at the concours d'elegance of the Royal Scottish Automobile Club's rally in June, 1935. He was unplaced in the competitive section, but he returned the car just in time for William Lyons to drive it to the SS Car Club's first national rally at Blackpool. Lyons wanted to show it off to 100 competitors and SS enthusiasts gathered from all over the country as well as abroad. Interest turned into excitement when he did a demonstration drive through the half mile "sprint with obstacles" on Blackpool promenade, and knocked 6.6sec off the fastest competitor's time.

The principal change from SS90 to SS100 was the introduction of an overhead valve rendering of the seven-bearing side valve engine. The design work, carried out by Harry Weslake, was a simple enough conversion to pushrod operation which involved covering the side-valve mechanism with a blanking plate and substituting pushrods for a new ohv head.

John Black, now in control at Standard Motor Company, agreed to manufacture the engines and the

BODY
Sports; 2-doors; 2-seats; weight 990.7kg (2184lb).

ENGINE
6-cylinders, in line; front; 73 x 106mm; compr 7:1; 2663cc; 76.1kW (102bhp) @ 4600rpm; 29.3kW/L (39.2bhp/L).

ENGINE STRUCTURE
Weslake ohv, pushrod; cast iron cylinder head; 7-bearing crankshaft; 2 SU 1.25in carburettors, water cooled.

TRANSMISSION
Rear wheel drive; clutch single dry plate; manual 4-speed gearbox, synchro on 2,3,4; spiral bevel final drive, ratio 4.0:1.

CHASSIS DETAILS
Steel with coachwork body; front suspension beam axle, semi-elliptic leaf springs, Luvax hydraulic dampers on Silentblocs; rear suspension live axle, semi-elliptic leaf springs, Luvax hydraulic dampers on Silentblocs;

Burman Douglas worm-and-nut steering; Girling rod operated drum brakes front and rear; fuel tank 63.6L(14 Imp gal)(16.8 US gal); 5.50 tyres, 18in rims.

DIMENSIONS
Wheelbase 264cm (104in); front track 137cm (54in); rear track 137cm (54in); ground clearance 14cm (5.5in); turning circle 11.6m (38ft); length 381cm (150in); width 160cm (63in); height 137cm (54in);

PERFORMANCE
Maximum speed 151.3kph (94mph); acceleration 0-96kph (60mph)12.8sec; standing quarter mile 18.6sec; 13kg/kW (9.7kg/bhp); average fuel consumption 14.1L/100km (20mpg).

Right: Flowing lines of Lyons's masterpiece tackling rally climb.

SS Jaguar 100 2½-litre 1936-1941 (2)

bodywork was based on the SS90 and the SS1 open tourer with the spare wheel now mounted more upright at the back on a slab petrol tank.

It was the archetypal sports car with two seats, large headlights properly braced with struts and a crossbar, graceful flared aluminium wings, and a long bonnet which its engine almost filled. Yet it remained a low-key production at the factory because its role, like that of the XK120 more than a decade later, was essentially image-building. Lyons expected little more of it.

It was described as "intended for competition work", although the chassis was relatively primitive compared with the 328 BMW which had independent suspension, disc wheels, and a smooth

ride, but it was a bargain at £385 against the Frazer Nash-BMW imported by AFN at £445.

The new saloon range took precedence, and except for the 1935 motor show car and a few others, the first SS100s were built at the beginning of 1936. The reluctance of Lyons to make large numbers of SS100s stemmed from the work entailed in amending the SS1 chassis and equipping it with the steering, brakes, and suspension of the new saloons. Unlike the 90, the 100's half-elliptic springs slid in trunnions instead of being suspended on shackles.

Only 190 2½-litre cars were made and 118 of the succeeding 3½-litre version before production ended in 1940.

SS Jaguar 1½-litre saloon sv 1608cc 4-cylinder 1936-1938

Now the real reason for all the excitement was revealed. The 1936 model year cars not only marked the first use of the Jaguar name, but also the company's arrival among fully fledged motor manufacturers. It gained official recognition as a car maker rather than a coachbuilder at the Olympia motor show in 1934 but now the appearance of the SS Jaguar range confirmed its integration into the motor industry.

It was a well integrated range. The 1½-litre did not aspire to an overhead valve engine just yet, but it had the appearance and the fine finish of the larger-engined cars despite being 11in (27.9cm) shorter.

The trade lunch at the Mayfair Hotel, London on the introduction of the SS Jaguar on 21 September 1935 has gone down in motor industry folklore. The guests were invited to say how much they thought the new 2½-litre car would sell for, and the difference between what they replied (£635) and the price fixed by SS Cars (£385) looked encouraging. The side valve 1½-litre was a mere £285. Also, by the time the Jaguar appeared, SS Cars felt less need for exotic colour schemes. The Mayfair launch car was a dignified black.

BODY
Saloon; 2-doors; 4-seats; weight 1066.8kg (2351.9lb).

ENGINE
4-cylinders, in line; front; 69.5 x 106mm; compr 6.1:1; 1608cc; 37.3kW (50bhp) @ 4000rpm; 23.3kW/L (31.3bhp/L); 11.98hp.

ENGINE STRUCTURE
Side valves; 2-valves per cylinder; 3-bearing crankshaft; aluminium cylinder head; chain-driven camshaft; cast iron block; Solex carburettor; coil ignition; water cooled.

TRANSMISSION
Rear wheel drive; clutch single plate; 4-speed gearbox, synchromesh on 2,3,4; final drive ratio 4.86:1.

CHASSIS DETAILS
Steel construction; front suspension beam axle, semi-elliptic leaf springs; rear live axle, semi-elliptic leaf springs; Luvax hydraulic dampers front and rear;

Burman Douglas worm-and-nut brakes, finned alloy brake drums, Girling mechanical brakes; 4.75 tyres, 18in rims.

DIMENSIONS
Wheelbase 274.3cm (108in); track 121.9cm (48in); ground clearance 17.8cm (7in); turning circle 12.2m (40ft); length 424.2cm (167in); width 156.2cm (61.5in); height 152.4cm (60in).

PERFORMANCE
Maximum speed 112.4kph (70mph); acceleration 96kph (0-60mph) 33secs; standing quarter mile 24sec; 28.6kg/kW (21.3kg/bhp); average fuel consumption 11.3L/100km (25mpg).

Right: All the style at half the price. "The long sweeping lines form a great attraction to prospective buyers", said *The Motor.*

The 1½ Litre Jaguar 4-Door Saloon

Although smaller than the 2½ Litre Saloon, this model is so perfectly proportioned as to bear the closest resemblance to the larger car.

Full accommodation is provided in an interior characterised by that high degree of comfort which is so marked a feature of every SS. Refinements usually associated only with larger and more expensive cars are incorporated in this model, which, with its "big car performance" is definitely in the forefront of moderately powered cars. As in the 2½ Litre model, the one piece rear back rest is furnished with a heavily padded central arm rest, which may be folded back to permit of a third passenger being carried in the rear compartment.

Details in Brief

1½ Litre four-cylinder side valve engine, 1608·5 c.c., 12 h.p. £9 Tax. Single downdraught carburetter. 12" 1½" Girling brakes. Burman Douglas steering gear with Bluemel Douglas steering wheel adjustable for height and rake. Special double action Luvax hydraulic shock absorbers. Four-speed improved synchro-mesh gear box—"finger tip" control. Four-door coachbuilt body in wide range of attractive colour schemes.

Price, £235, *ex works*.

For complete specification see overleaf.

SS Jaguar 2½-litre open 4-seater 1936-1937

The 2½-litre open four seater represented the last link with the SS series, and although it was based on William Heynes's redesigned chassis with the side members boxed-in to make it stiffer and had the ohv engine, the bodywork remained a close copy of the older car. It had cutaway doors and the familiar cramped interior, with the armrest in the middle of the rear seat. Large Lucas P100 headlights were the principal distinguishing features although the wide Jaguar radiator was shared with late-model SS1 tourers and Airline saloons. Only 105 SS Jaguar tourers were made between 1935 and 1937.

The wider chassis gave more footroom, and the front wings had a distinctive curve round the dumb-irons and radiator. Curiously it was not offered with the wind-up windows and substantial hood of the 1935 drophead coupe. At the back the spare wheel lay in the open protected by a full-width bumper. Engine power was increased to 104bhp at 4500rpm in 1937 by raising the compression to 6.8:1 in compensation for the model's increased weight.

BODY
Convertible; 2-doors; 4-seats; weight 1398kg (3082lb).

ENGINE
6-cylinders, in line; front; 73 x 106mm; compr 6.4:1; 2663cc; 76.1kW (102bhp) @ 4600rpm; 28.6kW/L (38.3bhp/L).

ENGINE STRUCTURE
Overhead valve pushrod operated; 2-valves per cylinder, detachable head; 7-bearing counter-weighted crankshaft; machined combustion chamber & ports; twin SU carburettors; water cooled by centrifugal pump & automatic by-pass thermostat.

TRANSMISSION
Rear wheel drive; clutch single dry plate; 4-speed gearbox, synchromesh on 2,3,4; spiral bevel final drive, 4.5:1.

CHASSIS DETAILS
Steel with coachbuilt body; suspension semi-elliptic leaf springs front & rear; worm-and-nut gear steering; rod-operated drum brakes front & rear; 63.6L (14Imp gal) (16.8US gal)fuel tank; 5.25 tyres, 18in rims.

DIMENSIONS
Wheelbase 286cm (112.5in); front track 132cm (52in); rear track 140cm (55in); turning circle 11.6m (38ft); length 457cm (180in); width 168cm (66in); height 152cm (60in).

PERFORMANCE
Maximum speed 141.7kph (88mph); acceleration 0-100kph (62mph) 16sec; standing quarter mile18.8sec; 18.4kg/kW (13.7kg/bhp); average fuel consumption 14.1L/100km (20mpg).

THE 2½ LITRE JAGUAR OPEN TOURER

For those who prefer an open car, the lithe grace of the SS Jaguar 2½ Litre Tourer will make instant appeal. Here is a car in which incredibly long distances can be covered at sustained high speeds with effortless ease. Superb road-holding, light yet positive steering, and brakes of the highest efficiency allow full advantage to be taken of the magnificent performance of which this SS is capable. Though essentially a car for the open road, such is the extraordinary flexibility of the powerful engine that all but the densest traffic can be negotiated in top gear—with abundant power in reserve for rapid acceleration.

£375

SS Jaguar 2½-litre saloon 1936-1937

At last, a car with power. SS customers had never known such vivid performance. With 102bhp (76.1kW) the 2½-litre reached 88mph (140.8kph) on road test which corresponded to 4,700rpm. Occupying 17.4sec to reach 60mph (approx 100kph) would have been respectable for a sports car let alone a well equipped luxury saloon. It would reach 27mph (43.2kph) in first gear, 46mph (73.6kph) in second, and 69mph (110.4kph) in third.

Yet MG still seemed a thorn in the flesh of SS, and after adapting its tiger for a jaguar, the advertising agency purloined its advertising slogan, Grace, Space, Pace. The agency also evolved SS's own stylised hexagonal radiator badge not unlike MG's octagon and (like MG) all SS office typewriters had to be made with one key incorporating the SS logo. SS had even backed the instruments with the hexagon much like MG did with the octagon. There was no real competition, for although MG announced its SA 2.0-litre ten days after the SS Jaguar and £10 cheaper, it was restricted and confined by the Nuffield Organisation, production was delayed and the challenge never materialised.

BODY
Saloon; 4-doors; 4-seats; weight 1473.2kg (3247.8lb).

ENGINE
6-cylinders, in line; front; 73 x 106mm; compr 6.4:1; 2663cc; 76.1kW (102bhp) @ 4700rpm; 28.6kW/L (38.3bhp/L).

ENGINE STRUCTURE
Overhead valves pushrod operated; 2-valves per cylinder; detachable head; 7-bearing counter-weighted crankshaft; machined combustion chamber; twin SU carburettors; water cooled by centrifugal pump & automatic by-pass thermostat.

TRANSMISSION
Rear wheel drive; clutch single dry plate; 4-speed manual gearbox, synchromesh on 2,3,4; spiral bevel final drive, ratio 4.5:1.

CHASSIS DETAILS
Steel with coachbuilt body; suspension semi-elliptic leaf springs front & rear; Girling rod-operated drum brakes front & rear; Burman Douglas worm-and-nut steering; 63.6L (14Imp gal) (16.8US gal); 5.50 x 18 tyres.

DIMENSIONS
Wheelbase 3.02cm (119in); front track 137cm (54in); rear track 137cm (54in); ground clearance 17.8cm(7in); turning circle 11.6m (38ft); length 452cm (178in); width 170cm (67in); height 147cm (58in).

PERFORMANCE
Maximum speed 141.3kph (88mph); acceleration 96kph (0-60mph) 19.0sec; 19.4kg/kW (14.5kg/bhp); average fuel consumption 13.3L/ 100km (21.3mpg).

I wanted a car that could stand the gruelling punishment of the Alpine Trial without losing a mark . . . a car that could win its class at Shelsley with ease . . . that could, with equal ease, lap Brooklands at 100 m.p.h. . . . carry off a Continental Grand Prix . . . win a string of coachwork awards . . . a true high performance car that wouldn't "cost the earth" . . .

. . *so I bought a* **Jaguar**

1½ LITRE MODELS FROM £295. 2½ LITRE, £375-£395. MANUFACTURERS: S.S. CARS LTD., HOLBROOK LANE, COVENTRY. LONDON SHOWROOMS: HENLYS LTD., DEVONSHIRE HOUSE, PICCADILLY, W.1

The SS2 (it was variously described as SSII and SS2 in the press and in SS Cars' advertising, but never consistently in either) continued to be made alongside the new SS Jaguars, but during 1936 it began to be phased out. It was almost the final fling of the ash-framed aluminium-panelled cars produced by Lyons, and for their final season suffered the indigity of a separate catalogue called "Sidevalve chassis for 1936." A total of 4254 cars were built on the SS1 chassis including the 23 SS90s. There were in all 1796 SS2s, and although neither model may have made a significant contribution to the technical evolution of the motor car, they certainly added to its aesthetic development. The long bonnet, tall engine, and low roofline generated by the super-sports cars of the era was brought into the popular domain.

Often euphemistically described as "overbodied", meaning too heavy, the SS2's competition record is sparse, although Norman Black, a notable racing driver of the era, did compete in the 1934 Alpine Rally in a factory-owned car but spoiled any chances of success by oversleeping on the fifth day and failing to start.

BODY
Saloon; 2-doors; 4-seats; 1028kg (2268lb).

ENGINE
4-cylinders, in line; front; 63.5 x 106mm, 1343cc [1608cc]; compr 6.0:1; 23.9kW (32bhp), [28.3kW (38bhp)] @ 4000rpm; 17.8kW/L (23.8bhp/L)[17.6kW/L (23.6bhp/L)].

ENGINE STRUCTURE
Side valve; 2-valves per cylinder; chain-driven camshaft; aluminium cylinder head; cast iron block; 3-bearing crankshaft; RAG carburettor; water cooled.

TRANSMISSION
Rear wheel drive; 4-speed gearbox, synchromesh 2,3,4; final drive 5.43:1.

CHASSIS DETAILS
Steel chassis with coachwork body; front suspension semi-elliptic leaf springs; rear suspension, semi-elliptic leaf springs; mechanical brakes; Marles Weller cam and lever steering; 54.6L (12 Imp gal) (14.4 US gal) fuel tank; tyres 4.75 x 18in.

DIMENSIONS
Wheelbase 264.2cm (104in), front track 118cm (46.5in), rear track 118cm (46.5in), ground clearance 17.8cm (7in), turning circle 11.88m (39ft), length 416.6cm (164in), width 142.2cm (56in).

PERFORMANCE
Maximum speed 97.9kph (61mph); standing quarter mile 27sec; 43kg/kW (32kg/bhp) [36.2kg/kW (27kg/bhp); average fuel consumption 10.5L/100km (27mpg).

SS Jaguar 2664cc coachbuilt cars 1936-1940

It was a measure of the respect that the SS Jaguar attained in the 1930s, that the chassis became popular with a number of bespoke coachbuilders of the sort that Swallow had been in the 1920s. Captain John Black, managing director of Standard which was responsible for so much of SS Cars' structural work, commissioned a Mulliner limousine with division for his wife in the "razor-edge" style popular with Bentleys of the 1930s. S H (Sammy) Newsome the Coventry SS agent, who not only competed successfully in rallies such as the Alpine and the RAC but also took an SS100 up Shelsley Walsh in 43 sec, recognised their burgeoning reputation with an elegant drophead coupe based on the SS100.

It was along the lines of the contemporary Atalanta, with enclosed rear wheels, and its body was built by Avon, once a Swallow rival. The Swiss coachbuilder Tuscher of Zurich produced a convertible top strongly reminiscent of the Mercedes-Benz autobahn cruisers popular on the Continent.

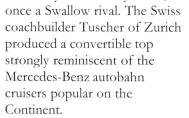
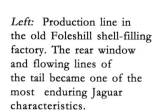

Left: Production line in the old Foleshill shell-filling factory. The rear window and flowing lines of the tail became one of the most enduring Jaguar characteristics.
Right: Door trim is applied to saloon bodies before they are mounted on their chassis.

SS 100 3485cc 1938-1941

The new 3½-litre engine produced for the 1938 model year saloons was also fitted into the 2-seater, producing a sports car that was not only among the fastest of its day, but was destined to become a classic. The SS100 accelerated to 60mph (approx 100kph) in just over the benchmark 10 sec regarded in the 1990s as marking the difference between lively and leisurely. In 1938 it was extremely fast. Its top speed of 100mph (160.9kph) (or something very close – contemporary road testers disagreed with one another) was also notable at a time when many cars were hard-pressed to reach 80mph (128.7kph).

The SS100 was not a specialist sports car that could scarcely be used as practical transport, as some Frazer Nash or Aston-Martin neo-racers were. It had a close-fitting hood and strong sidescreens; it was comfortably upholstered and carpeted, and there was space behind the seats for luggage. The ride was firm. *The Motor* felt sure the shock absorbers would need to be slackened off for driving over pavé, ..."because the car normally has a very stiff feeling, which settles down into a pleasant motion when higher speeds are reached."

BODY
Open sports; 2-seats; 2-door; weight 1180.7kg (2603lb).

ENGINE
6-cylinders, in line; front; 125 x 110mm; 3485cc; compr 7:1; 93.2kW (125bhp) @ 4250rpm; 26.6kW/L (35.7bhp/L).

ENGINE STRUCTURE
Ohv; 2-valves per cylinder; Weslake cast iron cylinder head; cast iron cylinder block; 7-bearing crankshaft; 2 1½in SU carburettors; water cooled.

TRANSMISSION
Rear wheel drive; single dry plate clutch; manual 4-speed gearbox, synchromesh on 2,3,4; spiral bevel final drive .

CHASSIS DETAILS
Steel with coachwork body; front suspension beam axle, semi-elliptic leaf springs, rear live axle, semi-elliptic leaf springs; rod operated drum brakes front & rear; 68.2L (15 Imp gal) (18 US gal)fuel tank; 5.50 x 18 tyres.

DIMENSIONS
Wheelbase 264cm (104in); front track133cm (52.5in); rear track 137cm (54in); ground clearance 13.97cm (5.5in); turning circle 11m (36ft); length 389cm (153in); width 160cm (63in); height 137cm (54in).

PERFORMANCE
Maximum speed 157.9 kph (98.1mph); acceleration 0-96kph (0-60mph) 10.4sec; standing quarter mile 17.1sec; 12.7kg/kW (9.4kg/bhp); average fuel consumption 13.5L/100km (21mpg).

Right: **The SS's greatest virtue was its flexibility and vigorous performance in top gear. Its swiftness from 30mph (48.3kph) to 50mph (80.5kph) would be praiseworthy in any age.**

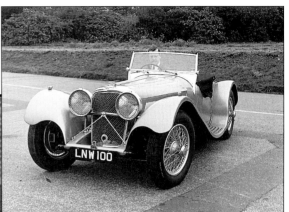

SS 100 coupe prototype Earls Court show car 1938

According to the late Andrew Whyte, the notable Jaguar historian, it was correct to call the SS100 an SS Jaguar 100, or even a Jaguar 100 after Jaguar Cars Ltd was registered in November 1937. SS Cars Ltd continued as an operating entity until 9 April, 1945. The policy of not becoming deeply involved in motor racing may have disappointed Brooklands, but while others over-reached themselves financially in it, prudent Lyons actively discouraged racing when he knew his cars would be outclassed.

His talent for publicity surfaced at the 1938 London motor show, the second held at the new Earls Court exhibition centre. The 100 had altered little in appearance for three years, and a show surprise would create fresh interest. Bugatti's Atalante was the archetypal Continental coupe and SS's response was a two-seat closed body with rounded wings, enclosed rear wheels, and a flowing tail which included luggage boot and spare wheel. The cockpit was beautifully furnished.

Only one was ever made. It had served its purpose. It enriched and enhanced Jaguar as much as any racing success.

BODY
Coupe; 2-doors; 2-seats.

ENGINE
6-cylinders, in line; front; 125 x 110mm; 3485cc; compr 7:1; 93.2kW (125bhp) @ 4250rpm; 26.6kW/L (35.7bhp/L).

ENGINE STRUCTURE
Ohv; 2-valves per cylinder; Weslake cast iron cylinder head; cast iron cylinder block; 7-bearing crankshaft; 2 1½in SU carburettors; water cooled.

TRANSMISSION
Rear wheel drive; single dry plate clutch; manual 4-speed gearbox, synchromesh on 2,3,4; spiral bevel final drive .

CHASSIS DETAILS
Steel with coachwork body; front suspension beam axle, semi-elliptic leaf springs, rear live axle, semi-elliptic leaf springs; rod operated drum brakes front & rear; 68.19L (15 Imp gal) (18 US gal) fuel tank; 5.50 x 18 tyres.

DIMENSIONS
Wheelbase 264cm (104in); front track133cm (52.5in); rear track 137cm (54in); ground clearance 13.97cm (5.5in); turning circle 11m (36ft); length 389cm (153in); width 160cm (63in).

PERFORMANCE
Maximum speed 160.5kph (100mph)approx; acceleration 0-100kph (62mph) 10.5sec approx; standing quarter mile 17.2sec approx.

Tommy Wisdom, motoring correspondent of the *Daily Herald*, enthused, "...beautiful car. Had I seen it at the Paris motor show I would have priced it at £1500. Mr Lyons tells me it is fixed at £595."

SS Jaguar 1½-litre steel saloon 1938-1939

The major innovation for the 1938 model year was the steel-bodied car. The company decided it had finally outgrown Swallow-style coachbuilding and panel-beating. It was simply too slow to keep up with the growing demand for the cars. Steel presswork was still an inexact science, but a structure made up of small spot-welded portions could be strong and more consistent than the coachbuilt job. It was not unusual for two hand-wrought bodies to be quite unalike.

SS commissioned its own chassis for the new range of 1½, 2½, and 3½-litre saloons in two wheelbase lengths (112.5in [285.75cm] for the 1½). Standard delivered engines and transmissions to the Holbrook Lane SS factory. Steel framed and panelled bodies were announced at the 1937 motor show, but their introduction was problematical, and it was spring 1938 before full production. Doors and roof were made by Rubery Owen, quarter panels by Sankey of Wellington, the bonnet and boot by Pressed Steel. Lead-loading (filling blemishes with molten lead) made a seamless, elegant car that embodied the composure of a Derby Bentley with the dash of a Delage.

BODY
Saloon; 4-doors; 4-seats; weight 1321kg (2912lb).

ENGINE
4-cylinders, in line; front; compr 7.2:1; 73 x 106mm; 1776cc; 48.5kW (65bhp) @ 4600rpm; 32.3kW/L (43.3bhp/L).

ENGINE STRUCTURE
Overhead pushrod; 3-bearing counter-weighted crankshaft; aluminium pistons; cast iron cylinder head, lozenge combustion chambers; chrome-iron cylinder block; downdraught SU carburettor; coil ignition; water cooled.

TRANSMISSION
Rear wheel drive; clutch single dry plate; 4-speed manual gearbox, synchromesh on 2,3,4; hypoid bevel final drive; 19.18:1.

CHASSIS DETAILS
Steel with steel body; front suspension beam axle, semi-elliptic leaf springs, rear live axle, semi-elliptic leaf springs; rod-operated drum brakes front & rear; Burman Douglas steering; 63.6l (14 Imp gal) (16.8 US gal) fuel tank; 5.25 tyres, 18in rims.

DIMENSIONS
Wheelbase 286cm (112.5in); front track 140cm (55in); rear track 140cm (55in); ground clearance 17.78cm (7in); turning circle 11.6m (38.ft); length 460cm (181in); width 168cm (66in); height 152cm (60in).

PERFORMANCE
Maximum speed 115.9kph (72mph); acceleration 0-96kph (0-60 mph) 25.1sec; 27.2kg/kW (20.3kg/bhp); average fuel consumption 11.2L/100km (25.3mpg).

Right: Drophead Coupe assembly. Pressed steel body panels were initially difficult to put in place, leading to much hand-finishing.

SS Jaguar 2½-litre steel saloon 1938-1940

The new cars were 5in (12.7cm) longer and the track 2in (5.08cm) wider, the 2½ and 3½-litre cars' longer bonnet accommodating the two extra cylinders. The radiator with its large flat filler cap underwent a further widening and reproportioning, and the larger cars had big Lucas P100 headlights. Large areas of chrome were in vogue, and besides the headlamps the front was adorned with twin horns and two so-called passlamps. Since there was more room in the back, the rear doors were made wider, and the front wings swept down towards an apron which filled the gap between the front of the chassis members. The spare wheel was moved from the sidemount to under the luggage compartment, and the boot lid carried the reassuringly complete toolkit.

SS Cars was profitable, making £24,209 in 1935, £27,367 in 1936, and £34,292 for the year ending in July 1937. But a year later the production difficulties of the steel body saw profits fall by £12,000. Henlys, which sold half the firm's output, saw its profits decline from £56,700 to £38,000. Lyons blamed his suppliers, yet by the autumn motor show, production had recovered sufficiently for the firm to record its first 5,000-car year.

BODY
Saloon; 4-doors; 4-seats; weight 1600.3kg (3528lb).

ENGINE
6-cylinders, in line; front; 73 x 106mm; compr 7.6:1; 2663cc; 78.3kW (105bhp) @ 4600rpm approx; 31.3kW/L (42bhp/L).

ENGINE STRUCTURE
Ohv; pushrod operated valves; 2-valves per cylinder; aluminium pistons; cast iron detachable cylinder head, machined combustion chamber; chrome iron cylinder block; 7-bearing crankshaft; twin SU carburettors with thermo-electric starting carburettor; Lucas coil & distributor ignition; water cooled.

TRANSMISSION
Rear wheel drive; clutch single dry plate; 4-speed manual gearbox, synchromesh on 2,3,4; hypoid bevel ratio 4.5:1.

CHASSIS DETAILS
Steel with steel body; front & rear suspension beam axle, semi-elliptic leaf springs; rod-operated drum brakes front & rear; Bluemel Douglas steering; 63.6L (14Imp gal) (16.8US gal); 5.50 tyres, 18in rims.

DIMENSIONS
Wheelbase 305cm (120in); front track 142cm (56in); rear track 142cm (56in); ground clearance 17.8cm (7in); turning circle 11.6m (38ft); length 472cm (186in); width 168cm (66in); height 155cm (61in).

PERFORMANCE
Maximum speed 140.1kph (87mph); kph (mph) @ 1000rpm; acceleration 0-96kph (0-60mph) 17 sec; standing quarter mile 20.6sec; 20.4kg/kW (15.2kg/bhp); average fuel consumption 14.9L/100km (19mpg).

SS Jaguar 3½-litre steel saloon 1938-1940

The cross-bracing of the new chassis for 1938 was by transverse members rather than in the form of an X, and it was a stiffer affair with box-sections 6in (15.2cm) deep, quite unlike that of the old SS. It still had half-elliptic springing but even here there were refinements, and they were mounted on sliding trunnions with self-lubricating sliding-roller anchorages at the back. The brakes remained mechanical however; SS was rather slow in accepting hydraulic operation. The drumming noises expected of a steel body were taken seriously and much sound-deadening was added with thick underfelt in the bulkhead, beneath the back seat, and ½in (1.27cm) under the carpet.

The new 3½-litre engine was not completely new, although it was sufficiently so to be promoted as such. The bottom end still ran on seven splendid main bearings, the top was an overhead valve adaptation by Weslake although the head material was cast iron, not light weight aluminium. The old RAG carburettors were long gone, and SS used two 1½in SUs for the 3½ bolted directly to the head.

BODY
Saloon; 4-doors; 4-seats;weight 1600.3kg (3528lb).

ENGINE
6-cylinders, in line; front; 82 x 110mm; 3485cc; compr 7.2:1; 93.2kW (125bhp) @ 4500rpm approx; 26.6kW/L (35.7bhp/L).

ENGINE STRUCTURE
Ohv; 2 large-diameter valves, pushrod operated; cast iron cylinder head; chrome-iron cylinder block; 7-bearing counter-weighted crankshaft; 2 SU 1.5in carburetters with automatic electronically controlled choke; forced lubrication distributor ignition; water cooled.

TRANSMISSION
Rear wheel drive; single dry plate clutch; 4-speed manual gearbox, synchromesh on 2,3,4; hypoid bevel final drive, ratio 4.25:1

CHASSIS DETAILS
Box-section steel with steel body; suspension semi-elliptic leaf springs front & rear; rod-operated drum brakes front & rear; Burman Douglas worm-and-nut steering; 63.6L (14 Imp gal) (16.8US gal) fuel tank; 5.50 tyres, 18in rims.

DIMENSIONS
Wheelbase 305cm (120in); front track 137.2cm (54in); rear track 142cm (56in); turning circle 11.6m (38ft); length 472cm (186in); width 168cm (66in); height 155cm (61in).

PERFORMANCE
Max speed 148kph (91.8mph); acceleration 0-80kph (50mph) 9sec; standing quarter mile 19.4sec; 17.2kg/kW (12.8kg/bhp); average fuel consumption 14.1-15.7L/100km (18-20mpg).

Above: The facia had
a symmetrical layout that
was to remain familiar with
Jaguars through the years,
with large speedometer
and rev counter on each
side of a group of
small instruments.
Right & far right: Broad chrome
stripe and war-time blackout
hoods date this car.

SS Jaguar 1½, 2½, and 3½-litre drophead coupe 1938-1939

The new strong frame brought about an open 4-seater but not along the lines of the cutaway door SS1. It followed the example of the 1935 Drophead Coupe, built more for comfort than speed. Open 2-seaters were essentially sports cars, but 4-seaters with sketchy hoods and small back seats came close. D H Coupes, by contrast, were expected to be as comfortable as saloons when the top was up, elegant when it was down, or furled in what was known as the "de ville" position. This exposed the chauffeur to the elements, leaving the occupants snug and dry in the back.

The new steel body was made differently from the saloon's. The dilemma of soft-top manufacturers, now that steel bodies gave beam strength to a car, was how to brace the structure once the roof was removed. The Jaguar needed all the stiffening it could get. It had two large doors and reverted to wood underpinnings for the rear of the body, providing a basis for the soft top, folding flush with the waistline. The hood was a marvellously substantial lined affair, filled with horsehair to insulate it almost as well as a saloon. It was also very private, with blind rear quarters and a tiny back window.

2½-litre Specifications

Body
Coupe; 2-doors; 4-seats; weight 1702kg (3752lb).

Engine
6-cylinders, in line; front; compr 6.9:1 or 7.6:1; 73 x 106mm; 2663cc; 78.3kW (105bhp) @ 4600rpm; 31.3kW/L (42bhp/L); 182.4Nm (18.8mkp) @ 2000rpm.

Engine Structure
Pushrod overhead valves; 2-valves per cylinder; overhead pushrod; chain-driven side camshaft; cast iron cylinder head and block; 7-bearing crankshaft; twin SU downdraught carburettors, water cooled.

Transmission
Rear wheel drive; single dry plate clutch; 4-speed manual gearbox, synchromesh on 2,3,4; hypoid bevel final drive, ratio 4.5:1.

Chassis Details
Steel with steel body; front and rear suspension beam axle, semi-elliptic leaf springs; rod-operated drum brakes front & rear; Burman Douglas worm-and nut steering; 63.6L (14 Imp gal) (16.8 US gal) fuel tank; 5.5 tyres, 18in rims.

Dimensions
Wheelbase 305cm (120in); front track 142cm (56in); rear track 142cm (56in); ground clearance 15.2cm (6in); turning circle 11.6m (38ft); length 472cm (186in); width 168cm (66in); height 152cm (60in).

Performance
Maximum speed 136.5kph (85mph); acceleration 0-96kph (0-60mph)17sec; 21.7kg/kW (16.2kg/bhp); average fuel consumption 14.9L/100km (19mpg).

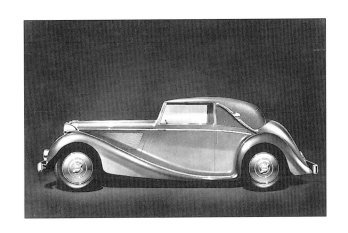

Jaguar 1½-litre saloon 1946-1949

Jaguar publicised its 1940 range in July 1939, more in hope than with any conviction that it would ever go into production. There were only detail changes, but among them was what was cheerfully described as "air conditioning" – literally true in that it did change the condition of the incoming air, but only to heat it.

When production resumed in 1945, nothing as frivolous as a drophead coupe was contemplated. Getting it under way at all was difficult enough and a statement of September 1945 said that, "...for the moment closed bodies only are available and the 100-series of open sports cars is temporarily out of production."

The 1776cc engine was still manufactured by Standard, and improvements were made to the manifolding. The biggest engineering change was the 1940 innovation of a Salisbury hypoid bevel back axle. Its pinion lay below the crown wheel centre, so it had the effect of lowering the propellor shaft by around 2in (5.08cm), which in turn gave a lower transmission tunnel. The extra room inside removed one of the disadvantages of the car's low build.

BODY
Saloon; 4-doors; 4-seats; weight 1270kg (2800lb).

ENGINE
4-cylinders, in line; front; 73 x 106mm; 1776cc; compr 7.5:1; 12.23hp; 48.5kW (65bhp) @ 4500rpm; 28.5kW/L (38.2bhp/L); 130Nm (13.4mkp) @ 2500rpm.

ENGINE STRUCTURE
Pushrod ohv; 2-valves per cylinder; chain-driven side camshaft; cast iron cylinder head and block; 3-bearing crankshaft; single SU horizontal carburettor; Lucas coil ignition; water cooled.

TRANSMISSION
Rear wheel drive; single plate Borg and Beck clutch; 4-speed synchromesh gearbox; hypoid bevel final drive, ratio 4.86:1.

CHASSIS DETAILS
Steel chassis, pressed steel body; front and rear suspension with semi-elliptic leaf springs; front, bronze bush and trunnion; rear, Silentbloc; Luvax dampers; Burman-Douglas worm-and-nut steering; Girling drum brakes front & rear; 63.6L (14Imp gal) (16.8US gal) fuel tank; 5.25 tyres, 18in rims.

DIMENSIONS
Wheelbase 285.75cm (112.5in); front track 132.1cm (52in); rear track 139.7cm (55in); ground clearance 17.8cm (7in); turning circle 11.6m (38ft); length 436.9cm (172in); width 166.4cm (65.5in); height 152.4cm (60in).

PERFORMANCE
Maximum speed 115kph (71.7mph); 27.6kph (17.2mph) @ 1000rpm; acceleration 0-96kph (62mph) 25.1sec; 26.2kg/kW (19.5kg/bhp); average fuel consumption 10.5-11.3L/100km (25-27mpg).

Right: The 1½-litre was the most numerous model of the immediate post-war period, 11952 being made between 1940 and 1948.
Below: Jaguar was one of the first manufacturers to standardise hypoid bevel final drive with the pinion well below the centre-line of the crown wheel, lowering the propellor shaft by 2in (5.1cm).

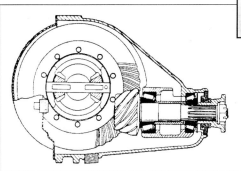

VA, VB

Jaguar's activities between 1939 and 1945 included making 10,000 sidecars for the military, including specialised ones for carrying RAF cameras and parachutes, before the sidecar business was sold in 1944. The firm worked on aircraft including Whitley and Stirling bombers, De Havilland Mosquitoes, Spitfires, and Lancasters. It also made some 50,000 trailers ranging from small two-wheeled lightweights to 6-ton affairs for carrying aircraft.

The VA and VB were experimental lightweight 4-seat personnel carriers designed to be dropped by parachute. The first was VA which had an air-cooled JAP V-twin engine at the back. The specification did not run to four wheel drive so it was mounted over the rear driving wheels to help traction on muddy ground.

The monocoque body was made from folded sheet steel and suspension was independent all round.

A more powerful development was VB which was built with a side-valve Ford 10 engine at the front, driving the rear wheels. The supple long-travel springing was by independent by coil springs with double wishbones at the front and swing-axles at the rear. To improve grip twin rear wheels could be used, which were carried as spares on the back. In the event aircraft were developed which were big enough to hold full-sized Jeeps, so the requirement to build VB did not arise.

Above, and middle right:
Severely practical
lines of VA and
(upper facing page) VB.

Jaguar 2½-litre saloon 1946-1949

By the time the range got into production in the autumn of 1945, Jaguar had undergone substantial change. John Black, believing the austere post-war dogma that a car company should concentrate on only one model, offered Lyons the production machinery for the 6-cylinder engines. Lyons could scarcely believe his luck. "Within a few days I sent transport to collect the plant and sent our cheque in payment for it." Black's Standard Vanguard was not a big success, while Jaguar went from strength to strength and exports to America began in earnest.

In an effort to improve braking, the post-war range had big Millenite cast iron drums with Girling two-leading shoes to give more even wear and better resistance to fade. Yet although hydraulic brakes were now widespread, Jaguar stuck with mechanical until the end of the model's life. A hydro-mechanical system of pull-rods for the back, and hydraulic operation for the front brakes was proposed but never went into production. The spare wheel was still below the boot floor and the Clayton heater had demisting ducts to the windscreen.

BODY
Saloon; 4-doors; 4-seats; weight 1600kg (3528lb).

ENGINE
6-cylinders, in line; front; 73 x 106mm; 2663cc; compr. 7.6:1; 19.84hp; 76.1kW (102bhp) @ 4600rpm; 30.4kW/L (40.8bhp/L); 182.4Nm (18.8mkp)@ 2500rpm.

ENGINE STRUCTURE
Pushrod overhead valve; 2-valves per cylinder; chain-driven camshaft; cast iron cylinder head and block; 7-bearing crankshaft; twin SU horizontal carburettors; Lucas coil ignition; water cooled.

TRANSMISSION
Rear wheel drive; single plate Borg and Beck clutch; 4-speed synchromesh gearbox; hypoid bevel final drive, ratio 4.55:1.

CHASSIS DETAILS
Steel chassis, pressed steel body; front and rear suspension with semi-elliptic leaf springs; front, bronze bush and trunnion; rear, Silentbloc; Luvax dampers; Burman-Douglas worm-and-nut steering; Girling drum brakes front & rear; 63.6L (14Imp gal) (16.8US gal) fuel tank; 5.25 tyres, 18in rims.

DIMENSIONS
Wheelbase 304.8cm (120in); front track 137.2cm (54in); rear track 142.2cm (56in); ground clearance 17.8cm (7in); turning circle 11.6m (38ft); length 472.4cm (186in); width 167.6cm (66in); height 154.9cm (61in).

PERFORMANCE
Maximum speed 139.6kph (87mph); 30.2kph (18.8mph) @ 1000rpm; acceleration 0-100kph (62mph) 19sec; 21kg/kW (39.2kg/bhp); average fuel consumption 14.9L/100km (19mpg).

Right: Non-standard mesh grille on Col Rixon Bucknall's 2½-litre, to assist cooling on mountain passes.
Far right: W (Bill) Rankin, Public Relations & Advertising Manager for SS and later Jaguar.

Jaguar 2½-litre drophead coupe 1947-1948

Introduced for the 1940 model year, the 2½-litre drophead coupe was priced at £415. Reintroduced in December 1947 in time for the first shipment of Jaguars for America, the price was inflated with the addition of purchase tax to £1189. Only 104 were built. Drophead customers were more likely to go for the 3½-litre at £1263 or its dollar equivalent, and 560 of them were made before the Mark IV (as the model became known retrospectively) was replaced by the Mark V. Left hand drive cars were introduced in 1947 (the first a 1½-litre), and between 1946 and 1949 35% of production went for export. Some concessions were made to foreign customers, such as bumper over-riders, fitted by US dealers if they had been overlooked by the factory.

Wire wheels were standard. American cars usually had black or polished aluminium Ace wheel discs, which could be painted to match the car at extra cost. Distinguishing colours for the radiator badges changed from pre-war pale grey enamel for 1½-litre cars, cream for 2½-litres and black for 3½s, to post-war pale lilac and black lettering for 1½s, cream and chome lettering for 2½s, and black and chrome for 3½s.

BODY
Coupe; 2-doors; 4-seats; weight 1730kg (3814lb).

ENGINE
6-cylinders, in line; front; 73 x 106mm; 2663cc; compr. 7.6:1; 19.8hp; 76.1kW (102bhp) @ 4600rpm; 30.4kW/L (40.8bhp/L); 182.4Nm (18.8mkp)@ 2500rpm.

ENGINE STRUCTURE
Pushrod overhead valve; 2-valves per cylinder; chain-driven camshaft; cast iron cylinder head and block; 7-bearing crankshaft; twin SU horizontal carburettors; Lucas coil ignition; water cooled.

TRANSMISSION
Rear wheel drive; single plate Borg and Beck clutch; 4-speed synchromesh gearbox; hypoid bevel final drive, ratio 4.55:1.

CHASSIS DETAILS
Steel chassis, pressed steel body; front and rear suspension with semi-elliptic leaf springs; front, bronze bush and trunnion; rear, Silentbloc; Luvax dampers; Burman-Douglas worm-and-nut steering; Girling drum brakes front & rear; 63.6L (14Imp gal) (16.8US gal) fuel tank; 5.25 tyres, 18in rims.

DIMENSIONS
Wheelbase 304.8cm (120in); front track 137.2cm (54in); rear track 142.2cm (56in); ground clearance 17.8cm (7in); turning circle 11.6m (38ft); length 472.4cm (186in); width 167.6cm (66in); height 154.9cm (61in).

PERFORMANCE
Maximum speed 139.6kph (87mph); 30.2kph (18.8mph) @ 1000rpm; acceleration 0-100kph (62mph) 20.1sec; 22.7kg/kW (17kg/bhp); average fuel consumption 14.9L/100km (19mpg).

Jaguar 3½-litre saloon 1947-1949

The shape of the Jaguar was much as it had been in 1939, with detail improvements. Yet big headlamps, the Bentley look of the tall grille, the sweeping tail, and the subtle curve by the rear window made a Jaguar unmistakable. The engine was still a pushrod, the brakes more surprisingly perhaps still mechanical, and the front suspension still not independent although there had been some improvements in damping.

It was a quite large car by the standards of the time. According to an unusually equivocal *The Autocar*: "Sizeable though it is, this Jaguar can be accommodated in a private garage not of exceptional dimensions, though perhaps above the average." The testers of 1948 found that: "On a straightaway main road journey it is naturally seen at its best, and only the nature of the route and other traffic can prevent average speeds in the order of 50 miles in the hour." Performance figures of the 1940s were affected by the poor quality of "pool" petrol, and Jaguars could be specified with low-compression engines to take account of its low octane rating. Petrol rationing remained in Britain until June 1950, and "pool" petrol for a further three years.

BODY
Saloon; 4-doors; 4-seats; weight 1600kg (3528lb).

ENGINE
6-cylinders, in line; front; 82 x 110mm; 3485cc; compr. 6.75:1; 25.01hp; 93.2kW (125bhp) @ 4250rpm; 26.6kW/L (35.7bhp/L); 246.7Nm (25.4mkp) @ 2000rpm.

ENGINE STRUCTURE
Pushrod overhead valve; 2-valves per cylinder; chain-driven camshaft; cast iron cylinder head and block; 7-bearing crankshaft; twin SU horizontal carburettors; Lucas coil ignition; water cooled.

TRANSMISSION
Rear wheel drive; single plate Borg and Beck clutch; 4-speed synchromesh gearbox; hypoid bevel final drive, ratio 4.55:1.

CHASSIS DETAILS
Steel chassis, pressed steel body; front and rear suspension beam axle, semi-elliptic leaf springs;

front, bronze bush and trunnion; rear, Silentbloc; Luvax dampers; Burman-Douglas worm-and-nut steering; Girling drum brakes front & rear; 63.6L (14Imp gal) (16.8US gal) fuel tank; 5.50 x 18 tyres.

DIMENSIONS
Wheelbase 304.8cm (120in); front track 137.2cm (54in); rear track 142.2cm (56in); ground clearance 17.8cm (7in); turning circle 11.6m (38ft); length 472.4cm (186in); width 167.6cm (66in); height 154.9cm (61in).

PERFORMANCE
Maximum speed 146.1kph (91mph); acceleration 0-96kph (60mph) 16.8sec; 32.1kph (20mph) @ 1000rpm; 17.2kg/kW (12.8kg/bhp); average fuel consumption 15.7-17.2L/100km (16-18mpg) .

Jaguar 3½-litre drophead coupe 1947-1948

External landau irons lent the drophead coupe an air of grandeur rare in the gloomy post-war era of austerity and parsimony. The walnut facia, the leather upholstery, the mellow air of a gentleman's club all added to Jaguar's coachbuilt image, in an era when the custom of buying a chassis and having one's coachbuilder construct a body on it was fast ebbing away.

Taking the top down was not a job undertaken lightly, and as American writer Rick O'Kane put it, "...something you wouldn't want to do twice in the same afternoon." Doing it single-handed involved a lot of walking round the car to fasten and unfasten things or push and pull at thick layers of fabric. O'Kane found the disadvantages of restricted visibility. "The padded inside of the top looms as darkly as the universe, effectively blocking out about 180 degrees of fellow motorists. If you're parked on the left, the only safe way to get across from the kerb is to get out, look, wait for the traffic to clear completely then quickly get back in the car and drive away before anything else comes."

BODY
Coupe; 2-doors; 4-seats; weight 1730kg (3814lb).

ENGINE
6-cylinders, in line; front; 82 x 110mm; 3485cc; compr. 6.75:1; 25.01hp; 93.2kW (125bhp) @ 4250rpm; 26.6kW/L (35.7bhp/ L); 246.7Nm (25.4mkp) @ 2000rpm.

ENGINE STRUCTURE
Pushrod overhead valve; 2-valves per cylinder; chain-driven camshaft; cast iron cylinder head and block; 7-bearing crankshaft; twin SU horizontal carburettors; Lucas coil ignition; water cooled.

TRANSMISSION
Rear wheel drive; single plate Borg and Beck clutch; 4-speed synchromesh gearbox; hypoid bevel final drive, ratio 4.55:1.

CHASSIS DETAILS
Steel chassis, pressed steel body; front and rear suspension beam axle, semi-elliptic leaf springs; front, bronze bush and trunnion; rear, Silentbloc; Luvax dampers; Burman-Douglas worm-and-nut steering; Girling drum brakes front & rear; 63.6L (14Imp gal) (16.8US gal) fuel tank; 5.50 x 18 tyres.

DIMENSIONS
Wheelbase 304.8cm (120in); front track 137.2cm (54in); rear track 142.2cm (56in); ground clearance 17.8cm (7in); turning circle 11.6m (38ft); length 472.4cm (186in); width 167.6cm (66in); height 154.9cm (61in).

PERFORMANCE
Maximum speed 146.1kph (91mph); acceleration 0-96kph (60mph) 18sec; 32.1kph (20mph) @ 1000rpm; 18.6kg/kW (13.8kg/bhp); average fuel consumption 15.7-17.2L/100km (16-18mpg) .

Gardner MG special with 4-cylinder XK engine 1948

In September 1948 a 2.0-litre 4-cylinder Jaguar engine propelled Lieut Col A T G Gardner's streamlined record-breaking car to over 176mph (109.3kph) on a Belgian Autoroute. The engine was reputed to date back to wartime Coventry when office staff took regular turns to 'fire-watch', report factory fires following air raids. When there were no raids it could be a long night doing nothing, so senior staff talked about an engine Jaguar might build after the war. It would have to sound and look like a racing engine yet be fit for a luxury car.

The reality was slightly different. The engine was a secret project of engineering staff in the later stages of the war. But diverting resources from war-work might have been thought unpatriotic, so the inspiration for the engine was attributed to the fire-watching sessions. A 1360cc 4-cylinder with two overhead camshafts was developed known as the XF, followed by the XG, a cross-pushrod design like the BMW based on the Standard 1776cc block. They were succeeded by the XJ 2.0-litre twin overhead cam used by Gardner in his special, formerly the MG Ex135, to break 2.0-litre class records.

BODY
Single-seater; lightweight tubular framework with formers and aluminium panelling.

ENGINE
4-cylinders, in line; front; 80.5mm x 98mm, 1995cc; compr 10:1; 108.9kW (146bhp) @ 6000rpm; 54.6kW/L (73.2bhp/L).

ENGINE STRUCTURE
Twin chain-driven ohc; 2-valves per cylinder; aluminium cylinder head; cast iron block; 5-bearing crankshaft; 2 SU carburettors; water cooled.

TRANSMISSION
Rear wheel drive; 4-speed gearbox; offset propellor shaft; various axle ratios.

CHASSIS DETAILS
Steel channel-section chassis; front suspension beam axle, semi elliptic springs; rear live axle with semi-elliptic springs; drum brakes on rear wheels only modified from Eyston's MG Ex 135 and Harton's offset-bodied MG Magnette.

PERFORMANCE
Maximum speed 283.64kph (176.69mph)with XJ engine.

Right: When Nuffield refused funds to subsidise record-breaking after the war, Gardner called the MG simply the Gardner record car, installed the Jaguar engine and reached 283.64kph (176.69mph) at Jabbeke in September 1948.

Jaguar Mark V 2½-litre saloon 1948-1951

The demands of export markets were apparent when the new luxury range made its appearance. Big bumpers and independent front suspension by torsion bars were combined with few compromises to the established Jaguar line. The sweeping wings remained, so did the long curved luggage boot, and the distinctive turn of the rear window echoed subtly in the shape of the side windows. Lyons's styling skill was well-tested with the Mark V. He had full-sized mock-ups set up behind the factory or taken to his home, where he fine-tuned them until he got exactly what he wanted. He knew his clientele. Interiors were unadulterated luxury, and although the free-standing headlamps were gone, the cars had a well-bred air that was exactly right for the buyers coming forward for a luxury car at a relatively moderate price.

William Heynes had long been an admirer of Citroën engineering, so Jaguar's first independent front suspension was based on low-stress torsion bars. There was no 1½-litre. The last 4-cylinder car was made in the spring of 1949, marking the end of the best part of two decades' association between Jaguar and Standard.

BODY
Saloon; 4-doors; 4-seats; weight 1676.5kg (3696lb).

ENGINE
6-cylinders, in line; front; 73 x 106mm; compr 7.3:1; 2663cc; 76.1kW (102bhp) @ 4600rpm; 30.4kW/L (40.8bhp/L).

ENGINE STRUCTURE
Ohv operated by pushrods; 2-valves per cylinder; counter-weighted 2½in diam crankshaft in 7 steel-backed bearings; cast iron cylinder head and block; twin SU carburettors with electrically controlled automatic choke; water cooled.

TRANSMISSION
Rear wheel drive; clutch 9in diam single dry plate; 4-speed manual gearbox, synchromesh on 2,3,4; hypoid bevel final drive, ratio 4.55:1.

CHASSIS DETAILS
Box-section with steel bodywork; independent front suspension with wishbones & torsion bar springs, hydraulic dampers, anti-sway bars; rear semi-elliptic leaf springs; hydraulic dampers; hydraulic 12in. dia. drum brakes front & rear; Burman worm & nut steering; 63.6L (14 Imp gal) (16.8 US gal) fuel tank; 6.70 tyres, 16in rims.

DIMENSIONS
Wheelbase 305cm (120in); front track 142cm (56in); rear track 146cm (57.5in); ground clearance 19cm (7.5in); turning circle 11.3m (37ft); length 476cm (187.5in); width 174cm (68.5in); height 159cm (62.5in).

PERFORMANCE
Maximum speed 139.7kph (87mph); 29.1kph (18.1mph) @ 1000rpm; acceleration 0-96kph (60mph) 17sec; standing quarter mile 20.6sec; 22kg/kW (16.4kg/bhp); average fuel consumption 14.9L/100km (19mpg).

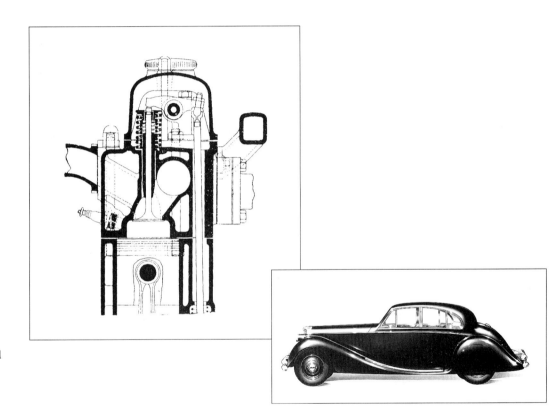

Right: Last
in line. Harry
Weslake's pushrod
overhead valve
conversion saw
service for the
last time in the
Mark V.

Jaguar Mark V 3½-litre saloon 1948-51

The Mark V saw the last of the venerable pushrod 7-bearing 6-cylinder, whose design roots went back 20 years to the original side-valve. In service for 14 years with overhead valves, it had been improved in detail, and with his keen eye for under-bonnet beauty, Lyons had the exhaust manifolding finely stove-enamelled.

The Mark V introduced a new substantial chassis frame with box-section side members, independent front suspension, and massive bumpers to cope with export market parking-by-ear. The original plan included the XK engine as well, but getting such a revolutionary new power unit into production at all stretched Jaguar to the utmost, although it scarcely mattered since none of its competitors had anything remotely as good. A new chassis, new engine and new body would have been too much to ask, so the Mark V was an interim model, while development of the Mark VII (there was no VI) proceeded at a pace the company could afford. The Mark V remained in production until June 1951, and proved to be a vital link between a traditional Jaguar with wings and running-boards and an upright old-style radiator, and the full-width shape of things to come.

BODY
Saloon; 4-doors; 4-seats; weight 1676.5kg (3696lb).

ENGINE
6-cylinders, in line; front; 82 x 106mm; 3485cc; compr 7.3:1; 93.2kW (125bhp) @ 4250rpm; 26.6kW/L (35.7bhp/L); 246.7Nm (25.4mkp) @ 2000rpm.

ENGINE STRUCTURE
Ohv operated by pushrods; counterweighted 2½in diam; 7-bearing crankshaft; cast iron cylinder head and block; twin SU carburettors with electrically controlled automatic choke; water cooled.

TRANSMISSION
Rear wheel drive; clutch 9in dia single dry plate; 4-speed manual gearbox, synchromesh on 2,3,4; hypoid bevel final drive, 4.3:1.

CHASSIS DETAILS
Box-section with steel bodywork; Suspension front independent with wishbones & torsion bar springs, hydraulic dampers, anti-sway bars; rear semi-elliptic leaf springs; hydraulic dampers; hydraulic 12in diam drum brakes front & rear; Burman worm & nut steering; 63.6L (14 Imp gal) (16.8 US gal) fuel tank; 6.70 tyres, 16 rims.

DIMENSIONS
Wheelbase 330.2cm (130in); front track 142cm (56in); rear track 146cm (57.5in); ground clearance 19.05cm (7.5in); turning circle 11.3m (37ft); length 476cm (187.5in); width 174cm (68.5in); height 159cm (62.5in).

PERFORMANCE
Maximum speed 146.1kph (91mph); 30.8kph (19.2mph) @ 1000rpm; acceleration 0-100kph (62mph)14.7sec; 18kg/kW (13.4kg/bhp); average fuel consumption 15.5L/100km (18.2mpg).

Jaguar **XK120** aluminium bodied prototypes 1948-1950

Two sports cars were designed for the new engines, an XK100 and an XK120, bodily alike the way the SS100 2½ and 3½-litre models were. They were intended less as a new product than as publicity vehicles for a new programme. Lyons sanctioned a limited production run of around 200 cars (240 were made), to be built on an abbreviated version of the chassis of the new Mk V range, and quickly evolved a sleek body which could be hand-beaten in aluminium for the short production run.

The 4-cylinder engine was discarded owing to an ineradicable vibration, and attention became focussed on the 6-cylinder, although it had to be increased in capacity owing to a shortage of pulling power. The stroke was increased and a classic engine was born. The XK120 was of such peerless beauty that it created a sensation at the first post-war motor show at Earls Court. Lyons's cautious judgement was that if public reaction was good he could put the car into production. If it was lukewarm, the XK120 would still fulfil its purpose and he could get on with introducing his new luxury saloon range.

BODY
Sports; 2-doors; 2-seats; weight 1295.4kg (2856lb).

ENGINE
6-cylinders, in line; front; 83 x 106mm; compr 8: 1 (opt 7:1 or 9:1); 3442cc; 119.3kW (160bhp) @ 5000rpm [comps 136.3kW (180bhp) @ 5300rpm]; 34.1kW/L (45.7bhp/L); 261.5Nm (27mkp) @ 2500rpm [comps 203Nm (20.9mkp) @ 4000rpm].

ENGINE STRUCTURE
Ohvs at 70deg, twin chain-driven ohc; aluminium cylinder head; cast iron block; aluminium alloy pistons, steel connecting rods, 7-bearing crankshaft; twin horizontal SU carburettors; water cooled.

TRANSMISSION
Rear wheel drive; 4-speed synchromesh gearbox; Borg and Beck single plate clutch, hypoid bevel final drive,opt ratios 3.27, 3.64, 3.92, 4.3, 4.56:1.

CHASSIS DETAILS
Box section steel, aluminium/ash frame body; ifs wishbones, torsion bar, anti-roll bar; rear susp live axle, semi-elliptic leaf springs; dampers lever arm Girling PV7 rear, Newton telescopic front; Lockheed hydraulic drum brakes, 2 LS front; Burman recirculating ball; 181.8L (40 Imp gal) (48 US gal) fuel tank; 6.00 tyres, 16in diam.

DIMENSIONS
Wheelbase 259.1cm (102in); track 129.5cm (51in); ground clearance 14cm (5.5in); turning circle 9.4m (31ft); length 398.8cm (157in); width 163.8cm (64.5in); height 97.8cm (38.5in).

PERFORMANCE
Max speed 200kph (124.6mph); 35.5kph (22.1mph) @ 1000rpm on 3.64:1 axle; 0-96kph (62mph) 9.8sec; standing quarter 17sec; 10.9kg/kW (8.1kg/bhp); av fuel cons 14.3L/100km (19.8mpg).

Above: Famous XK NUB120 tackles the Devil's Elbow between Glenshee and Braemar.

Right: The Jabbeke record car was restored to right-hand drive to win the newly instituted production car race at the Silverstone Daily Express meeting of 1949. Leslie Johnson leads from Peter Walker.

Jaguar **XK120** production 1949-1954

The chassis of the XK120 was not merely a shortened Mark V. There was no need for the larger car's cruciform bracing, which saved a great deal of weight, and the chassis was a simplified affair tapering in plan to a point adjacent to the driving seat, then kicking up over the rear axle. There was a wide cross-brace at the rear of the gearbox, with the Mark V's torsion bar independent front suspension and Burman recirculating ball steering. But tooling up for steel bodywork took time, and it was well into 1950 before production got under way.

Some of the old scepticism about Jaguar seemed to linger, and to deal with it a demonstration of the XK120's speed was mounted on 30 May 1949. A party of journalists flew on a chartered Sabena DC3 to watch R M V Sutton drive on the new Ostend-Jabbeke motorway at 132.596mph (213.386kph) with a small aero screen, and 126.594mph (203.727kph) with the hood and sidescreens erect. It was but a small subterfuge to flaunt the car as perfectly standard production. Strictly speaking it was, although it was not a production steel car like those which came out of the factory in 1950.

BODY

Sports 2-doors; 2-seats; weight 1321kg (2912lb).

ENGINE

6-cylinders, in line; front; 83 x 106mm; compr 8: 1 (optional 7:1 or 9:1); 3442cc; 119.3kW (160bhp) @ 5000rpm [special from 1951 136.3kW (180bhp) @ 5300rpm]; 34.1kW/L (45.7bhp/L); 261.5Nm (27 mkp) @ 2500rpm [special from 1951 203Nm (20.9mkp) @ 4000rpm].

ENGINE STRUCTURE

Ohvs at 70deg; twin chain-driven ohc; aluminium cylinder head; cast iron block; aluminium alloy pistons, steel connecting rods, 7-bearing crankshaft; twin horizontal SU carburettors; water cooled.

TRANSMISSION

Rear wheel drive; 4-speed synchromesh gearbox; Borg and Beck single plate clutch, hypoid bevel final drive,opt ratios 3.27, 3.64, 3.92, 4.3, 4.56:1 (early).

CHASSIS DETAILS

Steel construction; ifs, wishbones and torsion bar, anti-roll bar; rear susp live axle, semi-elliptic leaf springs; dampers lever arm Girling PV7 rear, Newton telescopic front; Lockheed hydraulic drum brakes, 2 LS front; Burman recirculating ball; 181.8L (40 Imp gal) (48 US gal) tank; 6.00 x 16 tyres.

DIMENSIONS

W/base 259.1cm (102in); front & rear track 129.5cm (51in); ground clearance 14cm (5.5in); turning circle 9.4m (31ft); length 398.8cm (157in); width 163.8cm (64.5in); height 97.8cm (38.5in).

PERFORMANCE

Max speed 200kph (124.6mph); 35.5kph (22.1mph) @ 1000rpm on 3.64:1 axle; 0-96kph (62mph) 10sec; standing quarter 17sec; 10.9kg/kW (8.1kg/bhp); av fuel cons 14.3L/100km (19.8mpg).

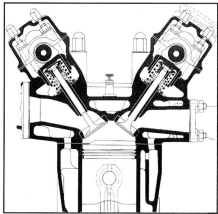

Above: Classic inclined valve twin ohc cylinder head of the XK engine. Jaguar engines followed the broad pattern for 50 years.

The aluminium car's light weight might not have made much difference to the top speed, but it certainly improved the acceleration of the cars prepared for the Production Car Race at the 1949 *Daily Express* Silverstone. They were driven by B Bira, Peter Walker, and Leslie Johnson, who won at the wheel of HKV 500, the Jabbeke car converted to right hand steering. It reappeared the following year painted red for the great Tazio Nuvolari to drive, and although he practised in the car, he was too ill to race it.

The XK120 nevertheless had a notable competition career. Stirling Moss showed his flourishing skill in the rain at Dundrod when he drove to victory in the 1950 Tourist Trophy. Two more XK120s were 2nd and 3rd. Johnny Claes, the Belgian band leader, won the endurance Marathon de la Route the Liège-Rome Liège rally. Ian Appleyard won the RAC Rally twice, although his four Alpine Cups were rather more praiseworthy. Four more owners won separate Alpine Cups in the rally that, more than any other at the time, brought celebrity status to Jaguar.

There were record-breaking runs, one by an early fixed-head coupe in 1952, which kept up 100mph for a whole week at the banked Montlhéry circuit near Paris (see p146). It was a fitting venue for quelling doubts, lingering perhaps among the old Brooklands set, about Jaguar as a manufacturer of splendid sports cars.

Its reputation was enhanced at Le Mans 1950, when Nick Haines came 12th in a fairly standard XK120; a sporting finish for a real sports car, even an aluminium-bodied example.

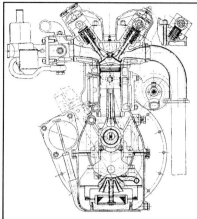

Left: Tall XK engine with shining cam covers filled the bonnet with excellent machinery.
Far right: William Lyons talks to one of motor racing's all-time great drivers. Tazio Nuvolari practised in a Jaguar XK120 for the Silverstone Production Car Race but was too ill to take part.
Right: Wire wheeled XK120 roadsters dispensed with rear spats.

Jaguar Mark V 3½-litre Drophead Coupe 1950-1951

Last in a long line of SS and Jaguar 4-seat convertibles with manually operated elaborately padded soft-tops and external hood-irons, this was virtually the end for the coachbuilder in Jaguar's post-war world. The collective skills that inaugurated Swallow Sidecars 28 years before had all but gone. Lacquered cellulosed and polished aluminium bodywork, with a framework of bent wood now seemed arcane, although Jaguars would still have a separate chassis for another five years. They were not yet made in sufficient numbers for a monocoque hull in pressed steel. Not that there was universal enthusiasm for such a change. It was still difficult to make a one-piece hull as quiet as a traditional car with a chassis. Jaguars were calm and refined by comparison with much of the competition and their most redoubtable rivals, Alvis, Armstrong Siddeley, Bentley, and Daimler still had chassis frames. The also-rans in terms of refinement, such as mass-production Wolseleys or Vauxhalls, reverberated disagreeably. The Drophead Coupe was an essential image-builder for the Californian market, where the bulk of them went, many gracing the homes of Hollywood.

BODY
Convertible; 2-doors; 4-seats; 1752.7kg (3864lb).

ENGINE
6-cylinders, in line; front; 82 x 106mm; 3485cc; compr 7.3:1; 93.2kW (125bhp) @ 4250rpm; 26.6kW/L (35.7bhp/L); 246.7Nm (25.4mkp) @ 2000rpm.

ENGINE STRUCTURE
Ohv operated by pushrods; counterweighted 2½in dia 7-bearing crankshaft; cast iron cylinder head and block; twin SU carburettors with electrically controlled automatic choke; water cooled.

TRANSMISSION
Rear wheel drive; clutch 9in dia single dry plate; 4-speed manual gearbox, synchromesh on 2,3,4; hypoid bevel final drive, 4.3:1.

CHASSIS DETAILS
Box-section with steel bodywork; Suspension front independent with wishbones & torsion bar springs, hydraulic dampers, anti-sway bars; rear semi-elliptic leaf springs; hydraulic dampers; hydraulic 12in diam drum brakes front & rear; Burman worm & nut steering; 63.6L (14 Imp gal) (16.8 US gal) fuel tank; 6.70 tyres, 16 rims.

DIMENSIONS
Wheelbase 305cm (120in); front track 142cm (56in); rear track 146cm (57.5in); ground clearance 19.05cm (7.5in); turning circle 11.3m (37ft); length 474.98cm (187in); width 174cm (68.5in); height 159cm (62.5in).

PERFORMANCE
Maximum speed 144.5kph (90mph); 30.8kph (19.2mph) @ 1000rpm; acceleration 0-96kph (60mph) 16secs; 18.8kg/kW (14kg/bhp); average fuel consumption 15.5L/100km (18.2mpg).

Emphasising the cars' suitability for export markets (Belgium the largest in the post-war period), was provision for a Radiomobile 100 set in the facia.

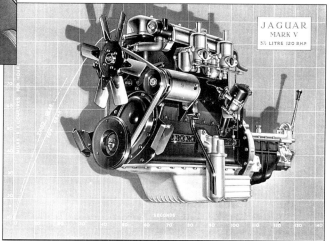

Jaguar Mark VII 1951-1954

From the moment of its introduction at the Earls Court motor show of 1950, the Mark VII was a triumph. It was a styling triumph because it captured the Jaguar vernacular perfectly with the re-entrant curve of the back window, the unmistakably good proportions, and the reworking of the traditional grille. It was a dynamic triumph because it handled better than any large saloon in America or anywhere else. It was a performance triumph with a top speed over 100mph (160kph) and acceleration to 60mph (96.55kph) in 12.5sec. It was a sales triumph when American dealers took $20,000,000's worth of orders at the New York motor show. It was even a competition triumph, with the Mark VII scoring some signal successes in production car racing, even though most of these were achieved with a handful of cars panelled not in steel but surreptitiously in aluminium.

The principal differences between the chassis of the Mark VII and the Mark V was that the engine was located some 7in (17.78cm) further forward in the chassis, and there was servo assistance, an important innovation, for the hydraulic brakes. The XK engine was

BODY
Saloon; 4-doors; 4/5-seats; weight 1752.7kg (3864lb).

ENGINE
6-cylinders, in line; front; 83 x 106mm; 3442cc; compr. 8:1; 119kW (160bhp) @ 5200rpm; 34.1kW/L (45.7bhp/L); 261.5Nm (27mkp) @ 2500rpm.

ENGINE STRUCTURE
Twin chain-driven ohc; 2-valves per cylinder; aluminium cylinder head; cast iron block; 7-bearing crankshaft; Lucas coil ignition; twin horizontal SU carburettors, water cooled.

TRANSMISSION
Rear wheel drive; single dry plate clutch; 4-speed manual gearbox, synchromesh on 2,3,4, or automatic 3-speed Borg-Warner; hypoid bevel final drive, ratio 4.3:1.

CHASSIS DETAILS
Box-section steel with pressed steel body; ifs by wishbones and torsion bars; hydraulic dampers, anti-roll bar; rear semi-elliptic leaf springs, hydraulic dampers; servo-assisted hydraulic 12in drum brakes front & rear; Burman re-circulating ball steering; 77.3L (17 Imp gal) (20.4 US gal) fuel tank; 6.70 tyres, 16in rims.

DIMENSIONS
Wheelbase 305cm (120in); front track 142.2cm (56in); rear track 146cm (57.5in); ground clearance 19cm (7.5in); turning circle 11.3m (37ft); length 499cm (196.5in); width 186.7cm (73.5in); height 160cm (63in).

PERFORMANCE
Maximum speed 168.4kph (104.6mph); acceleration 0-96kph (0-60mph)12.6sec; 31.1kph (19.35mph) @ 1000rpm; standing quarter mile 19.3sec; 14.7kg/kW (11kg/bhp); average fuel cons 14.9L/100km (19mpg).

The motoring public and the press of the world the competition drivers and suppliers acclaim

another **JAGUAR** *year*

Jaguar Mark VII 1951-1954 (2)

already 3in (7.62cm) longer than the pushrod and the Mark VII's radiator was 8in (20.32cm) further forward. The new car was altogether longer and wider, with 3in more legroom than its predecessor, and 5in (12.7cm) more elbow-room, thanks to the body extending out to the full width of the car. The rear seats were well ahead of the wheel arches and there was a huge luggage boot 30in (76.2cm) deep and 48in (121.9cm) long in the shapely tail. Two capacious fuel tanks had their own fillers in the rear wings.

The figured walnut of the facia, deep pile of the carpets, fine leather upholstery, and exquisite detailing that extended to subtle purple instrument lighting, contributed to well-rounded excellence.

The Mark VII was one of the most notable cars of the decade and proved pivotal for Jaguar at its introductory price of an astonishing £988 before tax. It put the company firmly in the forefront of the luxury car market, although it took the best part of two years to get it into production. The complexity of the body meant it could no longer be made up from a large number of small pressings and hand-finished to a high standard. The Pressed Steel company had to be enrolled, as with the XK120, to develop the specialised techniques for pressing and erecting the body which was shipped to the factory for final assembly. It was a necessary development, but it sowed the seeds for the loss of Jaguar's independence in the 1960s.

Jaguar XK120 F H Coupe 1951-1954

The 1938 SS100 Earls Court motor show Coupe was such an aesthetic success that it was natural for Lyons to repeat the recipe for the XK120. A snug 2-seat saloon with the distinguising curve of the back window and flowing tail, it was the acme of sporting car fashion. Some sports car owners valued quietness and refinement more than an open top with a noisy hood and draughty sidescreens. The XK120 sacrificed nothing in the way of comfort and equipment, enjoying the composure of a car with a separate chassis, wood and leather appointments, and framed winding windows, together with a lockable useful boot 41in x 12in x 37in (104.1cm x 30.5cm x 94cm) for luggage. Contemporary road testers enthused about the brakes and steering but could only report the gearshift as "positive" with "effective, not easily beaten" synchromesh. It was not one of the car's best features.

Jaguars in 1951 were still astonishingly low-priced. The XK120 cost only £988 in 1948, or £1263 3s 11d (£1263 19.6p) with purchase tax, and a special equipment 180bhp (134.23kW) Coupe with heater as standard (a radio was £33 extra) cost £1255.

BODY
Coupe; 2-doors; 2-seats; weight 1143kg (2520lb).

ENGINE
6-cylinders, in line; front; 83 x 106 mm; compr 8:1; 3442cc; 119kW (160bhp) @ 5000rpm (special 180bhp @ 5300rpm); 34.1kW/L (45.7bhp/L); 261.5Nm (27mkp) @ 2500rpm (special 272.2Nm @ 4000rpm).

ENGINE STRUCTURE
Twin chain-driven ohc; 2-valves per cylinder; aluminium cylinder head; cast iron block; 7-bearing crankshaft; Lucas coil ignition; twin horizontal SU carburettors, water cooled.

TRANSMISSION
Rear wheel drive; clutch 10in diam single dry plate; 4-speed manual gearbox, synchromesh on 2,3,4; semi-floating hypoid final drive, ratio 3.77:1.

CHASSIS DETAILS
Box-section steel with steel body; ifs, wishbone, torsion bar, anti-roll bar, rear axle, semi-elliptic leaf springs, hydraulic dampers; hydraulic drum brakes front & rear; 68.2L (15 Imp gal) (18 US gal) fuel tank; tyres 6.00 x 16 front, 6.50 x 16 rear.

DIMENSIONS
Wheelbase 259cm (102in); front track 130cm (51in); rear track 127cm (50in); ground clearance (7in); turning circle (31ft); length 427cm (168in); width 155cm (61in); height 127cm (50in)

PERFORMANCE
Max speed 193.4kph (120.5mph); acceleration 0-96kph (0-60mph) 9.9sec; standing quarter mile 17.3sec; 38.8kph (24.2mph) @ 1000rpm; average fuel consumption 16.4L/100km (17.2mpg).

Far right: Father
of the XK engine,
one of the war-time
firewatching team,
later Jaguar
chief engineer,
W M (Bill) Heynes.

Jaguar XK120C works Le Mans-winning car 1951

Even as the Mark VII saloon was making its debut at Earls Court, Lyons and Heynes concluded that the XK120 was never going to be competitive against pure sports-racing cars. Something had to be done to maintain the head of steam and the precious publicity it was accumulating. The great classic 24 Hours race at Le Mans had the right ingredients. It was technically demanding, it was famous in America, it was conveniently close, it had a tradition of British participation, and with factory entries from Aston-Martin, Ferrari, Frazer Nash, Bristol, Talbot, Allard, and some of the best private teams such as Cunningham, it promised keen competition.

Arrangements were made for work to begin in strict secrecy on a new lightweight XK120 with the suffix "C" for Competition. The XK120C, soon known as the C-type, had a tubular chassis frame based on Heynes's conviction that stiffness depended on a strong centre portion. The foundation was a drilled channel-section framework, but the strength lay in a triangulated box of tubes in the middle, with sub-frames carrying the engine and suspension in front, while at the back a live

BODY
Open sports racing car; 2-seats; 939.8kg (2072lb).

ENGINE
6-cylinders, in line; front; 83 x 106mm; 3442cc; compr 9:1; 156.6kW (210bhp) @ 5800rpm; compr 9:1; 174kW/L (233bhp/L).

ENGINE STRUCTURE
Ohv @ 70degrees operated by twin overhead camshafts driven by two-stage Duplex chain; aluminium cylinder head; cast iron cylinder block; 7-bearing crankshaft; twin horizontal SU carburettors; water cooled.

TRANSMISSION
Rear wheel drive; clutch single dry plate or Borg & Beck triple plate racing (introduced 1953); 4-speed synchromesh manual gearbox; hypoid bevel final drive, ratio 3.31:1, 3.54:1 variable.

CHASSIS DETAILS
Tubular frame with alloy body panels; front suspension wishbones, torsion bars, hydraulic dampers; rear live axle with torsion bar springs & torque reaction couplings, hydraulic dampers; hydraulic 12in drum brakes front & rear; 181.8L (40 Imp gal)(60 US gal) fuel tank; 6.50 x 16 tyres.

DIMENSIONS
Wheelbase 244cm (96in); front track 130cm (51in); rear track 130cm (51in); ground clearance 13.97cm (5.5in); turning circle 9.4m (31ft); length 399cm (157in); width 164cm (64.5in); height 98cm (38.5in).

PERFORMANCE
Maximum speed over 240.8kph (150mph); acceleration 0-96kph (60mph) 8.1sec; 6kg/kW (4.5kg/bhp); average fuel consumption 24.8L/100km (11.4mpg).

Jaguar XK120C works Le Mans-winning car 1951 (2)

axle was sprung on transverse torsion bars. The crucial centre section was braced laterally, longitudinally, and vertically, and contained the driver and passenger seats.

Secrecy was maintained up to the eve of the race. A resemblance to the XK120 was preserved in the waistline and the ovoid grille, but there was no doubt that this was a different car, and three were made ready with works-prepared 200bhp (149.14kW) engines for the 1951 Le Mans race. They were fast in practice, led convincingly at a fast pace, and although two went out with engine lubrication failure, the third driven by Peter Walker and Peter Whitehead coasted to victory leaving much of the opposition strewn by the wayside. A privately entered standard XK120 cruised into eleventh place. It could scarcely have been better.

Rebuilt with steel internal oil delivery pipes instead of the copper ones that had been responsible for the failure of two of the Le Mans cars, the three entered for the TT at Dundrod in Northern Ireland, finished fastest in race order and first, second, and fourth on handicap. The season was rounded off with Stirling Moss, a star of the Le Mans team and winner of the TT, scoring two more wins at Goodwood. Had there been a sports car world championship in 1951, as there would be in 1953, Jaguar would have won it.

Winning C-type sprints ahead of the Cunninghams at the start *(p135)*, shows off its tubular framework *(left)* and speeds through 24 hour's racing, 3610.94km (2243.8 miles) at an average speed of 150.08kph (93.495mph) to take the chequered flag *(right)*.

Jaguar XK120C production 1951

The transfer of all Jaguar production from the Foleshill factory to one bought from Daimler at Browns Lane, in the small rural town of Allesley, delayed the start of C-type production. There was also a shortage of high-grade steel tubes owing to the rearmament programme for the Korean War of 1950-1953.

It showed how seriously Jaguar took the spirit of regulations governing catalogued sports cars, that not only was the XK120C put into production, but it was road-tested by contemporary motoring magazines and sold to sporting all-comers, not just a chosen elite. Jaguar's open-ness extended to selling a C-type (chassis XKC 032) off the Brussels motor show stand to the 1950 world champion Dr Giuseppe Farina. He never intended to use it. The car went straight to Ferrari, which wanted to see how Jaguar did it at the price, and it was soon sold on to America. Fangio had a C-type he never used, and a third world champion Alberto Ascari, had a Mark VII which he did drive on the road.

Deliveries of production C-types began in August 1952 and continued for about a year. The price was £1495 plus £832 1s 1d (£832 5.4p). 53 were made.

BODY
Open sports car; 2-doors; 2-seats; 1016kg (2240lb).

ENGINE
6-cylinders; 83 x 106mm; 3442cc; compr 8:1; 149kW (200bhp) @ 5800rpm; compr 8:0; 43.3kW/L (58bhp/L).

ENGINE STRUCTURE
Overhead valves @ 70 degrees operated by twin overhead camshafts driven by two-stage Duplex chain; aluminium alloy detachable cylinder head; counterweighted crankshaft in seven 2∫in steel-backed bearings; twin horizontal SU carburettors; pump water circulation.

TRANSMISSION
Rear wheel drive; single dry plate clutch or Borg & Beck 10in single dry plate; 4-speed synchromesh manual gearbox; hypoid bevel final drive, ratio 3.31:1.

CHASSIS DETAILS
Tubular frame with alloy body panels; front suspension wishbones, torsion bars, hydraulic dampers, rear live axle, torsion bar springs, torque reaction couplings, hydraulic dampers; hydraulic 12in diam drum brakes front & rear; 181.8L (40 Imp gal) (60 US gal) fuel tank; tyres 6.00 x 16 front, 6.50 x 16 rear.

DIMENSIONS
Wheelbase 244cm (96in); front track 130cm (51in); rear track 130cm (51in); ground clearance 14cm (5.5in); turning circle 94.4m (31ft); length 399cm (157in); width 164cm (64.5in); height 98cm (38.5in).

PERFORMANCE
Max speed 231.8kph (144mph); accel 96kph (0-60mph) 8.1sec; 40.1kph (25mph) @ 1000rpm; 6.8kW/kg (5.1bhp/kg); av fuel cons 17.7L/100km (16mpg).

Jaguar XK120C Le Mans car 1952

Jaguar's expeditions to Le Mans were not invariably successful. Although its racing programme was expert by the standards of the time, in a firm where every cost was closely scrutinised, the racing budget was tight. All the personnel involved had a "real" job; the one they had in racing was regarded as something of a privilege. F R W England, the redoubtable and experienced team manager, was Jaguar's service director. The 1953 Le Mans was a disaster after attempts to improve the C-type's streamlining resulted in overheating. All the cars failed, one after only 16 laps. Mercedes-Benz, already Jaguar's rival in important markets, scored a spectacular 1-2 victory with the "gull-wing" 300SL, its first big post-war race win. Jaguar entered a C-type in the Mille Miglia in May, its first race with disc brakes, and it ran third before retiring. Stirling Moss won the Rheims sports car race in a C-type again with Dunlop disc brakes. An XK120 of Ecurie Ecosse, the Scottish team long faithful to Jaguar, finished third. The long-tailed Le Mans cars were never seen again, and a new competition department ensured that so long as Jaguar remained in racing, such a debacle was not repeated.

BODY
Open sports racing car; 2-seats; 939.8kg (2072lb).

ENGINE
6-cylinders, in line; front; 83 x 106mm; 3442cc; compr 9:1; 156.6kW (210bhp) @ 5800rpm; compr 9:1; 174kW/L (233bhp/L).

ENGINE STRUCTURE
Ohv @ 70degrees operated by twin overhead camshafts driven by two-stage Duplex chain; aluminium cylinder head; cast iron cylinder block; 7-bearing crankshaft; twin horizontal SU carburettors; water cooled.

TRANSMISSION
Rear wheel drive; clutch single dry plate or Borg & Beck triple plate racing (introduced 1953); 4-speed synchromesh manual gearbox; hypoid bevel final drive, ratio 4.27:1 variable.

CHASSIS DETAILS
Tubular frame with alloy body panels; front suspension wishbones, torsion bars, hydraulic dampers; rear live axle with torsion bar springs & torque reaction couplings, hydraulic dampers; hydraulic 12in drum brakes front & rear; 181.8L (40 Imp gal)(60 US gal) fuel tank; 6.50 x 16 tyres.

DIMENSIONS
Wheelbase 244cm (96in); front track 130cm (51in); rear track 130cm (51in); ground clearance 13.97cm (5.5in); turning circle 9.4m (31ft); length 424.2cm (167in); width 164cm (64.5in); height 98cm (38.5in).

PERFORMANCE
Maximum speed over 240.8kph (150mph); acceleration 0-96kph (60mph) 8.1sec; 6kg/kW (4.5kg/bhp); average fuel consumption 24.8L/100km (11.4mpg).

Jaguar XK120C series II C/D record car 1953

Still smarting perhaps from the 1952 imbroglio, in May 1953, a "Le Mans prototype" was shown to the press at the new Browns Lane factory. It was photographed outside the main office where the Coronation coat of arms was on proud display. Based on a C-type frame (XKC 054) it had a carefully shaped body, the work of the fine aerodynamicist Malcolm Sayer, recently joined from Bristol Aircraft and who called it an XK120C Mk II. Its engine had been used in the Moss TT car with Weber carburettors, and although it never ran at Le Mans, it was taken to Jabbeke in October 1953 to be driven with a bubble top over the cockpit at 179.817mph (289.379kph) by Norman Dewis who had replaced R M V Sutton as test driver.

The purpose of the C/D prototype was to run a test programme for the continuation of racing. Jaguar's racing success had finally demolished the old shibboleths about it being a "poor man's Bentley". It was no longer a poor man's anything; it was a shining example of British engineering enterprise, coupled with a prudent approach to competition which ranged it against the world's best.

BODY
Open sports racing car; 2-seats; 997.9kg (2200lb).

ENGINE
6-cylinders, in line; front; 83 x 106mm; 3442cc; compr 9:1; 162.6kW (218bhp) @ 5250rpm; compr 9:1; 47.2kW/L (63.3bhp/L).

ENGINE STRUCTURE
Ohv @ 70degrees operated by twin overhead camshafts driven by two-stage Duplex chain; aluminium cylinder head; cast iron cylinder block; 7-bearing crankshaft; 3 Weber 40mm twin-choke carburettors; water cooled.

TRANSMISSION
Rear wheel drive; clutch single dry plate or Borg & Beck triple plate racing (introduced 1953); 4-speed synchromesh manual gearbox; hypoid bevel final drive, ratio 4.27:1.

CHASSIS DETAILS
Tubular frame with alloy body panels; front suspension wishbones, torsion bars, hydraulic dampers; rear live axle with torsion bar springs & Panhard rod, hydraulic dampers; hydraulic 12in drum brakes front & rear; 181.8L (40 Imp gal)(60 US gal) fuel tank; 6.50 x 16 tyres.

DIMENSIONS
Wheelbase 244cm (96in); front track 130cm (51in); rear track 130cm (51in); ground clearance 13.97cm (5.5in); turning circle 9.4m (31ft); length 409cm (161in); width 164cm (64.5in).

PERFORMANCE
Maximum speed 286.4kph (178.38mph); acceleration 0-96kph (60mph) 8.1sec est; 6.1kg/kW (4.6kg/bhp); average fuel consumption 24.8L/100km (11.4mpg) est.

Jaguar XK120 SE 1953

The response by Jaguar to owners who wanted more speed was wide-ranging. By 1951, service bulletins were issued to dealers suggesting ways and means of increasing the XK's performance, but it was done in a uniquely discreet Jaguar way which made the fastidious owner feel cherished. Under F R W England, a culture was created in which speed enhancement was carried out with a deep obligation to safety.

As "Pool" was phased out and higher octane fuel became available, pistons giving 8:1 and 9:1 compression ratios came on offer. Modifications could be made to distributors and different jets fitted to SU carburettors. A high-lift camshaft giving 3/8th in (.952cm) lift instead of the standard cam's 5/16th in (.794cm) was available, together with a twin exhaust which gave the XK engine a deep throaty growl.

The Special Equipment package available throughout the range of roadster, Coupe, and DH Coupe varied. In North America the 180bhp (134.3kW) engine package was known as the 'M', and cost an extra $395 making $4460 for the Coupe tested in 1953 by

BODY
Coupe; 2-doors; 2-seats; weight 1370.7kg (3022lb).

ENGINE
6-cylinders, in line; front; 83 x 106mm, 3442cc; compr 8:1; 134kW (180bhp) @ 5300rpm; 38.4kW/L (51.4bhp/L).

ENGINE STRUCTURE
Twin chain-driven ohc; 2-valves per cylinder; aluminium cylinder head; cast iron block; 7-bearing crankshaft; Lucas coil ignition; twin horizontal SU carburettors.

TRANSMISSION
Rear wheel drive; clutch 10in diam single dry plate; 4-speed manual gearbox, synchromesh on 2,3,4; hypoid final drive.

CHASSIS DETAILS
Box-section steel with steel body; ifs, wishbone, torsion bar, anti-roll bar, rear axle, semi-elliptic leaf springs, hydraulic dampers; hydraulic drum brakes front & rear; 68.2L (15 Imp gal) (18 US gal) fuel tank; tyres 6.00 x 16 front, 6.50 x 16 rear.

DIMENSIONS
Wheelbase 259cm (102in), front track 129.5cm (51in), rear track 127cm (50in), ground clearance 19cm (7.5in), turning circle 9.44m (31ft), length 439cm (173in), width 157.5cm (62in), height 135.8cm (53.5in).

PERFORMANCE
Salisbury axle gear ratios were: 4.09:1, 3.77, 3.54, and 2.93. 3.54 produced 223kph (139mph)est @ 5800rpm.

Jaguar XK120 SE 1953 (2)

Auto Sport magazine, from Kjell Qvale's British Motor Car Distributors of San Francisco. *Auto Sport* liked the Coupe but found draughts from the side ventilator and through the brake and clutch holes in the floor. The XK "...moved off as smooth as silk, no roughness at idle, no spitting while waiting at stoplights, no flat spots in carburetion. The steering was light, the clutch firm but soft though it still has that dreadfully long stroke characteristic of Jaguars.... There are few if any production cars that can boast the combination of easy cruising at better than 100mph with complete docility around town, and all with virtually Detroit standards of ease of control."

Optional extras included stiffer front torsion bars and 7-leaf rear springs which reduced roll by 20%, alternative axle ratios, aero screens for racing, lightweight bucket seats, an undershield, and a metal tonneau cover.

Right: Special equipment on an XK120. Extra lights, wire wheels, bonnet straps and two-way radio featured on the historic Montlhéry record car. Reunited after 40 years, Stirling Moss (left) and Jack Fairman (centre), tell Jaguar chairman Nick Scheele about their record-breaking seven days in August 1952.

Jaguar XK120 D H Coupe 1953-1954

The XK's appeal was so wide that after the fixed-head coupe it seemed only logical to follow the pattern of the 1930s and produce a more luxurious alternative to the open 2-seater. The Convertible was pure XK120 fixed-head up to the waistline with winding windows and substantial fixed (but still split) windscreen with strong side-pillars. Interior trim was like the fixed-head with walnut veneer facia and door cappings. The metal window frames wound down into the doors diagonally so that the front edge of the window remained in contact with the swivelling quarter-lights to reduce draughts.

The hood clipped to three toggle fasteners on the top windscreen rail, and it was claimed that once they were released, folding the hood away was a one-person operation. It was possible, but the occupant had to get out to fasten down the cover . It did not fold flush with the rear deck because it was the traditional padded and lined mohair affair giving a smooth exterior and a saloon-like interior. The back window could be unzipped in hot weather and a novel item of equipment which extended to all Jaguars in 1953 was a screen washer.

BODY
Coupe; 2-doors; 2-seats; weight 1346kg (3629lb).

ENGINE
6-cylinders, in line; front; 83 106mm; compr 8:1; 3442cc; 141.7kW (190bhp) @ 5300rpm; 41.2kW/L (55.2bhp/L); 272Nm (28.1mkp) @ 4000rpm.

ENGINE STRUCTURE
Twin chain-driven ohc; 2-valves per cylinder; aluminium cylinder head; cast iron block; 7-bearing crankshaft; Lucas coil ignition; twin horizontal SU carburettors, water cooled.

TRANSMISSION
Rear wheel drive; clutch 1in diam single dry plate; 4-speed manual gearbox, synchromesh on 2,3,4; hypoid bevel final drive, 3.54:1.

CHASSIS DETAILS
Box-section steel with steel body; front independent wishbone, torsion bars, anti-roll bar, telescopic dampers, hydraulic drum brakes; rear live axle, semi-elliptic leaf springs, hydraulic dampers & drum brakes; fuel tank capacity 63.6L (14 Imp gal) (16.8 US gal); 6.00 tyres, 16in rims.

DIMENSIONS
Wheelbase 259cm (102in); front track 130cm (51in); rear track 127cm (50in); ground clearance 9.4m (31ft); turning circle 19.1cm 7.5in; length 427cm (168in); width 155cm (61in); height 133.4cm (52.5in).

PERFORMANCE
Maximum speed 194kph (120mph); 34.2kph (21.3mph) @ 1000rpm; acceleration 96kph (0-60mph)10.1sec; standing quarter mile 17.3sec; 9.5kg/kW (7.1kg/bhp); average fuel consumption 15.7-20.2L/100km (14-18mpg) DIN.

Jaguar XK120C works Le Mans-winning car 1953

Mercedes-Benz gratefully withdrew from racing after winning Le Mans in 1952. Victory was not a fluke, but the failure of the long-tailed C-type had left the door ajar. Ferrari was furious, convinced that the 300SL was not really very fast, challenged Mercedes to a duel but predictably was turned down.

For 1953 Jaguar reverted to a lightweight version of the C-type with the important innovations of three Weber carburettors and disc brakes. The brakes led to a lot of loose talk about going 200 metres deeper into corners, whereas their greater virtue was resistance to fade. Jaguar's aim was to win, and exceed the 300SL's speed of the previous year . Both objectives were met. The C-types finished 1st 2nd and 4th, Tony Rolt and Duncan Hamilton scoring their famous victory at 105.841mph (170.329kph), which was 9.145mph (14.7kph) faster than Lang and Reiss the year before. It was the first time the race had been won at over 100mph (160.93kph). Peter Walker and Stirling Moss were 2nd, Peter Whitehead and Ian Stewart 4th, and Roger Laurent and Guy De Tornaco 9th in a Belgian SU carburetted and drum-braked car.

BODY
Open sports racing car; 2-doors; 2-seats; weight 877.7kg (1935b).

ENGINE
6-cylinders, in line; front; 3442cc; compr 8:1; 164kW (220bhp) @ 5200rpm; 47.65kW/L (63.9bhp/L).

ENGINE STRUCTURE
Ohv @ 70degrees operated by twin overhead camshafts driven by two-stage Duplex chain; aluminium cylinder head; cast iron cylinder block; 7-bearing crankshaft; 3 double-choke horizontal Weber carburettors; Lucas coil ignition; water cooled.

TRANSMISSION
Rear wheel drive; clutch single dry plate or Borg & Beck triple plate racing (introduced 1953); 4-speed synchromesh manual gearbox; hypoid bevel final drive, ratio 4.27:1.

CHASSIS DETAILS
Tubular frame with alloy body panels; front suspension wishbones, torsion bars, hydraulic dampers; rear live axle with torsion bar springs & 40mm Panhard rod, hydraulic dampers; disc brakes front & rear; 227.3L (50Imp gal) (60US gal) fuel tank; 6.50 x 16 tyres.

DIMENSIONS
Wheelbase 244cm (96in); front track 130cm (51in); rear track 130cm (51in); ground clearance 13.97cm (5.5in); turning circle 9.4m (31ft); length 399cm (157in); width 164cm (64.5in); height 98cm (38.5in).

PERFORMANCE
Maximum speed 240.8kph (150mph)approx; 6kg/kW (4kg/bhp); average fuel consumption 20.2-28.3L/100km (10-14mpg).

Right: Hamilton-Rolt C-type in the pits. The scene is set for the famous Terence Cuneo painting which features the individuals on the pit counter including F R W (Lofty) England standing under the Jaguar banner on the left.

Jaguar XK140 open 2-seater 1954-1957

As the 1950s drew on, Jaguars tended to put on weight and accumulate decoration. It was done with the best of intentions and always in good taste, but when the XK140 succeeded the XK120 it seemed that some of the 120's purity of line and understatement were lost. A thick chrome stripe appeared on the bonnet and bootlid, the grille was coarser, the bumpers bigger, and it seemed to be aimed at comfort rather than speed.

The 140 was produced on the same underpinnings as the 120 with the 190bhp (141.68kW) Special Equipment XK120 engine. A C-type cylinder head was available with larger exhaust valves giving 210bhp (156.59kW). The engine was moved 3in (7.62cm) forward in the frame, providing more room inside, and improving the handling by balancing up the weight distribution front to rear. More significant was the adoption of rack and pinion steering instead of recirculating ball. The suspension was retuned using Special Equipment torsion bars and telescopic instead of lever arm dampers on the rear axle.

BODY
Sports; 2-doors; 2-seats; weight 1220kg (2690lb).

ENGINE
6-cylinders, in line; front; 83 x 106 mm; 3442cc; compr 8:1 (7:1, 9:1 optional); 141.7kW (190bhp) @ 5500rpm; 41.2kW/L (55.2bhp/L); 281.6Nm (29mkp) @ 2500rpm.

ENGINE STRUCTURE
Twin chain-driven ohc; 2-valves per cylinder; aluminium cylinder head; cast iron block; 7-bearing crankshaft; Lucas coil ignition; 2 1.75in SU carburettors, water cooled.

TRANSMISSION
Rear wheel drive; clutch 10in single dry plate; 4-speed manual gearbox, synchromesh on 2, 3, 4, overdrive optional, automatic Borg-Warner 3-speed optional from 1957; hypoid bevel final drive, 3.54:1, 3.19:1 overdrive.

CHASSIS DETAILS
Box-section steel with steel body; ifs, wishbone, torsion bars, telescopic dampers, anti-roll bar, rear live axle, semi-elliptic leaf springs, telescopic dampers; hydraulic 12in dia drum brakes; fuel tank 68.2L (15 Imp gal) (18 US gal); 6.00 x 16 tyres.

DIMENSIONS
Wheelbase 259cm (102in); front track 131cm (51.5in); rear track 128cm (50.5in); ground clearance 18cm (7.1in); turning circle 9.44m (31ft); length 447cm (176in); width 164cm (64.5in); height 136cm (53.5in).

PERFORMANCE
Max speed 197.5kph (123mph); 31.5kph (19.6mph)[36.4kph (22.7mph) overdrive] @ 1000rpm; accel 0-96kph (60mph) 8.4sec(SE); standing quarter mile 16.6sec (SE); 7.9kg/kW (5.9kg/bhp); av fuel cons 15.7-17.7L/100km (16-18mpg).

Jaguar Mark VIIM 1954-1957

Identification features of the Mark VIIM, introduced in September 1954 for the 1955 model year, included the relocation of the fog-lights or pass-lamps to the front bumper and their replacement with horn grilles, flashing indicators on the front wing, and J700 Lucas headlamps with a "J" motif in the centre. The tail lights were bigger, and the bumper reprofiled.

Widespread availability of high octane fuel allowed the high 8.0:1 compression to be standardised. Body roll was reduced by increasing torsion bar thickness to 1in (2.54cm) and raising the spring rate. The large boss on the steering column like a spear aimed at the driver's chest, was replaced by a flat horn button. Borg-Warner automatic was among the options, along with a Laycock de Normanville overdrive and a 4.55:1 axle. This improved refinement at speed, and fuel consumption by 8-10%. The price in Britain was now £1679.16s 6d (£1679 87.5p) with overdrive. *The Autocar* enthused, "... extremely good value for money; outstanding performance ... for its size does not have an excessive thirst for fuel ... very satisfactory for a driver desiring a large saloon with sports car performance."

BODY
Saloon; 4-doors; 4/5-seats; weight 1676.5kg (3696lb).

ENGINE
6-cylinders, in line; front; 83 x 106mm; 3442cc; compr 8:1; 141.7kW (190bhp) @ 5500rpm; 41.2kW/L (55.2bhp/L); 281.6Nm (29mkp) @ 2500rpm.

ENGINE STRUCTURE
Twin chain-driven ohc; 2-valves per cylinder; aluminium cylinder head; cast iron block; 7-bearing crankshaft; Lucas coil ignition; twin horizontal SU carburettors, water cooled.

TRANSMISSION
Rear wheel drive; clutch single dry plate; 4-speed manual gearbox, synchromesh on 2,3,4, overdrive optional, automatic 3-speed Borg-Warner; hypoid bevel final drive, ratio 4.27:1, overdrive ratio 4.55:1.

CHASSIS DETAILS
Box-section steel with pressed steel body; suspension front wishbones & torsion bars; rear semi-elliptic leaf springs; Girling hydraulic dampers; servo-assisted hydraulic 12in dia drum brakes front & rear; Burman recirculating ball steering; 77.3L (17 Imp gal) (20.4 US gal); 6.70 tyres, 16in rims.

DIMENSIONS
Wheelbase 305cm (120in); front track 144cm (56.5in); rear track 147cm (58in); ground clearance 19.05cm (7.5in); length 499cm (196.5in); width 185cm (73in); height 160cm (63in).

PERFORMANCE
Maximum speed 171kph (106.3mph); old direct: 31kph (19.3mph) @ 1000rpm; direct: (18.1mph)@ 1000rpm; old: 23.3mph @1000rpm; acceleration 0-96kph (0-60mph) 11.6sec; 11.8kg/kW (8.8kg/bhp); average fuel consumption 15L/ 100km (18.8mpg).

Jaguar D-type 'short-nosed' works prototype 1954

A preview of the Le Mans Jaguar in May 1954 showed its similarities to the C-type more than its differences. It was more obviously "streamlined", it was only 32in (81.28cm) tall, 2in (5.08cm) lower than a C, and it had dry-sump lubrication. The engine was canted 8 degrees to the left to clear the frame, and Jaguar overcame its reservations about Weber carburettors, again using three twin-chokes. Like the C-type, the chassis loads were concentrated in the centre, with the rear suspension and front sub-frame anchored in a stressed skin monocoque instead of a collection of welded tubes. The centre-section was a rivetted structure like an aircraft fuselage in magnesium alloy.

The body shape was breathtakingly beautiful, Malcolm Sayer's wind-tunnel confirming the efficiency of a design that was as elegant as it was finely proportioned. It used perforated centre-lock disc wheels, there was a headrest fairing with the fuel filler under a flap, a spare wheel compartment in the tail which had a headrest but not a fin, and the passenger seat, normally faired-over, was divided from the driver's by a structural member of the central hull.

BODY
Open 2-seater; 880kg (1940lb).

ENGINE
6-cylinders, in line; front; 83 x 106mm, 3442cc; compr 9:1; 186.4kW (250bhp) @ 6000rpm; 54.2kW/L (72.6bhp/L); 324.5Nm (33.5mkp) @ 4000rpm.

ENGINE STRUCTURE
Two chain-drive ohc; 2-valves per cylinder; aluminium cylinder head; cast iron block; 7-bearing crankshaft; 3 twin-choke Weber carburettors; water cooled.

TRANSMISSION
Rear wheel drive; triple plate clutch; 4-speed gearbox; hypoid final drive, 2.93:1, 3.31:1, 3.92:1, 3.54:1.

CHASSIS DETAILS
Alloy tubular front sub-frame; stressed skin magnesium centre-section; ifs by wishbones, torsion bars; rear axle on trailing arms, torsion bars; Girling telescopic dampers; Dunlop disc brakes with servo; rack and pinion steering; 163.7L (36 Imp gal) (43.2US gal) fuel tank; Dunlop light alloy disc wheels, 6.50 - 16 tyres.

DIMENSIONS
Wheelbase 229.4cm (90.3in), front and rear track 127cm (50in), ground clearance 13.3cm (5.25in), turning circle 10.7m (35ft), length 391.2cm (154in), width 165.9cm (65.3in), height 80cm (31.5in).

PERFORMANCE
Maximum speed 272.9kph (170mph); 38.8kph (24.2mph) @ 1000rpm on 3.54 axle; acceleration 0-96kph (60mph) 7.0sec approx; 4.7kg/kW (3.5kg/bhp); average fuel consumption 18.8-23.5L/100km (12-15mpg).

Right: First prototype D-type at the factory with some of the individuals chiefly concerned in its creation. The tall figure to the left is aero-dynamicist Malcolm Sayer, William Heynes has his hand on the car's head fairing, with Norman Dewis, chief test driver, in the cockpit. Behind Dewis (with glasses) is Bob Knight. Also pictured are *(left to right)* Joe Sutton, Arthur Ramsay, Keith Cambage, Philip Weaver, Gordon Gardner, Bob Penney and Len Haydon.

Jaguar XK140 FHC 1954-1957

Moving the engine forward allowed the XK140 drophead and fixed head versions to become a 2+2, and a back rest could be rearranged to form a corner seat transversely like the DB 18 Daimler 2½-litre Special Sports and its successors. The two small forward-facing seats with which it reached production were not satisfactory for grown-ups. The bulkhead behind folded down for additional luggage space when there were only two occupants, and the boot now had the spare wheel underneath a hinged part of the floor which measured 41in (104.14cm), 49.5in (125.73cm) with the flap open on the 2-seater, and 51in (129.54cm) on the Coupe.

The extended roofline of the Coupe enabled the rear window to be enlarged, and the doors width increased from 32½in (82.55cm), to 38in (96.52cm). The facia was walnut veneer and the interior trim owed a good deal to the style of the Mark VII. Jaguar sports car prices including purchase tax for the 1955 model year were XK140 open sports £1598 8s 4d (£1598 41.6p); XK140 fixed head coupe £1616 2s 6d (£1616 12.5p); XK140 drophead coupe £1644 9s 2d (£1644 45.8p); Jaguar D-type £2685 14s 2d (£2685 70.8p).

BODY

Coupe; 2-doors; 2+2-seats; weight 1295.5kg (2856lbs).

ENGINE

6-cylinders, in line; front; 83 x 106 mm; 3442cc; compr 8:1 (7:1, 9:1 optional); 141.7kW (190bhp) @ 5500rpm; 41.2kW/L (55.2bhp/L); 281.6Nm (29mkp) @ 2500rpm.

ENGINE STRUCTURE

Twin chain-driven ohc; 2-valves per cylinder; aluminium cylinder head; cast iron block; 7-bearing crankshaft; Lucas coil ignition; 2 1¾in SU carburettors, water cooled.

TRANSMISSION

Rear wheel drive; clutch 10in single dry plate; 4-speed manual gearbox, synchromesh on 2,3,4, overdrive optional, automatic Borg-Warner 3-speed optional from 1957; hypoid bevel final drive, 3.54:1, 3.19:1 overdrive.

CHASSIS DETAILS

Box-section steel with steel body; ifs, wishbone, torsion bars, telescopic dampers, anti-roll bar, rear live axle, semi-elliptic leaf springs, telescopic dampers; hydraulic 12in dia drum brakes; fuel tank 68.2L (15 Imp gal) (18 US gal); 6.00 x 16 tyres.

DIMENSIONS

Wheelbase 259cm (102in); front track 131cm (51.5in); rear track 128cm (50.5in); ground clearance 18.098cm (7.125in); turning circle 944.88cm (31ft); length 447cm (176in); width 164cm (64.5in); height 137.2cm (54in).

PERFORMANCE

C-type head: Max speed 208kph (129mph); 31.5kph (19.6mph) [overdrive 40.3kph (25.1mph)] @ 1000rpm; 0-96kph (0-60mph) 11sec; standing quarter mile 17.4sec; 8.6kg/kW (6.4kg/bhp); average fuel consumption 13L/100km (21.7mpg).

Jaguar XK140 DHC 1954-1957

The embodiment of all the best in Jaguar tradition, luxury, elegance, speed, and style, the 140 drophead coupe did not benefit as much as the fixed-head from the extra space gained by moving the engine forward. The front seats moved an extra 3 in (7.62cm) to 7in (17.78cm) but there was not as much room in the back owing to the space taken up by the hood when stowed. Putting the substantial top up was still something of a chore before the days of near-universal power operation. *The Motor* was relieved to report: "Another detail which will be much appreciated is the incorporation of spring assistance in the head linkage, the counterbalancing effect being sufficient to enable the hood to be erected single-handed from the driving seat."

The interiors of XK140s followed the pattern set by the 120, with the Roadster facia covered in leather, and a padded roll round the coaming. The two Coupes had wood door cappings and facia. The 140 dropped the traditional sporting fly-off handbrake for a conventional pattern in deference to export taste. A medallion in the tail carried the legend "Winner Le Mans 1951-53", perhaps implying three victories rather than two.

BODY
Coupe; 2-doors; 2-seats; weight 1346.3kg (2968lb).

ENGINE
6-cylinders, in line; front; 83 x 106 mm; 3442cc; compr 8:1 (7:1, 9:1 optional); 141.7kW (190bhp) @ 5500rpm; 41.2kW/L (55.2bhp/L); 281.6Nm (29mkp) @ 2500rpm.

ENGINE STRUCTURE
Twin chain-driven ohc; 2-valves per cylinder; aluminium cylinder head; cast iron block; 7-bearing crankshaft, damper; Lucas coil ignition; 2 1¾in SU carburettors, water cooled.

TRANSMISSION
Rear wheel drive; clutch 10in dia single dry plate; 4-speed manual gearbox, synchromesh on 2,3,4, overdrive optional; automatic 3-speed Borg-Warner optional from 1957 model year; hypoid bevel final drive, 3.54:1 standard, 4.09 with overdrive.

CHASSIS DETAILS
Box-section steel with steel body; front suspension wishbones & torsion bars; telescopic dampers, rear semi-elliptic leaf springs, telescopic dampers; hydraulic brakes front & rear; fuel tank capacity 63.6L (14 Imp gal) (16,8US gal); 6.00 tyres, 16in rims.

DIMENSIONS
Wheelbase 259cm (102in); front track 131cm (51.5in); rear track 128cm (50.5in); ground clearance 19cm (7.5in); length 447cm (176in); width 164cm (64.5in); height with hood erect 133.4cm (52.5in).

PERFORMANCE
C-type head: Max speed 208kph (129mph); 31.5kph (19.6mph) @ 1000rpm; 0-96kph (0-60mph) 11sec; standing quarter mile 17.4sec; 8.6kg/kW (6.4kg/bhp); average fuel consumption 12.3-15.7L/100km (18-23mpg).

Jaguar production D-Type 1955

There was feverish activity in the Jaguar competitions department early in 1954. In April two cars went to Rheims for private testing, astonishingly conducted on a public road course in secret. For a small fee the local gendarmes closed the circuit and Jaguar made a commitment to enter a team for the forthcoming 12-hour sports car race. Jaguar had won at Rheims twice and had already made up its mind to take part. Mercedes-Benz was about to make its comeback in the French Grand Prix the same week-end, and it was felt that Jaguar should try to win the sports car race, as a counter-attraction.

The debate lay between the XK120C Mk II, the C/D hybrid (cf p142) and the "pure" D-type prototype with the magnesium monocoque (cf p156). In May the cars were tried out at Le Mans where the circuit was in use for a rally event. They were driven at the Motor Industry Research Association (MIRA) test track at Lindley near Nuneaton, and at Gaydon, still a Royal Air Force airfield with an unusually long runway. The D-type was a runaway success, and although it only managed 2nd place at Le Mans behind the 4.9-litre

BODY
Open 2-seater; 880kg (1940lb).

ENGINE
6-cylinders, in line; front; 83 x 106mm, 3442cc; compr 9:1; 186.4kW (250bhp) @ 6000rpm; 54.2kW/L (72.6bhp/L); 324.5Nm (33.5mkp) @ 4000rpm.

ENGINE STRUCTURE
Two chain-drive ohc; 2-valves per cylinder; aluminium cylinder head; cast iron block; 7-bearing crankshaft; 3 twin-choke Weber carburettors; water cooled.

TRANSMISSION
Rear wheel drive; triple plate clutch; 4-speed gearbox; hypoid final drive, 2.93:1, 3.31:1, 3.92:1, 3.54:1.

CHASSIS DETAILS
Steel tubular front sub-frame; stressed skin magnesium centre-section; ifs by wishbones, torsion bars; rear axle on trailing arms, torsion bars; Girling telescopic dampers; Dunlop disc brakes

with servo; rack and pinion steering; 163.7L (36 Imp gal) (43.2US gal) fuel tank; Dunlop light alloy disc wheels, 6.50 - 16 tyres.

DIMENSIONS
Wheelbase 229.4cm (90.3in), front and rear track 127cm (50in), ground clearance 13.3cm (5.25in), turning circle 10.7m (35ft), length 391.2cm (154in), width 165.9cm (65.3in), height 80cm (31.5in).

PERFORMANCE
Maximum speed 272.9kph (170mph); 38.8kph (24.2mph) @ 1000rpm on 3.54 axle; acceleration 0-96kph (60mph) 7.0sec approx; average fuel consumption 18.8-23.5L/100km (12-15mpg).

Jaguar production D-Type 1955 (2)

Ferrari of Froilan Gonzalez and Maurice Trintignant (the Belgian C-type finished 4th), it and not the C/D represented the future.

The engine was a dry-sump development of the XK 6-cylinder with its single iron casting forming the block and crankcase. The bore-stroke ratio was 0.788:1 in deference to the long-standing British obligation to a taxation system that seemed to bind designers to long-stroke engines many years after flat-rate taxation had arrived. The engine was structurally stiff, its seven-main-bearing philosophy plausibly inherited from the old Standard engine of pre-war. The crankshaft was made of EN16 steel and had big-end bearings of indium-coated lead bronze. There was no flywheel, but there was a substantial torsional vibration damper at the front, and

some measure of flywheel effect was produced by the mass of the triple dry-plate clutch and starter ring.

There were two oil pumps, pressure on the right, and scavenge on the left of the engine. Oil was drawn from the tank on the left of the engine compartment through an oil cooler and thence to the crankcase. Dry-sump lubrication not only reduced the height of the engine, but decreased the risk of oil surge and starvation during fast cornering, by keeping the bearings pressure-fed at all times.

The close-ratio gearbox had single helical gears. There was a short Hardy Spicer propellor shaft and the Salisbury rear axle (except for a different ratio and different-length axle tubes) was, like many of the car's components, derived directly from the standard XK unit.

Right: The first
unpainted D-type had
a head fairing but no
tail fin.
Left: Customer car
chassis XKD 517 raced
by Gilbert Tyrer, Alex
McMillan, Henry
Taylor and Jim Clark.

Jaguar XK140 SE 1955-1957

All three XK140s were offered in Special Equipment (SE) mode, which provided wire wheels and Lucas foglamps. Additionally, S E cars could be ordered with a C-type cylinder head with high-lift camshafts and crankshaft damper, a dual exhaust system, and the option of an 8.0:1 or 9.0:1 compression.

Jaguar took care that when *The Autocar* tested a 140 in late 1955 it was a special equipment model with C-type head and overdrive and the customary 4.09:1 instead of the standard 3.54:1 axle ratio. It cost £1830 7s 11d (£1830 39.58p) excluding the radio at £47 5s 3d (£47 26.25p), and was the same RHP 576 as John Bolster had tested a month earlier for *Autosport*, at only 121.6mph (195.69kph). He claimed 135mph (217.25kph) on the "slightly optimistic," speedometer.

The Autocar managed 129.25mph (208kph), not quite the magic 130mph but doubtless more pleasing to Jaguar, which was jealous of its status among the fastest production cars on the market. "When its qualities are related to its price, there is no other car which can approach it ... a fine advertisement for the British automobile industry," said the testers.

BODY
Coupe; 2-doors; 2+2-seats; weight 1295.5kg (2856lbs).

ENGINE
C-type head: 6-cyl, in line; front; 83 x 106 mm; 3442cc; compr 8:1 (9:1 opt); 156.6kW (210bhp) @ 5750rpm; 45.5kW/L (61bhp/L); 285Nm (29.5mkp) @ 4000rpm.

ENGINE STRUCTURE
Twin chain-driven ohc; 2-valves per cylinder; aluminium cylinder head; cast iron block; 7-bearing crankshaft, damper; Lucas coil ignition; 2 1¾in SU carburettors, water cooled.

TRANSMISSION
Rear wheel drive; clutch 10in single dry plate; 4-speed manual gearbox, synchromesh on 2,3,4, overdrive optional, automatic Borg-Warner 3-speed optional from 1957; hypoid bevel final drive, 3.45:1, 4.09:1 overdrive.

CHASSIS DETAILS
Box-section steel with steel body; ifs, wishbone, torsion bars, telescopic dampers, anti-roll bar, rear live axle, semi-elliptic leaf springs, telescopic dampers; hydraulic 12in dia drum brakes; fuel tank 68.2L (15 Imp gal) (18 US gal); 6.00 x 16 tyres.

DIMENSIONS
W/b 259cm (102in); front track 131cm (51.5in); rear track 128cm (50.5in); g c 18cm (7in); turning circle 9.5m (31ft); length 447cm (176in); width 164cm (64.5in); height 137.2cm (54in).

PERFORMANCE
With C-type head: Max 208kph (129.3mph); 31.5kph (19.6mph)[36.4kph (22.7mph) overdrive] @ 1000rpm; 0-96kph (60mph) 8.4sec(SE); standing quarter mile 16.6sec (SE); 7.9kg/kW (5.9kg/bhp); av fuel cons 15.7-17.7L/100km (16-18mpg).

Right: **Lean lines of 140 2+2. SE cars had wire wheels.**

Jaguar D-Type works Le Mans-winner 1955

The 1955 Le Mans race saw the worst disaster in the history of the sport. What should have been a rousing three-way battle between Jaguar, Ferrari, and Mercedes-Benz in one of the most important sporting events of the season, was overwhelmed by the inhumanity of an accident in which over 80 spectators died.

By the middle 1950s Le Mans surpassed even grand prix racing in importance for many enthusiasts on both sides of the Atlantic. Mercedes-Benz engaged some of the best drivers in the world, such as Juan Fangio and Stirling Moss, for its 300SLR cars equipped with an air-brake devised to offset Jaguar's advantage in disc brake technology. Ferrari had its magnificent 121LMs driven by Umberto Maglioli, Phil Hill, and Eugenio Castellotti. Jaguar had a team of D-types driven by Mike Hawthorn and Ivor Bueb, 1953 winners and 1954 runners-up Tony Rolt and Duncan Hamilton, and Don Beauman with works test driver Norman Dewis. Sleek beautiful green Jaguars, stark efficient silver Mercedes-Benzes, passionate red Ferraris – ingredients surely for the race of a lifetime.

The D-types had a new 'wide angle' cylinder head

BODY
Open 2-seater; 880kg (1940lb).

ENGINE
6-cylinders, in line; front; 83 x 106mm, 3442cc; compr 9:1; 212.5kW (285bhp) @ 5750rpm; 61.7kW/L (82.8bhp/L); 324.5Nm (33.5mkp) @ 4000rpm.

ENGINE STRUCTURE
Two chain-drive ohc; 2-valves per cylinder; aluminium cylinder head; cast iron block; 7-bearing crankshaft; 3 twin-choke Weber carburettors; water cooled.

TRANSMISSION
Rear wheel drive; triple plate clutch; 4-speed gearbox; hypoid final drive, 2.93:1, 3.31:1, 3.92:1, 3.54:1.

CHASSIS DETAILS
Steel tubular front sub-frame; stressed skin magnesium centre-section; ifs by wishbones, torsion bars; rear axle on trailing arms, torsion bars; Girling telescopic dampers; Dunlop disc brakes with servo; rack and pinion steering; 163.7L (36 Imp gal) (43.2US gal) fuel tank; Dunlop light alloy disc wheels, 6.50 - 16 tyres.

DIMENSIONS
Wheelbase 229.4cm (90.3in), front and rear track 127cm (50in), ground clearance 13.3cm (5.25in), turning circle 10.7m (35ft), length 391.2cm (154in), width 165.9cm (65.3in), height 80cm (31.5in).

PERFORMANCE
Maximum speed 281.9kph (175.6mph), official timed speed on Mulsanne straight; 38.8kph (24.2mph) @ 1000rpm on 3.54 axle; acceleration 0-96kph (60mph) 7.0sec approx; 4.14kg/kW (3.08kg/bhp); average fuel consumption 18.8-23.5L/100km (12-15mpg).

and exhaust for increased power, a supplementary fuel tank, and aerodynamic alterations to improve stability on the 175.6mph (281.9kph) Mulsanne Straight. They also had some subtle changes to the all-important central structure, the elliptical aluminium-magnesium fabricated tube encompassing the cockpit. The upper portion of the 50-ton high-tensile steel triangular tubular frame, attached to the forward bulkhead and accommodating the engine and front suspension, could now be unbolted in the event of accident damage.

There were revisions to the tail, a stressed-skin fabrication with internal diaphragms, containing aircraft-style flexible fuel tanks. The torsion bar springing was much as before and the principal identification features lay in a nose stretched by 7.5in (19.05cm) to accommodate air ducting, and a closer wrap-round windscreen to reduce wind-buffeting for the driver.

Hawthorn and Fangio were engaged in close racing more like a 10 lap sprint than a 24 hour Grand Prix d'Endurance, when the accident that changed motor racing took place. Pierre Levegh, driving a 300SLR, hit an Austin Healey, and crashed over a wattle fence into the crowd. The Mercedes team was withdrawn and Hawthorn, whose car had been pulling into the pits at the time, went on to a cheerless victory.

It was cheerless too for William Lyons whose only son John Michael Lyons (25) died the same week-end in a road accident.

Right: Hawthorn
drove again for
Jaguar in 1956,
finishing 6th.

Jaguar 2.4 1955-1959

The most fundamental innovation in the history of Jaguar saloon cars came with the introduction of unitary construction for the 2.4. It was scarcely surprising that it did not turn out to be a masterpiece. It broke new ground technically; the production procedures that accompanied its introduction stretched Jaguar Cars to the limit. It aimed at a clientele from whom Jaguar had grown remote with the sports cars and the Mark VII, and although the engine was based on the XK with the same 83mm bore and a shorter (76.5mm) stroke, it was Jaguar's smallest engined car since the 2½-litre Mark V.

There was no doubt that it met a demand when it went on the market at £1269 0s 10d (£1269 4.16p) exactly the same price as the Rover 75. It was undercut by the slower Riley 1½-litre and Wolseley 6/90 at £1205 5s 10d (£1205 29.16p), but it was cheaper than the dull Riley Pathfinder. Its closest real rival, the 2½-litre Daimler Conquest, cost £1511 5s 10p (1511 29.16p), so-called because its basic price before tax was a neat £1066. The Rover was of excellent quality but looked staid; the Daimler was well-made but heavy. The 2.4 Jaguar looked like meeting the needs of customers who

BODY
Saloon; 4-doors; 4-seats; weight 1270.1kg (2800lb).

ENGINE
6-cylinder, in line; front; 83 x 76.5mm; compr 8:1 (7:1 optional); 2483cc; 83.5kW (112bhp) @ 5720rpm; 33.6kW/L (45.1bhp/L).

ENGINE STRUCTURE
Twin chain-driven ohc; 2-valves per cylinder; aluminium cylinder head; cast iron block; 7-bearing crankshaft, damper; Lucas coil ignition; 2 1¾in SU carburettors, water cooled.

TRANSMISSION
Rear wheel drive; clutch 9in Borg-Beck single dry plate; 4-speed manual gearbox, synchromesh on 2,3,4, overdrive optional, automatic 3-speed Borg-Warner optional from 1958 model year; hypoid bevel fd, 4.55:1, overdrive 3.55:1).

CHASSIS DETAILS
Monocoque steel body; ifs, wishbones, coil springs, telescopic dampers, rear trailing link with cantilever semi-elliptic springs & radius arms, telescopic dampers; servo-assisted hydraulic, 11.1in diam drum front brakes (discs optional from 1958), rear brakes 11.1in diam drums; 6.40 tyres, 15in rim.

DIMENSIONS
Wheelbase 273cm (107.4in); front track 139cm (54.7in); rear track 127cm (50in); ground clearance 17.8cm (7in); turning circle 11.5m (33ft 6in); length 459cm (180.75in); width 170cm (66.75in); height 146cm (57.5in).

PERFORMANCE
Maximum speed 162.1kph (101mph); 27.3kph (17mph) @ 1000rpm; 15.2kg/kW (11.3kg/bhp).

Right and following page: By 1958, 2.4 models had the wide grille of the 3.4.

wanted something sporty and stylish without losing any of the woody-leathery milieu to which they wanted to become accustomed.

The 2.4 may have turned out to be something of a disappointment requiring second thoughts in quick time, but it played an essential role in the creation of an important and distinctive ingredient in Jaguar culture. It demonstrated conclusively that a fast luxury car was not the same as a large luxury car. Lyons had shown it before with small-engined versions of his large cars, but the 2.4 reversed the old order by being a small Jaguar in its own right before graduating to a larger engine. It would not be seen as any sort of poor relation to a larger model.

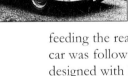

Jaguar aimed to make it in larger numbers than any model hitherto. The 1937 change from coachbuilt to all-steel, and the 1951 innovation of pressed steel was now followed by the change to monocoque construction. A new set of difficulties emerged, including making the body sufficiently stiff, and damping down the resonating noises that came with making it like a drum. Sub-frames for the suspension and heavy applications of sound-damping were put in hand. A 4-cylinder was considered like the one at the start of the XK programme, but discarded although a number of engine sets were made. The 4-cylinder never was sufficiently smooth-running, and since the 6-cylinder 2.4 used the same cylinder head as all the other Jaguars, it offered useful economies of scale.

There were compromises. Torsion bar springs were rejected in favour of coil springs for the front suspension, and to try and save weight in rear body reinforcement, the D-type solution of feeding the rear suspension loads into the centre of the car was followed. A cantilever arrangement was designed with half-elliptic springs, Panhard rod, and trailing arms in conjunction with a narrow-track rear axle, which made the car look sleek with its enclosed rear wheels but which was one of the first items of design that would be subject to revision.

HWM-Jaguar 1955

The XK engine had a reputation that transcended its successes in Jaguar cars. It was used in speed boats such as Christof von Mayenberg's Mathea VII and Norman Buckley's Miss Windermere, adapted for light tanks and fire engines, and enhanced its motor sporting reputation in a number of racing and hill-climb cars.

An early example was Frank Le Gallais's rear engined LGS-Jaguar sprint car. A Jersey man, Le Gallais took a number of records at Bouley Bay and Shelsley Walsh. In 1953 Jaguar sanctioned the use of XK engines in HWM sports cars, its first official non-Jaguar application in racing. HWM had earned respect in Formula 2 against Continental opposition.

By 1954 John Heath and former SS 100 driver George Abecassis had done almost as much as they could with the Formula 2 HWMs, and wanted to get back into 2-seater sports car racing. They built three cars on the popular basis, for the time, of a twin parallel tube chassis with independent front suspension and a De Dion back axle. HWM Jaguars continued racing succesfully until the late 1950s and encouraged the works team to use Weber carburettors.

BODY
Open sports; 2-doors; 2-seats; 864kg (1905lb).

ENGINE
6-cylinders, in line; front; 83 x 106mm, 3442cc; compr 9:1; 179kW (240bhp) @ 5700rpm; 52kW/L (69.7bhp/L).

ENGINE STRUCTURE
Twin ohc; 2-valves per cylinder; aluminium cylinder head; cast iron block; 7- bearing crankshaft; 3 twin-choke Weber carburettors; Lucas coil & distributor; water cooled.

TRANSMISSION
Rear wheel drive; Borg and Beck racing multi-plate clutch; 4-speed gearbox with short central remote control lever; final drive by straight spur gears, spiral bevel, 3.48:1, 4.11:1, 4.17:1, 4.93:1.

CHASSIS DETAILS
Twin tube frame; ifs, transverse spring and wishbone, anti-roll torsion bar, helical springs; Girling dampers, telescopic behind, auxiliary Andre friction dampers front; de Dion rear axle.

PERFORMANCE
Max speed 233kph (145.1mph) with 3.48:1; acceleration 0-96kph (62mph) 6.5sec; standing quarter mile 15sec; 4.8kg/kW (3.6kg/bhp); average fuel consumption 18.8L/100km (15mpg).

Right: HWM-Jaguar-in-waiting. The 1948 Alta GP1, auctioned by Coy's in 1996, was among the first Formula I cars made in Britain after the war. Owned and driven by George Abecassis, it raced for the British Empire Trophy in 1948. Phil Scraggs had it converted to a narrow-bodied sports car by HWM, which replaced the supercharged Alta engine with a 3.4-litreXK.

Cooper-Jaguar 1955

The biggest and last front-engined car made by Charles and John Cooper was inspired by Jaguar works driver and Le Mans winner Peter Whitehead. The D-type never handled as well on tight circuits as the contemporary Aston Martin, and it was in an effort to redress the balance that Whitehead commissioned the Cooper. By contrast with the popular formula for specialist racing cars in the 1950s, of two large-section tubes for the main members and a lot of little tubes built into strong triangles, Cooper rarely suffered a straight tube anywhere. In common with almost all the cars from the tiny workshop in Surbiton, it had independent front suspension using the arrangement its creators knew best, transverse leaf springs along the geometrical lines of the Fiat suspension used for the first 500cc racing cars suitably reinforced. On this occasion it had tubular double wishbones. Wider and lighter than a D-type, the first Cooper-Jaguar used a wet-sump C-type engine, and although it should have been faster it rarely posed a real threat. Later ones had a dry-sump D-type engine. Four Mark II cars were sold, to Peter Whitehead, Tommy Sopwith, Michael Head, and Bernard Ecclestone.

BODY
Open body, nominal 2-seats; 865kg (1907lb)approx.

ENGINE
6-cylinders, in line; front; 83 x 106 mm; 3442cc; compr 8:1 (9:1 optional); 167.8kW (225bhp) @ 5500rpm; 48.7kW/L (65.4bhp/ L); 281.6Nm (29mkp) @ 2500rpm.

ENGINE STRUCTURE
Two chain-drive ohc; 2-valves per cylinder; aluminium cylinder head; cast iron block; 7-bearing crankshaft; 3 twin-choke Weber carburettors; water cooled.

TRANSMISSION
Rear wheel drive; triple plate clutch; 4-speed gearbox; cast magnesium final drive casing, 2.93:1, 3.31:1, 3.92:1, 3.54:1.

CHASSIS DETAILS
Multi-tubular structure, 1˚in tubes main lower members 13swg, remainder 16swg; independent susp front and rear

by double wishbones all round, transverse leaf springs; drum brakes; rack and pinion steering; 181.8L (40 Imp gal) (48 US gal) fuel tank; tyres 6 x 16 front, 6.50 x 16 rear.

DIMENSIONS
Wheelbase 231.1cm (91in), front and rear track 129.5cm (51in), ground clearance 15.2cm (6in).

PERFORMANCE
5.2kg/kW (3.8kg/bhp).

Jaguar Mark VII Monte Carlo Rally-winner 1956

If Le Mans was the biggest event in international motor racing, the most glamorous road event of the year was the Monte Carlo Rally. Like the Olympic Games, victory here transcended anything else. The "Monte" could be unpredictable, with much depending on the weather at the different starting points, and the results of curiously indeterminate tests. Enforcement of the rules could be quirky and there was doubt about the impartiality of the organisers.

Yet in an era when car travel was well established but the continental motorway network was at best incomplete and at worst non-existent, driving long distances in the depths of winter at all looked daunting, and doing so competitively downright heroic. The rally was exhausting for crews who had to drive without sleep or rest, and demanding for cars, many of which could not officially complete the distance without a major service. Winners were usually nimble, although Cecil Vard finished 3rd in a Mark V Jaguar in 1951, another Mark V was 4th in 1952, Ian and Pat Appleyard came 2nd in 1953 in a Mark VII, and Ronnie Adams 6th in 1954.

BODY
Saloon; 4-doors; 4/5-seats; weight 1676.5kg (3696lb).

ENGINE
6-cylinders, in line; front; 83 x 106mm; 3442cc; compr 8:1; 141.7kW (190bhp) @ 5500rpm; 41.2kW/L (55.2bhp/L); 281.6Nm (29mkp) @ 2500rpm.

ENGINE STRUCTURE
Twin chain-driven ohc; 2-valves per cylinder; aluminium cylinder head; cast iron block; 7-bearing crankshaft; Lucas coil ignition; twin horizontal SU carburettors, water cooled.

TRANSMISSION
Rear wheel drive; clutch single dry plate; 4-speed manual gearbox, synchromesh on 2,3,4, overdrive optional, automatic 3-speed Borg-Warner; hypoid bevel final drive, ratio 4.27:1, overdrive ratio 4.55:1.

CHASSIS DETAILS
Box-section steel with pressed steel body; suspension front wishbones & torsion bars; rear semi-elliptic leaf springs; Girling hydraulic dampers; servo-assisted hydraulic 12in dia drum brakes front & rear; Burman recirculating ball steering; 77.3L (17 Imp gal) (20.4 US gal); 6.70 tyres, 16in rims.

DIMENSIONS
Wheelbase 305cm (120in); front track 144cm (56.5in); rear track 147cm (58in); ground clearance 19.05cm (7.5in); length 499cm (196.5in); width 185cm (73in); height 160cm (63in).

PERFORMANCE
Maximum speed 171kph (106.3mph); 29.1kph (18.1mph) @ 1000rpm; acceleration 0-96kph (0-60mph) 11.6sec; 11.8kg/kW (8.8kg/bhp); average fuel consumption 15L/100km (18.8mpg).

Accordingly when Ronnie Adams and Frank Biggar entered a Mark VIIM in 1956 starting from Glasgow, it was with serious intent. Although a large car could be a handful in ice and snow, it did have some advantages over smaller cramped cars in a rally like the Monte, in offering generous living room. It was possible to stretch out in the back of a Mark VII and get some sleep, the car was quiet and restful, there was a useful reserve of power for the competitive stretches, and the handling was superior to quite

a lot of so-called sports cars.

The comfort also helped the navigator, who had to be fairly adroit at map-reading in pre-motorway days and nights, with indifferent sign-posting. The crew also had to be responsible for careful timing and "regularity tests" which involved stopwatches and much calculation.

The Mark VII performed well on the new timed stretches which were the forerunners of special stages.

Jaguar D-Type Ecurie Ecosse Le Mans winners 1956, 1957

Wagers on the 1956 Le Mans race would have received short odds on the works Jaguar D-types driven by Hawthorn/Bueb, Fairman/Wharton, and Frère/Titterington. Their record was formidable. They were running with the 1955 35-40 cylinder heads, so-called because the inlet valves were inclined at 35 deg and the exhausts at 40 deg. Two team cars had Lucas fuel injection, raising the power from 250bhp (186.42kW) to 275bhp (205.07kW), but the privately-entered Ecosse cars had the previous year's Weber carburettors.

Yet within five minutes of the start, two of the cars were out. Paul Frère's and Jack Fairman's crashed at the Esses. A third car suffered misfiring due to a fault in the new Lucas fuel injection and dropped back to finish 6th. Fortunately Jaguar had a second string. Old works cars were disposed of to the Scottish team Ecurie Ecosse, a compliment to its organiser David Murray, and acknowledgement for his loyalty to Jaguar since 1951. Ninian Sanderson and Ron Flockhart saved the day by winning in the "old" cars in 1956, Flockhart again leading a clean sweep of four D-types in 1957 with yet another in 6th place.

BODY
Open 2-seater; 880kg (1940lb).

ENGINE
(1957) 6-cylinders, in line; front; 87 x 106mm, 3781cc; compr 9:1; 212.5kW (285bhp) @ 5750rpm; 56.2kW/L (75.4bhp/L); 324.5Nm (33.5mkp) @ 4000rpm.

ENGINE STRUCTURE
Two chain-drive ohc; 2-valves per cylinder; aluminium cylinder head; cast iron block; 7-bearing crankshaft; 3 twin-choke Weber carburettors; water cooled.

TRANSMISSION
Rear wheel drive; triple plate clutch; 4-speed gearbox; hypoid final drive, 2.54:1.

CHASSIS DETAILS
Steel tubular front sub-frame; stressed skin magnesium centre-section; ifs by wishbones, torsion bars; rear axle on trailing arms, torsion bars; Girling telescopic dampers; Dunlop disc brakes with servo; rack and pinion steering; 163.7L (36 Imp gal) (43.2US gal) fuel tank; Dunlop light alloy disc wheels, 6.50 - 16 tyres.

DIMENSIONS
Wheelbase 229.4cm (90.3in), front and rear track 127cm (50in), ground clearance 13.3cm (5.25in), turning circle 10.7m (35ft), length 391.2cm (154in), width 165.9cm (65.3in), height 80cm (31.5in).

PERFORMANCE
Maximum speed 281.9kph (175.6mph), official timed speed on Mulsanne straight; 38.8kph (24.2mph) @ 1000rpm on 2.54 axle; acceleration 0-96kph (60mph) 4.2sec approx; 4.14kg/kW (3.08kg/bhp); average fuel consumption 18.8-23.5L/100km (12-15mpg).

Right: Winning
form. Ecurie Ecosse
followed up the works
cars' win in 1955 with
victories in 1956 and
1957. Ivor Bueb,
Flockhart's co-driver,
(above) at the wheel
of 1957 winner.

Jaguar MkVII automatic 1956

Automatic transmission was available on export Jaguars for two years before it went on sale in Britain. Strapped for foreign currency, the Board of Trade refused to relax exchange controls allowing the Borg-Warner units to be imported from the United States. Only those which would be re-exported installed in cars were tolerated. The situation only changed when Borg Warner built a factory in Letchworth and two-pedal motoring could be introduced by Jaguar in Britain.

The new transmission consisted of a torque converter and a hydraulically controlled three speed epicyclic gearbox. In 1955 *The Motor* had to explain to readers exactly what kickdown and PNDLR meant (R was only separated from the sequence later to avoid unwanted selection on the move). Gearshifts were smooth and the only real criticism that early testers could level was that with the parking pawl engaged, the selector became difficult to move. The extra cost for automatic transmission was £181 6s 8d (£181 33.3p) and the option was soon extended to the XK140. Laycock de Normanville overdrive continued to be an option on manual Mk VIIs.

BODY
Saloon; 4-doors; 4/5-seats; weight 1765kg (3891lb).

ENGINE
6-cylinders, in line; front; 83 x 106mm; 3442cc; compr 8:1; 119kW (160bhp) @ 5200rpm; 34.6.1kW/L (46.5bhp/L).

ENGINE STRUCTURE
Twin chain-driven ohc; 2-valves per cylinder; aluminium cylinder head; cast iron block; 7-bearing crankshaft; Lucas coil ignition; twin horizontal SU carburettors, water cooled.

TRANSMISSION
Rear wheel drive; clutch single dry plate; 4-speed manual gearbox, synchromesh on 2,3,4, overdrive optional, automatic 3-speed Borg-Warner; hypoid bevel final drive, ratio 4.27:1.

CHASSIS DETAILS
Box-section steel with pressed steel body; suspension front wishbones & torsion bars, hydraulic dampers; rear semi-elliptic leaf springs, hydraulic dampers; servo-assisted hydraulic 12in dia drum brakes front & rear; 77.3L (17 Imp gal) (20.4 US gal); 6.70 tyres, 16in rims.

DIMENSIONS
Wheelbase 305cm (120in); front track 144cm (56.5in); rear track 147cm (58in); ground clearance 19.05cm (7.5in); length 499cm (196.5in); width 185cm (73in); height 160cm (63in).

PERFORMANCE
Maximum speed 160.5kph (100mph); old direct: 31kph (19.3mph) @ 1000rpm; direct: (18.1mph)@ 1000rpm; old: 23.3mph @1000rpm; acceleration 0-96kph (0-60mph) 14.3sec; 14.8kg/kW (11kg/bhp); average fuel consumption 15.3L/100km (18.5mpg).

Jaguar Mark VIII 1957-1959

When the Mark VIII was introduced in the autumn of 1956, it was depicted as a sort of special equipment VII costing an extra £79. It was very little of the kind. The subterfuge was only invoked to clear dealers' unsold stock. It was a replacement, and underwent all the excesses of chrome strips and accessory jewellery that befell so many Jaguars. It was as though Lyons (by New Year 1956 *Sir* William), with a deft touch in creating lilies, was unsure how to gild them.

A one-piece curved windscreen and the option of two-colour paintwork did little for the car's dignity, although picnic tables and deeper upholstery more than lived up to the maker's claims that the interior was a match for anything. Tradition has it that Lyons presented the Mark VII designers with a Mark VI Bentley and instructed them to match it at less than half the price. Automatic transmission cars normally had a bench front seat on which occupants tended to slither on corners. Like the works D-types with the 35-40 cylinder head, the Mark VIII had the inlet valve angle at 45 degrees, and the inlet manifold water gallery was no longer cast integrally.

BODY
Saloon; 4-doors; 4/5-seats; weight 1830kg (4034lb).

ENGINE
6-cylinders, in line; front; 83 x 106mm; 3442cc; compr. 8:1; 156.6kW (210bhp) @ 5500rpm; 45.5kW/L (61bhp/L); 289.7Nm (29.9mkp) @ 3000rpm.

ENGINE STRUCTURE
Twin chain-driven ohc; 2-valves per cylinder; aluminium cylinder head; cast iron block; 7-bearing crankshaft; Lucas coil ignition; twin horizontal SU carburettors, water cooled.

TRANSMISSION
Rear wheel drive; clutch single dry plate; 4-speed manual gearbox, synchromesh on 2,3,4, overdrive optional, automatic 3-speed Borg-Warner; hypoid bevel final drive, 4.27:1.

CHASSIS DETAILS
Box-section steel with pressed steel body; suspension front wishbones & torsion bars, hydraulic dampers; rear semi-elliptic leaf springs, hydraulic dampers; servo-assisted hydraulic 12in dia drum brakes front & rear; 77.3L (17 Imp gal) (20.4 US gal); 6.70 tyres, 16in rims.

DIMENSIONS
Wheelbase 305cm (120in); front track 144cm (56.5in); rear track 147cm (58in); ground clearance 19.05cm (7.5in); length 499cm (196.5in); width 185cm (73in); height 160cm (63in).

PERFORMANCE
Maximum speed 171kph (106.5mph); old direct: 31kph (19.3mph) @ 1000rpm; direct: (18.1mph) @ 1000rpm; old: 23.3mph @ 1000rpm; acceleration 0-96kph (0-60mph) 11.6sec; 11.7kg/kW (8.7kg/bhp); average fuel consumption 15.8L/100km (17.9mpg).

Charges to pay
s.   d.
RECEIVED

A 196

TELEGRAM

POST **O** +✠ TS O

No.
OFFICE STAMP

Prefix. Time handed in. Office of Origin and Service Instructions. Words.

31

D At 328

K127 12.55 . BUCKINGHAM PALACE OHMS 44

SIR WILLIAM LYONS CHAIRMAN JAGUAR CARS LIMITED

CCOVENTRY

I AM SO SORRY TO LEARN OF THE TERRIBLE FIRE A

THE JAGUAR WORKS AND I HOPE THAT YOUR FACTORY

WHICH MY HUSBAND AND I VISITED LAST YEAR WILL

SOON BE IN PRODUCTION AGAIN= ELIZABETH R +

at office of delivery. Other enquiries should be accompanied by this form, and, if possible, the envelope. B or C

Mark VIIIs and 2.4s
were among the cars
destroyed in the
February 1957 fire
(see also p195) which
drew a sympathetic
message from the
Queen. The factory
was back in limited
operation within
36 hours.

189

Jaguar 3.4 1957-1959

Spring 1957 saw the second stage in the development of the small unitary-structure Jaguar, with the introduction of the 3.4-litre engine. It was a sombre time. A fire at the factory in February stopped production for six weeks and destroyed several hundred cars including much of the the launch stock of 3.4s, identifiable by the broad grille of the XK150 (soon to be revealed) instead of the narrow 140 one.

The engine was a full 210bhp (156.59kW) unit with the B-type cylinder head, providing formidable speed and acceleration, faster than an XK120 and almost a match for an XK140. The transmission was fortified to take the additional power, and the Salisbury 4HA back axle was located by a more robust and better-anchored Panhard rod. Disc brakes were an option before the end of 1957. Sporting character was enhanced by a choice of wire wheels (chromed or painted) and modifications to provide more power. The handling was exemplary for the time, although at speed it could catch out even the most experienced. Mike Hawthorn crashed his much-modified car to his death on the Guildford by-pass.

BODY
Saloon; 4-doors; 4-seats; weight 1422.5kg (3136lb).

ENGINE
6-cylinders, in line; front; 83 x 106mm, 3442cc; compr 8:1; 156.6kW (210bhp) @ 5500rpm; 44.7kW/L (60bhp/l); 289.7Nm (29.9mkp) @ 3000rpm.

ENGINE STRUCTURE
Twin chain-driven ohc; 2-valves per cylinder; aluminium cylinder head; cast iron block; 7-bearing crankshaft; Lucas coil ignition; 2 1¾in SU carburettors, water cooled.

TRANSMISSION
Rear-wheel drive; single dry plate clutch, 9in diam; 4-speed manual gearbox, synchromesh on 2,3,4, overdrive optional; hypoid bevel final drive, 3.54:1, overdrive 3.77:1.

CHASSIS DETAILS
Monocoque steel body; front suspension wishbones & coil springs, telescopic dampers; rear trailing link with cantilever semi-elliptic springs and radius arms, telescopic dampers; front servo-assisted disc brakes, 11.75in dia; rear hydraulic drum brakes, 11.1in dim; 6.40 tyres, 15in rim.

DIMENSIONS
Wheelbase 273cm (107.4in); front track 139cm (54.6in); rear track 127cm (50.13in); ground clearance 17.8cm (7in); turning circle 10.6m (34.75ft); length 459cm (180.8in); width 170cm (66.8in); height 146cm (57.5in).

PERFORMANCE
Maximum speed 192.6kph (120mph); 35.2kph (21.9mph)@ 1000rpm; 0-96kph (60mph) 9.1sec manual transmission; 9.1kg/kW (6.8kg/bhp); average fuel consumption 12.8-18.8L/ 100km (15-22mpg).

Jaguar XKSS 1957

The factory fire in February 1957 extinguished the career of the XKSS, a road-going sports car based on the D-type. As a result of the hiatus in production, and dislocation of plans for new product lines as important as the 3.4 saloon, the XKSS was abandoned. It was a cruel fate for a car that was a true thoroughbred, made in the image of the Le Mans winner, and one of the classic might-have-beens of motoring history. It took Jaguar four years to recover its poise with a car that became a 20th century icon, the E-type.

Yet if the E-type represented the best in refinement and road-going elegance, the XKSS had the raw swagger of a race-bred sports car, related to the track in appearance and in accomplishment. It was an open 2-seater with a sketchy hood and a sparkling performance that could be driven to the track, raced, and driven home again. It was a dying breed; a sports car that could be used equally for sport and for transport without elaborate preparation for either. It was a sports car in the mould of the Bugattis, which could do double duty as grand prix racers, or be equipped with wings and headlights to compete

BODY
Sports/racer; 2-doors; 2-seats; weight 920.8kg (2030lb).

ENGINE
6-cylinders, in line; front; 83 x 106mm, 3442cc; compr 9:1; 186.4kW (250bhp) @ 5750rpm; 54.8kW/L (73.5bhp/L); 324.5Nm (33.5mkp) @ 4000-4500rpm.

ENGINE STRUCTURE
Twin chain-driven ohc; 2-valves per cylinder; aluminium cylinder head; cast iron block; 7-bearing crankshaft; Lucas coil ignition; 3 Weber carburettors, water cooled.

TRANSMISSION
Rear wheel drive; clutch triple plate; 4-speed manual synchromesh gearbox; hypoid bevel final drive, ratio 3.54:1.

CHASSIS DETAILS
Semi-monocoque alloy and steel frame; suspension front unequal length wishbones with torsion bars, telescopic dampers, anti-roll bar; rear trailing links & torsion bars, live axle, telescopic dampers; Servo-assisted Dunlop disc brakes front & rear; 168.2L (37 Imp gal) (44.4 US gal); 6.50 tyres, 16in rims.

DIMENSIONS
Wheelbase 230cm (90.6in); front track 127cm (50in); rear track 122cm (48in); ground clearance 13.3cm (5.25in); turning circle 10.7m (35ft); length 399cm (157in); width 166cm (65.5in); height 112cm (44in).

PERFORMANCE
Maximum speed 231.8kph (144mph); 38.5kph (24mph) @1000rpm; acceleration 0-96kph (0-60mph) 5.2sec; standing quarter mile 14.3sec; 4.9kg/kW (3.7kg/bhp); average fuel consumption 15.7-14L/100km (18-20mpg).

at Le Mans and still be driven home.

The XKSS was devised with two objectives. On the one hand a number of D-type monocoques remained unsold, and on the other American owners were keen to have a car eligible for Class C Production racing. The regulations required a road-equipped car, so a road-going D-type looked up to the job. Before the fire the XKSS was not selling well, even at a bargain $6,900, and after the production facility was destroyed in the blaze, only 16 were built.

It was pure production D-type, without the tail fin, and with a full-width windscreen and bumpers. The interior was fully trimmed in leather, and there was a complete set of instruments, but no luggage boot. The occupants had to climb in over a wide sill, after the style of the Mercedes-Benz 300SL, and there was no seat adjustment. Small drivers needed extra cushioning; tall drivers had to crouch. There was not much room for passengers' legs. By way of a concession to the carriage of anything other than two people there was a suitcase grid on the back.

Maximum speeds in gears were 66mph (106.2kph), 85mph (136.79kph), 109mph (175.41kph), and 144mph (231.74kph) at 6000rpm on the 3.54:1 axle, using the middle of the range of axle ratios on offer, which encompassed 2.93, 3.31, 3.92 and 4.09:1. On the highest ratio the maximum on a long straight would be close to 160mph (257.49kph). The handling was not nimble. The D-type was designed to keep going straight at high speeds at Le Mans and that was what the XKSS did best.

Jaguar XK150 3.4 FHC 1957-1961

Third and last of the XK sports cars, the 150 remained true to its stout chassis frame, its broad silhouette, and its twin overhead camshaft engine. But its character was more touring than ever and it renounced some of the 140's luxury trappings. Its body was built out to give more elbow room inside, even though the enamel plaque on the bootlid added 1955, 1956, and 1957 to the proclaimed Le Mans victories 1951-53. It seemed content to fulfil the role of grand tourer.

Its greatest asset was the catalogued inclusion of disc brakes, a legacy of motor racing. Research into discs began in 1951, in conjunction with Dunlop who made them for aircraft, to try and improve the raceworthiness of the C-type. Discs had been used successfully at Rheims in 1952, been crucial in winning Le Mans in 1953, and even though Jaguar was not first to offer them as standard equipment on a road car, the firm was instrumental in their development. A demerit of the XK150 was a failure to develop an effective handbrake. An exclusive Jaguar feature in the optional Borg Warner automatic was an intermediate gear hold to give the driver jurisdiction over upward shifts.

BODY
Coupe; 2-doors; 2+2-seats; weight 1320.9kg (2912lb).

ENGINE
6 cylinders, in line; front; 83 x 106mm; 3442cc; compr 8:1 (7:1, 9:1 optional); 141.7kW (190bhp) @ 5500rpm; 41.7kW/L (55.9bhp/L); 281.6Nm (29mkp) @ 2500rpm.

ENGINE STRUCTURE
Twin chain-driven ohc; 2-valves per cylinder; A-type cylinder head; cast iron block; 7-bearing crankshaft; Lucas coil ignition; 2 1¾in SU carburettors, water cooled.

TRANSMISSION
Rear wheel drive; 10in dia single dry plate clutch; 4-speed manual synchromesh gearbox, overdrive optional, automatic 3-speed Borg Warner; hypoid bevel final drive, ratio 3.54:1, (overdrive 4.09:1).

CHASSIS DETAILS
Box-section with steel body; front suspension independent wishbones, torsion bars, telescopic dampers, anti-roll bar, rear live axle, semi-elliptic leaf springs, telescopic dampers; servo-assisted 12 in dia disc brakes front & rear; rack & pinion steering; 64L (14 Imp gal) (16.8 US gal) fuel tank; 6.00 tyres, 16in rims.

DIMENSIONS
Wheelbase 259cm (102in); front track 131cm (51.63in); rear track 131cm (51.63in); ground clearance 18cm (7.1in); turning circle 10.1m (33ft); length 450cm (177in); width 164cm (64.5in);height 140cm (55in).

PERFORMANCE
Maximum speed 201.3kph (125mph; acceleration 0-96kph (60mph) 8.9sec; standing quarter mile 16.9sec (SE); 9.3kg/kW (7kg/bhp); average fuel consumption 13.8L/100km (20.5mpg).

Jaguar XK150 3.4 DHC 1957-1961

The XK150 was the heaviest XK, even though the bonnet and boot lid were made of aluminium in an effort to keep the weight under 1½tons. The Drophead Coupe with its lined and trimmed hood was the heaviest at 29½ cwt (1498.6Kg). Jaguars tended to put on weight, as they reached middle age, and the XK150 was over 50kg more than the 140. The stouter body increased frontal area although the one-piece windscreen and sleek front disciplined the airflow.

The new windscreen was less of a success in the rain, the wiper blades failing to sweep to the curved edges. It was the sort of anomaly that symbolised the XK150, for by 1957 the basic design was more than ten years old, and in order to handle the increased weight it needed more power. The Blue Top cylinder head, with what was known as the segmental combustion chamber, was brought in to make good the balance. XK quality had improved, the detailing had been enriched, it was a car with some presence, and it was commercially successful yet the lithe appearance and youthful image had gone. Maturity, in the case of the Drophead Coupe at least, could be confused with dullness.

BODY
Convertible; 2-doors; 2-seats; weight 1364kg (3000lb).

ENGINE
6-cylinders, in line; front; 83 x 106mm; 3442cc; compr 8:1 (7:1, 9:1 optional); 157kW (210bhp) @ 5500rpm; 44.7kW/L (60bhp/L); 289.7Nm (29.9mkp) @ 3000rpm.

ENGINE STRUCTURE
Twin chain-driven ohc; 2-valves per cylinder; A-type cylinder head; cast iron block; 7-bearing crankshaft; Lucas coil ignition; 2 1¾in SU carburettors, water cooled.

TRANSMISSION
Rear wheel drive; single dry plate clutch 10in diam; 4-speed synchromesh gearbox, overdrive optional, automatic 3-speed Borg-Warner; hypoid bevel final drive, ratio 3.54:1(overdrive 4.09:1).

CHASSIS DETAILS
Box-section with steel body; independent front suspension, wishbones, torsion bars, telescopic dampers, anti-roll bar; rear live axle, semi-elliptic leaf springs, telescopic dampers; servo-assisted 12in diam disc brakes front & rear; rack & pinion steering; 64.0L (14Imp gal) (16.8US gal) fuel tank; 6.00 tyres, 16in rim.

DIMENSIONS
Wheelbase 259cm (102in); front track 131cm (51.6in); rear track 131cm (51.6in); ground clearance 18cm (7.1in); turning circle 10.1m (33ft); length 450cm (177in); width 164cm (64.5in); height 137cm (54in).

PERFORMANCE
Maximum speed 201.3kph (125mph); 36.3kph (22.6mph) @ 1,000rpm; acceleration 0-96kph (62mph) 8.9sec; 8.7kg/kW (6.5kg/bhp); average fuel consumption 13.8L/100km (20.5mpg).

Lister-Jaguar 1957-1958

Following accomplishments with Bristol engines in 1954-1955 and disappointments with a Maserati unit in 1956, Brian Lister of Cambridge built probably the most successful series of Jaguar-engined non-factory sports-racing cars. Lister's main driver, the remarkable Archie Scott Brown, raced MVE 303 with a dry-sump 3.4-litre XK engine (later a 3.8) in a chassis that formed the basis not only of many Lister designs, but also numerous contemporary small-production cars designed on small budgets for the highly active British sports car racing scene. It consisted of two large-diameter (usually 3in) (7.62cm) steel tubes forming the main frame with three similar-sized cross-members. The driver sat within the frame and the separate aluminium body was mounted on tubular formers. Suspension was equal-length wishbones front and rear. The brakes were Girling single-caliper disc, 11in (27.94cm) at the front and 10in (25.4cm) inboard at the back; steering was by Morris Minor rack and pinion; wheelbase 89in (226.06cm); track 52in (132cm); length 156in (396.24cm); and the height to the scuttle was only 29in (73.66cm). The engine was bought from the factory in

BODY
Sports racing; nominal 2-seats; weight 880kg (1940lb).

ENGINE
6-cylinders, in line; front; 83 x 106mm; 3442cc; compr 9:1; 186.4kW (250bhp) @ 6000rpm; 54.2kW/L (72.6bhp/L); 324.5Nm (33.5mkp) @ 4000rpm.

ENGINE STRUCTURE
Two chain-drive ohc; 2-valves per cylinder; aluminium cylinder head; cast iron block; 7-bearing crankshaft; 3 twin-choke Weber carburettors; water cooled.

TRANSMISSION
Rear wheel drive; clutch triple plate racing; 4-speed synchromesh manual gearbox; Salisbury hypoid bevel final drive.

CHASSIS DETAILS
Tubular construction, aluminium body on tubular formers; front suspension independent equal length wishbones, coli springs; rear DeDion with trailing arms,

coil springs; Girling disc brakes front & rear; rack & pinion steering; 163.7L (36 Imp gal) (43.2 US gal) fuel tank; Dunlop racing tyres & wheels, 6x16in front, 6.50 x16 rear.

DIMENSIONS
Wheelbase 230.2cm (90.6in); front track 132cm (52in); rear track 135.9cm (53.5in); ground clearance 13.3cm (5.25in); length 411.5cm (162in); height 99.1cm (39in) to headrest.

PERFORMANCE
Maximum speed 224.7kph (140mph) or more according to gearing; acceleration 0-96kph (60mph) 4.6sec; 4.1kg/kW (3kg/bhp); average fuel consumption 28.25 (racing)-18.8 (touring)L/100km (10mpg racing, 15mpg touring).

the normal way (later ones were furnished free of charge), tuned by Don Moore and probably gave more than the catalogued 3.4 D-type output of 250bhp (186.43kW). There was a ZF differential in the Salisbury back axle casing. MVE 303 weighed some 812 kg (1791.9lb) which was less than a D-type, so it reached 60mph (96.56kph) in 4.6sec, 80mph (128.74kph) in 8.0sec, 100mph 160.93kph) in 11.2sec, and 120mph (193.12kph) in 15.2sec. John Bolster tested the car and described the acceleration to 140mph (225.3kph) as breathtaking, guessing a top speed of around 190mph (305.77kph) with higher gearing than the standard 3.73:1.

The Lister-Jaguar was a triumph, winning 12 races out of 14 and setting lap records wherever it went in its first season. Its successors were equally formidable and were campaigned by Scott Brown until his death in 1958, Masten Gregory, Bruce Halford, Briggs Cunningham, Walt Hansgen, Peter Whitehead, and Carroll Shelby.

The Border Reivers also bought a Lister-Jaguar as a replacement for its D-type Jaguar on which the young Jim Clark began serious racing. "The Lister taught me a great deal about racing..." he wrote. "...a beast of a thing... but more fun than any except maybe the Aston Martins I drove later."

A Lister-Jaguar single-seater was built following the success of the Ecurie Ecosse D-types at Monza against Indianapolis roadsters. An invitation to Ecosse to race a D-type-derived car in America was on the cards, and a fund was set up to pay for it, so an offset single-seater was commissioned notwithstanding the antipathy between Brian Lister and David Murray, the team's owner. Ecosse ran it in the 1958 repeat race at Monza where it proved slower than the D-types before its engine failed. It weighed 762Kg (1680lb) so it had little advantage to offer over a sports Lister and was only 101.6kg (224.13lb) under a production D-type.

It was later turned it into a 2-seater sports car.

Right: Archie Scott Brown racing the familiar green and yellow Lister-Jaguar with dry-sump engine.

Jaguar E-Type prototype E1A 1957

Only ten years elapsed between the XK120 and the gestating E-type yet an automotive age had passed. In many essentials the XK120 remained a car of the 1930s, more refined, smoothly styled, with a magnificent engine, but with a chassis rooted in a vernacular that Panhard might have recognised and Porsche would have scoffed at. To Panhard the E-type might have been a space-ship; to Porsche it would have been a source of wonder.

There were two main prototypes. The first E1A was small, made of aluminium, and followed the pattern of the D-type with a central monocoque, deep side sills, and a magnesium forward framework for the engine. It had a 2.4-litre short-block engine to fit under the low bonnet, and its main purpose was to evaluate the independent rear suspension, evolving under W M Heynes and R J Knight, an outstanding experimental engineer. The main lesson it taught was that the production car should have the suspension mounted in its own cradle sub-frame, one of the key ingredients in a design, some elements of which lasted three times as long as the production run of the XK.

BODY
Sports; 2-doors; 2-seats; weight 812.9kg (1792lb).

ENGINE
XK 2.4-litre; 6-cylinders, in line; front; 83 x 76.5mm, 2483cc; compr 8:1; 89.5kW (120bhp) @ 5750rpm; 36kW/L (48.3bhp/L); 193.1Nm (19.9mkp) @ 2000rpm.

ENGINE STRUCTURE
Twin chain-driven ohc; 2-valves per cylinder; aluminium cylinder head; cast iron block; 7-bearing crankshaft, damper; Lucas coil ignition; twin SU HD8 carburettors; water cooled.

TRANSMISSION
Rear wheel drive; single dry plate clutch; 4-speed gearbox; hypoid bevel final drive.

CHASSIS DETAILS
Aluminium monocoque; ifs, wishbone & coil springs; independent experimental rear suspension; servo-assisted disc brakes outboard at front, inboard at rear; Dunlop road or racing tyres.

DIMENSIONS
Length 432cm (170in); width 160cm (63in).

Christopher Jennings wrote in 1958 in a confidential memo: "Production is expected to begin in the autumn and the target is 100 cars per week. With a 3-litre engine it will develop 285bhp and I visualise a road test speed not very far short of 150mph". On a secret Sunday morning test run Jennings covered the 20 miles from Carmarthen to Llandovery at an average speed of just over 70mph. He reached Brecon in 43 minutes giving an average for 48.5 miles of 67.7mph. "At no time did we exceed 120mph".

Above: Bob Knight, mastermind behind the E-type rear suspension, developments of which Jaguar used for many years.

Jaguar Mark IX 1958-1961

Except for its badges the Mark IX was outwardly identical to the Mark VIII. The appliqué chrome was not allowed to spread further than it already had, and some useful changes were incorporated for the London Motor Show of 1958. The Mark IX was the first Jaguar to have standard disc brakes, and power steering which allowed the turns from lock to lock to be reduced to 3½. Early Mark VIIs had an arm-twirling 4¾ turns and the reduction was welcome. The brakes were Dunlop, enabling the lively performance of this large and heavy car to be used with confidence. Road testers were unimpressed by some aspects, notably brake pad knock-off after corners and an ineffective handbrake.

The Mark IX was also first with the 3.8-litre engine. This had a new cylinder block which was not simply a 3.4 bored-out from 83mm to 87mm. It had dry cylinder liners for a 10bhp (7.5kW) increase in power and 11% more torque. There was an improvement in the mixture distribution from the SU auxiliary starting carburettor. Road testers grumbled about wind noise and the meagre output from the heater, an endemic problem with Jaguars well into the 1960s.

BODY
Saloon; 4-doors; 4/5 seats; weight 1803.5kg (3976lb).

ENGINE
6-cylinder, in line; front; 3781cc; 87 x 106mm; compr 8:1; 164kW (220bhp) @ 5500rpm; 43.2kW/L (57.9bhp/L); 321.6Nm (33.2mkp) @ 3000rpm.

ENGINE STRUCTURE
Twin chain-driven ohc; 2-valves per cylinder; aluminium cylinder head; cast iron block; 7-bearing crankshaft; Lucas coil ignition; twin horizontal SU carburettors, water cooled.

TRANSMISSION
Rear wheel drive; clutch single dry plate; 4-speed manual synchromesh gearbox, overdrive optional; automatic 3-speed Borg-Warner; hypoid bevel fd, 4.27:1, 3.54:1 overdrive, auto 4.27:1.

CHASSIS DETAILS
Steel box-section with pressed steel body; front suspension wishbones & torsion bars, telescopic dampers; rear semi-elliptic leaf springs, telescopic dampers; Burman recirculating ball worm-and-nut power-assisted steering; servo-assisted disc brakes front & rear; 77.3L (17 Imp gal)(20.4 US gal) fuel tank; 6.70 tyres, 16in rim.

DIMENSIONS
Wheelbase 305cm (120in); front track 144cm (56.5in); rear track 147cm (58in); ground clearance 19cm (7.5in); turning circle 11.3m (37ft); length 499cm (196.5in); width 185cm (73in); height 160cm (63in).

PERFORMANCE
Maximum speed 183.5kph (114mph); acceleration 0-96kph (60mph) 11.9sec; 31.1kph (19.35mph) @ 1000rpm; standing quarter mile 18.1sec; 11kg/kW (8.2kg/bhp); average fuel consumption 20.9L/100km (13.5mpg).

Tojeiro-Jaguar 1958

John Tojeiro came from much the same empirical engineering background as Brian Lister. The chassis of his Tojeiro-Jaguar was a multi-tube affair, with front suspension by unequal length wishbones and a De Dion axle at the back. The wheelbase was 87in (220.9cm) and at 787 kg (1735lb) it was among the lighter Jaguar-engined sports-racers. In 1956 it had a wet-sump D-type engine and although it had good traction, it had less satisfactory roadholding than its Lister rivals.

By 1958, with a dry-sump engine and lightened to 711kg (1567.4lb), it was competitive although less successful than the Listers. The De Dion rear suspension was abandoned for a Watts linkage to try and improve the handling, and it ran at Le Mans with an 86mm x 86mm engine which predictably failed with a warped cylinder head. Apart from a victory by Ron Flockhart in the 1959 BARC Goodwood Whit Monday meeting, it was not an achiever. Ecurie Ecosse entered it for Masten Gregory and Jim Clark in the 1959 TT, Clark's sole drive with the rival to the Reivers, only for Gregory to write it off by driving headlong into the bank at Woodcote.

BODY
Sports; 2-doors; nominal 2-seats; weight 762kg (1680lb).

ENGINE
6-cyl, in line; front; 83 x 106mm, 3442cc; compr 9:1; 186.4kW (250bhp) @ 5750rpm; 54.8kW/L (73.5bhp/L); 324.5Nm (33.5mkp) @ 4000-4500rpm.

ENGINE STRUCTURE
2 chain-drive ohc; 2-valves per cyl; aluminium cylinder head; cast iron block; 7-bearing crankshaft; 3 twin-choke Weber carburettors; water cooled.

TRANSMISSION
Rear wheel drive; 4-speed; Salisbury hypoid final drive, ZF diff.

CHASSIS DETAILS
Multi-tubular with ifs by unequal length double wishbones, coil springs; rear suspension de Dion axle on parallel trailing arms and central bronze slide block, coil springs *(see text)*; disc brakes inboard at rear; Dunlop racing tyres 600, 16in rims front, 650, 16in rear, light alloy wheels.

DIMENSIONS
Wheelbase 220.9cm (87in), front and rear track 127cm (50in); height 81.3cm (32in).

PERFORMANCE
Maximum speed 244.8kph (152.5mph); acceleration 0-100kph (62mph) 5.4sec; standing quarter mile 13.6sec; 4kg/kW (3kg/bhp); average fuel consumption 18.8L/100km (15mpg).

Right: Short-lived. The Ecurie Ecosse Tojeiro-Jaguar at the Goodwood TT of 1959, [W E (Wilkie) Wilkinson alongside in attendance] where it was driven by Jim Clark and Masten Gregory. It was wrecked by Gregory in spectacular fashion at Woodcote.

Jaguar XK150S 3.4 2-seater roadster 1958-1960

The chassis of the XK150 retained the modifications for the XK140 such as the telescopic rear dampers and modified cross-member making room for the overdrive and twin exhaust. The roadster was not announced until the spring of 1958, and rejected wood veneer for the door cappings and facia. It was trimmed in leather instead, which had the advantage of safety padding, but tended to soil easily.

The extra weight of the XK150 threatened its performance advantage, a jealously guarded Jaguar feature. The S model was given a third SU 2in carburettor and what was known as a "straight port" cylinder head with the ports rearranged to improve engine breathing. Borg-Warner automatic transmission was available only with the less powerful versions. When the full 250bhp (186.43kW) engine was specified it was strictly manual with overdrive only. The Roadster also broke with tradition by having wind-up windows instead of sidescreens, and the hood was more draught-and-weather proof than before. Demerits included the old XK grievance about the gearbox, and a handbrake that was at best only 25% effective.

BODY

Sports; 2-doors; 2-seats; weight 1432.6kg (3158lb).

ENGINE

6-cylinder, in line; front; 83 x 106mm; 3442cc; compr 9:1; 186kW (250bhp) @ 5500rpm; 53.1kW/L (71.4bhp/L); 322Nm (33.2mkp)@ 4500rpm.

ENGINE STRUCTURE

Twin chain-driven ohc; 2-valves per cylinder; A-type cylinder head; cast iron block; 7-bearing crankshaft; Lucas coil ignition; 2 1¾in SU carburettors, water cooled.

TRANSMISSION

Rear wheel drive; clutch 10in dia single dry plate; 4-speed synchromesh manual gearbox, overdrive standard; hypoid bevel final drive, limited-slip differential, ratio 3.54:1.

CHASSIS DETAILS

Box-section with steel body; ifs, wishbone, torsion bars, telescopic dampers, anti-roll bar, rear live axle, semi-elliptic leaf springs, telescopic dampers; servo-assisted 12in diam disc brakes front & rear; 64L (14 Imp gal) (16.8 US gal) fuel tank; 6.00 tyres, 16in rim.

DIMENSIONS

Wheelbase 259cm (102in); front track 131cm (51.6in); rear track 131cm (51.6in); ground clearance 18cm (7.1in); turning circle 10.1m (33ft); length 450cm (177in); width 164cm (64.5in); height 140cm (55in).

PERFORMANCE

Maximum speed 219kph (136mph); acceleration 0-97kph (0-60mph) 7.9 sec; 7.7kg/kW (20kg/bhp); standing quarter mile 15.1sec; average fuel consumption 14.9-20L/100km (14-19mpg).

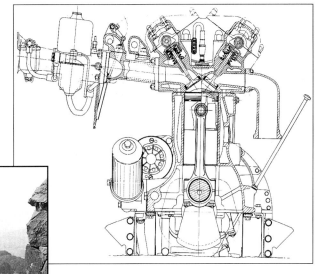

Above: Jaguar remained faithful to the classic twin-cam XK cylinder head with its hemispherical combustion chambers throughout. Only detailed changes to the valve angles and porting were carried out throughout its life.

Jaguar XK150S 3.8 FHC 1959-1961

The fastest standard XK of 1959 was almost a match for the road-going C-type. When *The Motor* tested a fixed head coupe in March 1959, it enthused about yesterday's racing car being today's road car, perhaps the last time such an assertion could truthfully be made. The XK150 had certainly benefitted from Jaguar's racing experience, both in details such as the crack-tested connecting rods that followed a 1950 failure of Biondetti's XK120, to the steel engine-oil pipe brought in after a failure at Le Mans. Like many evolving Jaguars however it had put on weight.

The 150S was faster than the C-type to 60mph (96.56kph) but neither was swifter to 100mph (160.93kph) which they reached in a fraction over 20sec. Their standing quarter mile times were identical at 16.2sec, and the road car's top gear and overdrive performance was superior thanks to the improvement in mid-range pulling power. The 150's top speed of 132mph (212.43kph) was the same as that achieved by the aluminium XK120 of 1949, yet only 11mph (17.7kph) short of a C-type, a tribute to the XK engine, a far-sighted design, which still had a long way to go.

BODY
Coupe; 2-doors; 2-seats; weight 1609kg (3548lb).

ENGINE
6-cylinder, in line; front; 87 x 106mm; 3781cc; compr 9:1 (8:1 optional); 197.6kW (265bhp) @ 5500rpm; 52kW/L (69.8bhp/L); 348.7Nm (36mkp)@ 4000rpm.

ENGINE STRUCTURE
Twin chain-driven ohc; 2-valves per cylinder; A-type cylinder head; cast iron block; 7-bearing crankshaft; Lucas coil ignition; 2 1¾in SU carburettors, water cooled.

TRANSMISSION
Rear wheel drive; 10in diam single dry plate clutch; 4-speed synchromesh manual gearbox, overdrive standard; hypoid bevel final drive, ratio 3.10:1.

CHASSIS DETAILS
Box section with steel body; ifs, wishbone, torsion bars, telescopic dampers, anti-roll bar; rear live axle, semi-elliptic leaf springs, telescopic dampers; hydraulic vaccum servo-assisted 12in diam disc brakes front & rear; 64L (14 Imp gal) (16.8 US gal) fuel tank; 6.00 tyres 16 rim.

DIMENSIONS
Wheelbase 259cm (102in); front track 131cm (51.6in); rear track 131cm (51.6in); ground clearance 18cm (7.1in); turning circle 10.1m (33ft); length 450cm (177in); width 164cm (64.5in); height 137cm (54in).

PERFORMANCE
Maximum speed 212.4kph (132mph); acceleration 0-96kph (60mph) 7.6sec; standing quarter mile 16.2sec; 8.1kg/kW (6kg/bhp); average fuel cons 20.9L/100km (13mpg) hard driving.

The 3.8 engine and 'S' modifications on 3.4 and 3.8 were also available on DHC and roadster.

Above: Early
XK works driver
Stirling Moss talks
to the boss, Sir
William Lyons.

Jaguar E-Type prototype E2A 1959

After E1A's test programme, which included a celebrated secret week-end in the hands of Christopher Jennings, editor of *The Motor*, a second prototype was made in steel. It was closer to the production E-type and in due course emerged as a fully-welded road-going test vehicle. Its gestation occupied fully four years.

E2A was something of a diversion, and although its appearance was close to how the E-type emerged, its nearest relative was the D-type. It had a light alloy centre section, which instead of finishing behind the driver, included a shapely tail to house a prototype of the E-type's independent rear suspension. The engine was a 3.0-litre fuel injected dry-sump D-type, with an aluminium block and steel cylinder liners, saving some 80lb (36.28kg), although the car as a whole was heavier than a D-type by about the same amount. Briggs Cunningham saw E2A in Jaguar's experimental department and persuaded the factory, by now out of racing, to let him enter it for the 1960 Le Mans. It was fast but not a success. Re-equipped with a 3.8-litre Weber-carburetted engine, it won memorably in America ahead of a Lister-Jaguar and a Birdcage Maserati.

BODY
Open Sports racing; 2-doors; nominal 2-seats; weight 952.6kg (2100lb).

ENGINE
XK 3.0-litre (later 3.8-litre with Weber carburettors, 294bhp); 6-cylinders, in line; front; 85 x 88mm, 2997cc; compr 10.0:1; 218.5kW (293bhp) @ 6750rpm; 72.9kW/L (97.8bhp/L); 308.4Nm (31.8mkp) @ 6000rpm.

ENGINE STRUCTURE
Twin chain-driven ohc; 2-valves per cylinder; aluminium cylinder head and block with pressed-in liners; 7-bearing crankshaft; Lucas fuel injection; water cooled.

TRANSMISSION
Rear wheel drive; triple-plate racing clutch; 4-speed all synchromesh manual gearbox; hypoid bevel final drive, limited-slip differential, 3.1:1.

CHASSIS DETAILS
Aluminium alloy monocoque; front suspension, wishbones & torsion bars, telescopic dampers; rear independent, lower wishbones, drive-shaft as top link, twin coil spring/damper units; Dunlop 10.75in disc brakes at front, 10.25in disc brakes at rear; tyres 6.50, 16in rims.

DIMENSIONS
Wheelbase 244cm (96in); front track 122cm (48in); rear track 122cm (48in); length 432cm (170in); width 159cm (62.75in); height 135cm (53.25in).

Top right: E2A in its raw state as a works prototype and (*far right*) resplendent in Cunningham's American blue and white, posed by the old Brown's Lane gatehouse.

Jaguar Mark 2 2.4 1959-1967

Jaguar's second thoughts on appearance and handling became the most successful Jaguar until the XJ6. Over 100,000 Mark 2s were made, and it established such a reputation among what used to be called sports saloons, that its recipe was reformulated in the 1990s.

    The same size and much the same shape as its predecessor, Sir William transformed the gloomy interior and enriched the appearance at a stroke, which not only proved he had a deft touch for styling but had not lost his cost-cutting cunning. The transformation was achieved by little more than replacement of the upper door pressings with chromed frames for the windows. The windscreen was deeper too, and the effect was a brighter airier interior, and a lighter sleeker look. The rear track was widened, and reshaping the back improved the proportions of the car, but increased the weight by around 50kg. As a result the 2.4 was unable to reach 100mph (160.93kph), although with high-lift cams, a D-type head and 8bhp (5.96kW) extra, it just might. Jaguar declined all attempts to provide one for press road test. Exasperated, *The Autocar* tried a second-hand one, which achieved 96.3mph (154.97kph).

BODY
Saloon; 4-doors; 4-seats; weight 1447.8kg (3192lb).

ENGINE
6-cylinder, in line; front; 83 x 76.5mm, 2483cc; compr 8:1; 89.5kW (120bhp) @ 5750rpm; 16.5kW/L (50bhp/L); 193Nm (19.9mkp) @ 2000rpm.

ENGINE STRUCTURE
Twin chain-driven ohc; 2-valves per cylinder; aluminium cylinder head; cast iron block; 7-bearing crankshaft, damper; Lucas coil ignition; twin Solex carburettors, water cooled.

TRANSMISSION
Rear wheel drive; 4-speed gearbox; final drive, 4.27:1, overdrive 3.54:1.

CHASSIS DETAILS
Steel unitary construction; ifs, double wishbones, coil springs, anti-roll bar; rear cantilevered live axle, parallel radius arms, Panhard rod, semi-elliptic leaf springs; telescopic dampers; Dunlop disc brakes front and rear, vacuum servo; Burman recirculating ball steering; PAS optional; 54.6L (12 Imp gal) (14.4US gal) fuel tank; Dunlop 6.4, 15in rim.

DIMENSIONS
Wheelbase 273cm (107.4in); front track 139.7cm (55in); rear track 135.6cm (53.4in); ground clearance 17.8cm (7in); length 459cm (180.75in); width 169.5cm (66.75in); height 147cm (57.75in).

PERFORMANCE
Maximum speed 154.6kph (96.3mph); 27.3kph (17.0mph) @ 1000rpm [35.2kph (21.9mph) with overdrive]; acceleration 0-100kph (62mph) 17.3sec; standing quarter mile 20.8sec; 36.7kg/kW (12.1kg/bhp); average fuel consumption 15.7L/100km (18mpg).

Jaguar Mark 2 3.4 1959-1967

The wider back axle contributed to the Mark 2's good behaviour. The axle casing extended outwards by one and five-eighths of an inch (4.13cm) on each side to make the track 3¼in (8.25cm) wider. The front track was still one and five-eighths of an inch (4.13cm) more; Jaguar claimed that to make them both the same would have been expensive and spoiled the sleek tail. The wider track meant the rear wheelarch cover was cut away in the centre. Among other detail changes which altered the car's appearance was a larger, curved back window, and scooped-out portions in the rear quarters to accommodate bigger side windows.

Mechanical changes included angling the front wishbones downwards, to lift the roll centre and reduce body roll on corners. The Mark 2 felt more stable partly owing to the wider rear, partly to the improved front suspension, and partly to having a fraction more weight on the front wheels. The additional overall weight affected acceleration compared with the 'Mark I', adding 0.5sec to the 0-60mph time. Jaguar tried to improve the heater, which had a claimed output of 3.9kW, but against the competition it remained woefully inadequate.

BODY
Saloon; 4-doors; 4-seats; weight 1498.7kg (3304lb).

ENGINE
6-cylinder, in line; front; 83 x 106mm 3442cc; compr 8:1; 156.6kW (210bhp) @ 5500rpm; 46.1kW/L (61.8bhp/L); 289.7Nm (29.9mkp) @ 3000rpm.

ENGINE STRUCTURE
Twin chain-driven ohc; 2-valves per cylinder; aluminium cylinder head; cast iron block; 7-bearing crankshaft; Lucas coil ignition; 2 1¾in SU carburettors, water cooled.

TRANSMISSION
Rear wheel drive; single dry plate 9in diam clutch; 4-speed manual synchromesh gearbox, overdrive optional, automatic 3-speed Borg-Warner; hypoid bevel final drive, 3.54:1, 3.77:1 overdrive.

CHASSIS DETAILS
Monocoque steel body; front wishbones, coil springs, telescopic dampers; rear trailing link with cantilever semi-elliptic springs & radius arms, telescopic dampers; servo-assisted disc brakes front & rear; 54.6L (12 Imp gal) (14.4US gal) fuel tank; 6.40 tyres, 15in rim.

DIMENSIONS
Wheelbase 273cm (107.4in); front track 140cm (55in); rear track 136cm (53.4in); ground clearance 17.8cm (7in); turning circle 10.6m (34.75ft); length 459cm (180.75in); width 170cm (66.75in); height 146cm (57.5in).

PERFORMANCE
Maximum speed 192.6kph (120mph); 34.4kph (21.4mph) @ 1000rpm; acceleration 0-100kph (62mph) 11.9sec; standing quarter mile 19.1sec; 9.6kg/kW (7.1kg/bhp); average fuel consumption 17.7L/100km (16mpg).

219

Jaguar Mark 2 3.8 1959-1967

The flagship Mark 2 3.8-litre was often supplied with optional wire wheels which could be chromed, silver enamelled, or painted in body colour. Slightly showy, with a *basso profundo* exhaust note, the 3.8 was equally at home in a concours d'elegance or the rough and tumble of a saloon car race. Now that the handling had been put right, ("...a more stable ride with increased resistance to roll," *The Motor* confirmed), it was a formidable performer on the racetrack. America voted it Best Imported Car for several years.

Power steering was overdue however. It did not appear on home-market cars until 1960, and while five turns lock to lock and the poor response in the mid-sector of the manual rack and pinion was still acceptable in America, it was unpopular elsewhere. An optional steering box with 3½ turns was available but it was heavy. Mark 2 3.8s had Powr-Lok limited slip differentials as standard, eliminating the 'Mark I' tendency to axle tramp. The device made in Britain, under licence from the Thornton Axle Company of America, had small multi-plate clutches which released the supply of torque to the wheel with least grip.

BODY
Saloon; 4-doors; 4-seats; weight 1525kg (3362lb).

ENGINE
6-cylinders, in line; front; 87 x 106mm, 3781cc; compr 8:1; 164kW (220bhp) @ 5500rpm; 43.2kW/L (57.9bhp/L); 321.8Nm (33.2mkp) @ 3000rpm.

ENGINE STRUCTURE
Twin chain-driven ohc; 2-valves per cylinder; aluminium cylinder head; cast iron block; 7-bearing crankshaft; Lucas coil ignition; two 1¾in SU carburettors, water cooled.

TRANSMISSION
Rear wheel drive; single dry plate 9in dia clutch; 4-speed manual synchromesh gearbox, overdrive optional, automatic 3-speed Borg-Warner; hypoid bevel final drive, limited slip differential, 3.54:1, 3.77:1 overdrive.

CHASSIS DETAILS
Monocoque steel body; front suspension wishbones & coil springs, telescopic dampers; rear trailing link with cantilever semi-elliptic springs & radius arms, telescopic dampers; servo-assisted disc brakes front & rear; 6.40 tyres, 15in rim.

DIMENSIONS
Wheelbase 273cm (107.4in); front track 140cm (55in); rear track 136cm (53.4in); ground clearance 17.8cm (7in); turning circle 10.6m (34.75ft); length 459cm (180.75in); width 146cm (66.75in); height 146cm (57.5in).

PERFORMANCE
Maximum speed 200.7kph (125mph); acceleration 0-96kph (60mph) 8.8sec; 34.4kph (21.4mph) @ 1000rpm; standing quarter mile 16.3sec; 9.3kg/kW (6.9kg/bhp); average fuel consumption 18L/100km (15.7mpg).

Jaguar Mark X 3.8 1961-1964

The early 1960s was the era of Kennedy and Kruschev, Macmillan's wind of change, the first man in space, and Jaguar's takeover of Daimler and introduction of the Mark X. It had a unitary structure, E-type independent rear suspension, voluptuous curves, and an interior of great luxury and immense space. It was wider than a Rolls-Royce Silver Cloud, with generous elbow-room and leg-room. It had an exemplary ride and well-mannered handling even though it covered the road area of a small bus. It was also roughly the weight of a small bus, at getting on for two tons, so it needed all the power it could get from the now venerable XK engine. It was the first saloon Jaguar to be equipped with the "straight port" cylinder head, in which the ports were not so much straight as slightly less crooked, giving better cylinder filling with more control of turbulence. This engine also pioneered equal length inlet tracts, subsequently reinvented.

It was Jaguar's biggest car and at less than £2500 including tax maintained the company's reputation for astonishingly good value although its quality was probably not up to the standards of its predecessors.

BODY
Saloon; 4-doors; 5-seats; weight 1892kg (4171lb).

ENGINE
6-cylinders; front; 87 x 106mm; 3781cc; compr 8:1 (7:1,9:1 opt); 197.6kW (265bhp) @ 5500rpm; 52.3kW/L(70.1bhp/L); 348.7Nm (36mkp)@ 4000rpm.

ENGINE STRUCTURE
Twin chain-driven ohc; 2-valves per cyl; aluminium cyl head; cast iron block; 7-bearing crankshaft; Lucas coil ignition; 2 1¾in SU carburettors, water cooled.

TRANSMISSION
Rear wheel drive; sdp clutch; 4-spd synchromesh, auto 3-spd Borg-Warner DG; hypoid bevel final drive, limited-slip diff; 3.54:1, 2.933:1 overdrive.

CHASSIS DETAILS
Monocoque steel body; ifs with wishbones & coil springs, telescopic dampers; irs, drive shafts & lower tansverse links; twin coil spring/damper units; servo assisted disc brakes, rear inboard; Burman recirculating ball PAS; 90.9L (20 Imp gal) (24US gal) fuel tank; tyres 7.50 x 14 RS5.

DIMENSIONS
Wheelbase 305cm (120in); front & rear track 147cm (58in); ground clearance 13.3cm (5.25in); turning circle 10.3m (34ft) [11.3m (37ft) right]; length 513cm (202in); width 193cm (76in); height 138cm (54.5in).

PERFORMANCE
Max speed 192.6kph (120mph); 33.9kph (21.1mph) @ 1000rpm in top gear; 0-96kph (0-60mph) 10.4sec; standing quarter mile 17.4sec; 9.6kg/kW (7.1kg/bhp); av fuel cons 20.8L/100km) (13.6mpg).

Far right: **Sir William Lyons with Mark Xs at Browns Lane headquarters.**

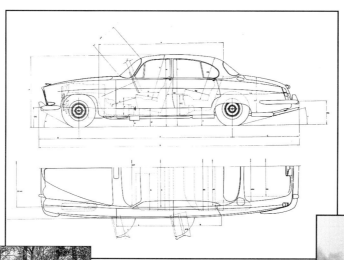

Jaguar E-Type 3.8 FHC 1961-1964

An automotive classic, the E-type Jaguar was the epitome of the modern sports touring car. The successor to the XK, it evoked the lines and style of the D-type, slimmed and refined to create a beautiful car that became a symbol of the 1960s. More attainable than a Ferrari, more charismatic than a Rolls-Royce, racier than a Mercedes-Benz, the E-type stamped its image on a generation and its shape became an icon of the so-called swinging sixties.

Its basis was straightforward. Both the open and closed versions had a cockpit made up of welded steel pressings, with the independent rear suspension carried in its cradle underneath. The front of the car was constructed of Reynolds 541 square section steel tubing, containing the engine, and carrying the front suspension. A smaller tubular sub-frame was bolted to the front of this, supporting the radiator and front bonnet anchor. The bonnet hinged upwards for access to the engine and front suspension, and comprised the entire nose-section of the car, with complicated ducts and electrical connections. It was an elaborate and expensive item of equipment, as anybody unfortunate enough to

BODY
Coupe; 2-doors; 2-seats; weight 1219.2kg (2688lb).

ENGINE
6-cylinders, in line; front; 87 x 106mm; 3781cc; compr 9:1 (8:1 optional); 197.6kW (265bhp) @ 5500rpm; 348.7Nm (36mkp) @ 4000rpm.

ENGINE STRUCTURE
Twin chain-driven ohc; 2-valves per cylinder; aluminium cylinder head; cast iron block; 7-bearing crankshaft; Lucas coil ignition; 3 x 2in SU carburettors, water cooled.

TRANSMISSION
Rear wheel drive; single dry plate clutch; 4-speed manual gearbox, synchromesh 2,3,4; hypoid bevel final drive, limited-slip differential, ratio 3.31:1, options 4.09:1, 3.77:1, 3.07:1, 3.27:1.

CHASSIS DETAILS
Monocoque steel; ifs, wishbone, torsion bars, telescopic dampers, anti-roll bar, independent rear susp by lower wishbone, upper driveshaft link, radius arms, twin coil spring/damper units, anti-roll bar; servo-assisted discs front & rear; 63.6L (14 Imp gal) (16.8US gal) fuel tank; 7.50 x 14, or 6.40 x 15 RS5 tyres.

DIMENSIONS
Wheelbase 244cm (96in); front track 127cm (50in); rear track 127cm (50in); ground clearance 12.7cm (5in); turning circle 12.3m R (40.4ft), 11.7m L (38.4ft); length 444cm (175in); width 165cm (65in); height 122cm (48in).

PERFORMANCE
Maximum speed 243.1kph (151mph); acceleration 0-96kph (60mph) 7.0sec; 36.9kph (23mph) @ 1000rpm; standing quarter mile 14.7sec; 6.2kg/kW (4.6kg/bhp); average fuel consumption 15.8L/100km (17.9mpg).

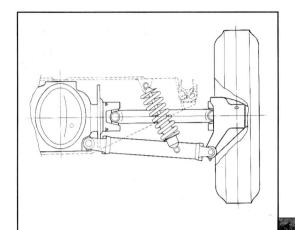

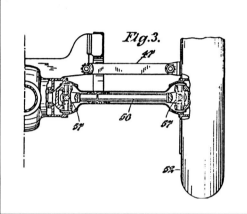

Fig.3.

Above: Key ingredient in the success of the E-type, Bob Knight's clever adaptation of Georges Roesch's 1933 proposal *(top right)* which used the driveshaft as integral part of suspension. Inboard brake discs proved problematical.

damage one soon found out.

The E-type was introduced at the Geneva motor show, its official unveiling in the Parc des Eaux Vives, within sight of the famous jet d'eau fountain. It created shock-waves throughout the European motor industry. Its UK price was less than £1500, its projected top speed was 150mph (241.39kph), and it looked the quintessence of quality.

The Autocar and *The Motor* road tested E-Types at 150mph, but it soon emerged that there had been some duplicity. Production E-Types seldom got near 150mph, their reputation was sullied with overheating inboard disc brakes and, as the years passed they tended to rust.

Yet in 1961 they changed the world. They set standards in ride and handling that lasted throughout the decade. They arrived at the dawn of the motorway age in Britain, when people could still dream of dashing from one end of the country to the other at unfettered speed. Nervous ministers of transport impatient to impose the 70mph limit were years away.

Jaguar was delighted with the reception given the E-Type. The social elite of Geneva queued up – literally – to be whisked up a hill-climb course by test driver Norman Dewis, and Jaguar PRO Bob Berry, who raced a D-type. So many turned up that the police were called to keep order.

Top right: One of the author's first E-type tests was on the occasion of the Scottish Motor Show following the car's introduction in Geneva. He is seen *(right)* with Jaguar apprentice Clive Martin.

227

Jaguar E-Type 3.8 2-seat roadster 1961-1964

Although the E-type Coupe was sleek, practical, exquisitely proportioned, and had useful luggage space in the tail, the Roadster had splendour. The build of the Coupe was certainly stiffer although the open car never suffered scuttle shake. But it had meagre luggage space, and the hood was a heavy mohair affair that called for a certain agility. The Roadster was graceful. The curved screen with its three wipers, the glitter of the optional chrome wire wheels, the long bonnet with the bulge in the top made it a cynosure wherever it went. It was also curiously classless, inspiring praise at all levels rather like the other emblem of the 1960s, the Mini.

The oval centre section was immensely strong. It was constructed from a large number of small pressings – one of Jaguar's ways of keeping costs down. The transmission tunnel, wide sills, and a transverse member running beneath the seats all contributed to its solid feel. Among the first changes was footwells in the welded steel floor. The interior trim was stylish rather than luxurious, and the only jarring note was struck by the old Moss gearbox, with its weak synchromesh and ponderous shift.

BODY
Sports; 2-doors; 2-seats; weight 1206kg (2658.7lb).

ENGINE
6-cylinders, in line; front; 87 x 106mm; 3781cc; compr 9:1 (8:1 optional); 197.6kW (265bhp) @ 5500rpm; 348.7Nm (36mkp) @ 4000rpm.

ENGINE STRUCTURE
Twin chain-driven ohc; 2-valves per cylinder; aluminium cylinder head; cast iron block; 7-bearing crankshaft; Lucas coil ignition; 3 x 2in SU carburettors, water cooled.

TRANSMISSION
Rear wheel drive; single dry plate clutch; 4-speed manual gearbox, synchromesh 2,3,4; hypoid bevel final drive, limited-slip differential, ratio 3.31:1, options 4.09:1, 3.77:1, 3.07:1, 3.27:1.

CHASSIS DETAILS
Monocoque steel; ifs, wishbone, torsion bars, telescopic dampers, anti-roll bar, independent rear susp by lower wishbone, upper driveshaft link, radius arms, twin coil spring/damper units, anti-roll bar; servo-assisted discs front & rear; 63.6L (14 Imp gal) (16.8US gal) fuel tank; 7.50 x 14, or 6.40 x 15 RS5 tyres.

DIMENSIONS
Wheelbase 244cm (96in); front track 127cm (50in); rear track 127cm (50in); ground clearance 12.7cm (5in); turning circle 12.3m R (40.4ft), 11.7m L (38.4ft); length 444cm (175in); width 165cm (65in); height 119.4cm (47in).

PERFORMANCE
Maximum speed 239.4kph (149.1mph); acceleration 0-96kph (60mph) 7.0sec; 36.9kph (23mph) @ 1000rpm; standing quarter mile 14.7sec; 6.1kg/kW (4.6kg/bhp); average fuel consumption 14.3L/100km (19.7mpg).

Left: FSN1, Dumbuck Garage's E-type demonstrator, helped launch career of Jackie Stewart. A "flat floor" Mark 1, the author and Jackie's brother Jimmy drove it many miles in Scotland and the north of England.
Below: Drawing shows how strong door sills stiffened structure.

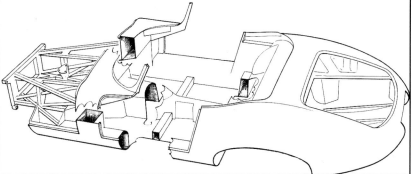

Jaguar S-Type 3.4 1963-1968

The first aspect of the Mark 2 to be outmoded was the rear suspension. The E-type and the Mark X led in ride comfort, and independent springing to all four wheels improved handling and roadholding. A live rear axle seemed out of place in an up-market sports saloon.

The S-type turned out to be something of an interim model and looked like a compromise from the start. It was based on the Mark 2, with an extended rear a little like a Mark X containing the independent suspension, and a new front which parodied the Mark X with vogueish hooded headlamps. The Mark 2's tail was not designed to carry suspension loads, so what amounted to a substantial redesign of the monocoque structure became necessary. *Road and Track* was not alone in being dubious about the new proportions. "We always admired the taut compact look of the Mark 2." Yet if the S-type gave the impression of being conceived in something of a hurry, it was still distinguished. Luggage space was enlarged, and the promise of the independent suspension was amply fulfilled. Once again however weight increased and there was to be no 2.4 S-type.

BODY
Saloon; 4-doors; 4-seats; weight 1627kg (3587lb).

ENGINE
6-cylinders, in line; front; 83 x 106mm; 3442cc; compr 8:1 (7:1,9:1 optional); 156.6kW (210bhp) at 5500rpm; 46kW/L (61.8bhp/L); 289.7Nm (29.9mkp) @ 3000rpm.

ENGINE STRUCTURE
Twin ohc; 2-valves per cylinder; ohc; B-type aluminium alloy cylinder head, hemispherical combustion chambers; cast iron block; 2 SU 1.75in HD6 carburettors; water cooled.

TRANSMISSION
Rear wheel drive; single dry plate clutch; manual 4-speed synchro, overdrive optional; automatic 3-speed Borg-Warner; final drive options 4.09, 3.77, 3.07, 3.27.

CHASSIS DETAILS
Monocoque steel; ifs, semi-trailing double wishbones & coil springs, telescopic dampers, anti-roll bar; independent rear susp by lower wishbone/upper driveshaft link, radius arms, twin coil spring/damper units; servo-assisted disc brakes, rear inboard; worm & nut steering, PAS optional; 63.6L (14 Imp gal) (16.8US gal)fuel tank; 6.40 tyres,15in rims, 185x15 optional.

DIMENSIONS
Wheelbase 273cm (107.4in); front track 140cm (55.25in); rear track 138cm (54.25in); ground clearance 14.6cm (5.75in); turning circle 11m (36ft); length 477cm (187.75in); width 170cm (66.75in); height 142cm (55.75in)

PERFORMANCE
Max speed 183.5kph (114mph); 34.7kph (21.6mph) @ 1000rpm; accel 0-96kph (60mph) 14.2sec; standing quarter mile 19.2sec; 10.4kg/kW (7.7kg/bhp); average fuel consumption 16.6-20.1L/ 100km (14-17mpg).

Jaguar Lightweight E-Type 1963

The E-type began racing almost at once, and a requirement arose for a competition version. Its principal adversaries were the Aston Martin DB4GT, DB4 Zagato, Ferrari 250GT and the renowned Ferrari GTO, all lightweight aluminium-bodied specialist racing coupes. The standard E-type could scarcely be expected to keep up, although it managed manfully, driven by Graham Hill and Roy Salvadori. Accordingly Jaguar set about making its own lightweight aluminium-bodied racing coupes with something more than the 290bhp (216.25kW) already available, a close-ratio 5-speed gearbox, and a weight reduction of 150lbs (68kg).

Around a dozen competition E-types were made to special order and all were different. They were based on roadsters usually with some kind of hardtop, or tapering roofline like that of the Coupe, to stiffen the structure. The centre section monocoque and all the outer skin panels were re-made in aluminium, and some of the rear suspension components replaced by similar lighter, or stronger ones from the Mark X. The suspension was stiffened; only 2in (5cm) of bump and rebound being permitted.

BODY
Roadster; 2-doors; 2-seats; 1151.2kg (2538lb).

ENGINE
6-cylinders, in line; front; 85 x 88mm, 2997cc; compr 10.0:1; 218.5kW (293bhp) @ 6750rpm; 72.9kW/L (97.8bhp/L); 308.4Nm (31.8mkp) @ 6000rpm

ENGINE STRUCTURE
Twin chain-driven ohc; 2-valves per cylinder; aluminium cylinder head and block with pressed-in liners; 7-bearing crankshaft; Lucas fuel injection; water cooled.

TRANSMISSION
Rear wheel drive; triple-plate racing clutch; 4 or 5-speed all synchromesh manual gearbox; hypoid bevel final drive, limited-slip differential, 3.1:1, variable.

CHASSIS DETAILS
Aluminium monocoque; ifs, wishbone, torsion bars, telescopic dampers, anti-roll bar, independent rear susp by lower wishbone, upper driveshaft link, radius arms, twin coil spring/damper units, anti-roll bar; servo-assisted discs front & rear; 63.6L (14 Imp gal) (16.8US gal) fuel tank; Dunlop R5 6.50 x 15 tyres.

DIMENSIONS
Wheelbase 244cm (96in); front track 127cm (50in); rear track 127cm (50in); ground clearance 12.7cm (5in); turning circle 12.3m R (40.4ft), 11.7m L (38.4ft); length 444cm (175in); width 165cm (65in); height 119.4cm (47in).

Jaguar E-Type 'series I' 4.2 Coupe 1964-1968

The E-type's minor defects were dealt with by detail changes in the course of production, some made at the time of the first major variation in October 1964. Together with the 4.2-litre engine came a welcome change to all-synchromesh gears. The old Moss gearbox was pensioned off. There was now a light diaphragm spring clutch and the gearbox had a smooth crisp shift.

Motor industry culture in the 1960s allowed rather more in the way of customer-prompted development than would be contenanced by the 1990s, and the E-type came in for continuous modification. The inboard rear brake discs were made thicker. Handbrake cables stretched. Battery capacity was inadequate. Exposed rear universal joints wore out, and the exhaust system had problems. Light scatter from the enclosed headlights meant that the car's speed was not much use after dark. The Coupe's rear window misted up quickly in wet weather.

Improvements including the change to sealed-beam headlights, waited for what came to be known as the "Series 1½"; something between the original 3.8 and 4.2, and the true Series 2 which came in 1968.

BODY
Coupe; 2-doors; 2-seats; weight 1275kg (2811lb).

ENGINE
6-cylinders, in line; front; 92.07 x 106mm; 4235cc; compr 9:1; 197.6kW (265bhp) @ 5400rpm; 47.1kW/L (63.1bhp/L); 380Nm (39.1mkp) @ 4000rpm.

ENGINE STRUCTURE
Twin chain-driven ohc; 2-valves per cylinder; aluminium cylinder head; cast iron block; 7-bearing crankshaft; Lucas coil ignition; 3 x 2in SU carburettors, water cooled.

TRANSMISSION
Rear wheel drive; single dry plate clutch; 4-speed synchromesh manual gearbox; hypoid bevel final drive, limited slip differential.

CHASSIS DETAILS
Monocoque steel; front suspension by wishbone, torsion bar, anti-roll bar, telescopic dampers; independent rear suspension, lower wishbone, upper drive shaftlink, radius arms, coil springs, anti-roll bar; front brakes servo-assisted discs, rear servo-assisted inboard discs; 63.6L (14 Imp gal) (16.8US gal) fuel tank; 7.50 tyres, 14in rims.

DIMENSIONS
Wheelbase 244cm (96in); front track 127cm (50in); rear track 127cm (50in); ground clearance 14cm (5.5in); turning circle 10.9m L, 11.7m R (35.75ft L, 38.5ft R); length 444cm (175in); width 165cm (65in); height 122cm (48in).

PERFORMANCE
Maximum speed 241.5kph (150mph); acceleration 0-96kph (60mph) 7.1sec; 39.2kph (24.4mph) @ 1000rpm; standing quarter mile 14.9sec; 6.5kg/kW (4.8kg/bhp); average fuel consumption 15.3L/100km (18.5mpg).

Jaguar E-Type 4.2 Roadster 1964-1968

William Lyons may have been inspired by the 1940 Mille Miglia BMW for the XK120 but there was no such exemplar for the E-type. Every other sports car disappeared into a medieval dark age after its arrival, and although its decline began with the "Series 1½", there was still almost nothing in the world to match it. There was certainly nothing remotely like it at the price.

The 4.2 was a slightly more solemn car, red-lined at 5,000rpm instead of 5,500rpm, so a little of the original car's zest was gone. The engine was rearranged rather than redesigned and it was not simply a bored-out 3.8. The roadster's mohair hood was replaced by a plastic one, yet the E-type was still matchless and the words of Charles Bulmer in *The Motor* writing about 77RW the first press 3.8 roadster still held good: "Its very close connection in design and appearance with competition Jaguars gives the impression that this is essentially a racing car. Nothing could be further from the truth. The roadholding is entirely capable of handling the power, the springing is more comfortable than many touring cars and the engine is extremely flexible and devoid of temperament."

BODY
Coupe; 2-doors; 2-seats; weight 1206kg (2658.7lb).

ENGINE
6-cylinders, in line; front; 92.07 x 106mm; 4235cc; compr 9:1; 197.6kW (265bhp) @ 5400rpm; 47.1kW/L (63.1bhp/L); 380Nm (39.1mkp) @ 4000rpm.

ENGINE STRUCTURE
Twin chain-driven ohc; 2-valves per cylinder; aluminium cylinder head; cast iron block; 7-bearing crankshaft; Lucas coil ignition; 3 x 2in SU carburettors.

TRANSMISSION
Rear wheel drive; single dry plate clutch; 4-speed manual gearbox, synchromesh 2,3,4; hypoid bevel final drive, limited-slip differential, ratio 3.31:1, options 4.09:1, 3.77:1, 3.07:1, 3.27:1.

CHASSIS DETAILS
Monocoque steel; ifs, wishbone, torsion bars, telescopic dampers, anti-roll bar, independent rear susp by lower wishbone, upper driveshaft link, radius arms, twin coil spring/damper units, anti-roll bar; servo-assisted discs front & rear; 63.6L (14 Imp gal) (16.8US gal) fuel tank; 7.50 x 14, or 6.40 x 15 RS5 tyres.

DIMENSIONS
Wheelbase 244cm (96in); front & rear track 127cm (50in); ground clearance 12.7cm (5in); turning circle 12.3m R (40.4ft), 11.7m L (38.4ft); length 444cm (175in); width 165cm (65in); height 119.4cm (47in).

PERFORMANCE
Maximum 243.1kph (151mph); 0-96kph (60mph) 7.0sec; 36.9kph (23mph) @ 1000rpm; standing quarter 14.7sec; 6.1kg/kW (4.6kg/bhp); av fuel cons 15.8L/100km (17.9mpg).

Right: 'Series 1½' lost flush-fitting headlamps and had small air intake.

Jaguar Mark X 4.2 1964-1966

In America there was an unofficial competition among the domestic manufacturers to see who could offer the most horsepower. The winners were generally those with the most cubic inches of engine capacity. Jaguar was not specifically drawn in, but it did enjoy being the fastest or the mostest, and it looked to its flagship Mark X to maintain its prestige. Following its takeover of Daimler, it considered the Majestic Major's splendid Edward Turner 90 degree 4.56-litre V8. It would have fitted. Jaguar introduced the 2½-litre version in a Mark II saloon successfully; why not try it in the Mark X?

Experiments showed it to be astonishingly fast, quicker than any XK-engined saloon, but the V8 was not tooled up for large production numbers and the plan was dropped. In any case, by 1964 the V12 was on the drawing board, with a far longer potential life-span than a V8, already five years old. Instead the 4.2-litre was installed in the Mark X. The internal changes, which accompanied the 5.07mm increase in cylinder bore, meant rearranging the cylinder centres with 1 and 6 moved outwards, and 3 and 4 closer together.

BODY

Saloon; 4-doors; 5 -seats; weight 1778kg (3920lb).

ENGINE

6-cylinders, in line; front; 92.07 x 106mm; 4235cc; compr 8:1 (7:1, 9:1 optional); 197.6kW (265bhp) @ 5400rpm; 47kW/L (63.1bhp/L); 380Nm(39.1mkp)@ 4000rpm.

ENGINE STRUCTURE

Two chain-driven ohc; 2 valves per cylinder; 'straight port' aluminium alloy cylinder head, hemispherical combustion chambers; cast iron cylinder block; 3 SU 2ins HD8 carburettors; 7-bearing crankshaft; water cooled.

TRANSMISSION

Rear wheel drive; diaphragm single dry plate clutch; 4-speed all synchromesh manual gearbox, automatic 3-speed Borg-Warner Model 8; hypoid bevel final drive, limited slip differential, 3.54:1.

CHASSIS DETAILS

Steel monocoque; ifs wishbones, coil springs, telescopic dampers; independent rear susp, hubs located by drive shafts & lower transverse links; twin coil spring/damper units; servo-assisted disc brakes, inboard at rear; 90.9L (20 Imp gal) (24 US gal); tyres 205, 14in rim.

DIMENSIONS

Wheelbase 305cm (120ins), front and rear track 147cm (58in); ground clearance 14.4cm (5.75in); turning circle 10.9 L, 11m R(35.75ft L, 36ft R); length 513cm (202ins); width 193cm (76cm); height 138cm (54.5in).

PERFORMANCE

Max speed 189.7kph (118.2mph) auto; 34.7kph (21.6mph) @ 1000rpm in top; accel 0-96kph (60mph) 10.3sec auto; standing quarter mile 17.4sec; 8kg/kW (6.7kg/bhp); av fuel cons 21.1L/100km (13.4mpg)auto.

Jaguar E-Type racers 1964

One of the best drivers of lightweight Jaguars, Peter Lindner the German Jaguar distributor, was killed in his at the end of 1964. The factory's interest in racing was once again on the wane, and it did not even carry on its surreptitious involvement in the sport, through support for John Coombs or Briggs Cunningham. Sir William Lyons was of the firm opinion that there were times to be in racing and times to be out, and there was a lot to think about back at the factory in 1965. Jaguar was contemplating the merger with the British Motor Corporation (BMC), following an approach by Sir John Black and Lord Stokes. It was no time to squander resources in motor racing.

Left: Cunningham car, Le Mans 1963, finished 9th. *Right:* Lightweight E-type raced by the German duo of Peter Lindner and Peter Nocker. Only 12 of these special aluminium-bodied competition machines were ever built, and this one, with its modified Sayer tail section, boasted one of the most potent XK engines ever to have powered an E-type.

241

Jaguar S-Type 3.8 1964-1968

Jaguar was obliged to produce more power to offset the increasing weight of each new model. The 3.8-litre S-type almost exactly matched the 3.4-litre Mark II in straight-line performance. The S-type's burden was increased by some 3cwt (around 152kg, 336lb) with the new rear suspension and heavier bodywork. It was also less aerodynamic since the headlamp hoods intruded at a critical point in the airflow, so although acceleration was about the same, the Mark 2 enjoyed an advantage in top speed owing to a smoother profile and narrower tyres.

The 3.8 outsold the 3.4, with 15,000 against 10,000, the greater part of its advantage coming from left hand drive export cars. By June 1968 the S-type had run its course and, together with the 420, production was halted to make way for the XJ6 that would in various forms take Jaguar to the threshold of the 21st century.

BODY
Saloon; 4-door; 4-seats; weight 1676kg (3587lb).

ENGINE
6-cylinders, in line; front; 87 x 106mm; 3781cc; compr 8:1 (7:1, 9:1 optional); 164kW (220bhp) @ 5500rpm; 43.2kW/L (58bhp/L); 322Nm (33.2mkp) @ 3000rpm.

ENGINE STRUCTURE
2 chain-driven ohc; 2-valves per cylinder; cylinder head 'B-type' aluminium alloy, hemispherical combustion chambers; cast iron cylinder block; 7-bearing crankshaft; 2 SU 1ʃin HD6 carburettors; water cooled.

TRANSMISSION
Rear wheel drive; single dry plate clutch; manual 4-sp synchromesh, overdrive optional; automatic 3-speed Borg-Warner; hypoid bevel limited-slip differential final drive, 3.77:1.

CHASSIS DETAILS
Steel monocoque steel; ifs semi-trailing double wishbones, coil springs, anti-roll bar; rear independent, lower wishbone/ upper driveshaft link, radius arms, twin coil springs; servo-assisted disc brakes, inboard at rear; worm & nut steering, PAS optional; 63.6L (14 Imp gal) (16.8US gal) fuel tank; tyres 185, 15in.

DIMENSIONS
Wheelbase 273cm (107.4in); front track 140cm (55.25in); rear track 138cm (54.25in); ground clearance 17.8cm (7in); turning circle 12m R, 11.6m L(39.3ft L, 38.25ft R); length 477cm (187.75in); width 170cm (66.75in); height 142cm (55.75in).

PERFORMANCE
Max speed 194.8kph (121mph); 41.6kph (25.9mph) @ 1000rpm; accel 0-96kph (0-60mph)10.5sec; 10.2kW/kg (7.6kg/bhp); av fuel cons 18.3L/100km (15.4mpg).

Jaguar E-Type series I 4.2 2+2 1966-1970

In due course even the magnificent "E" suffered adornment, complication, and middle-age spread. The American market in particular seemed to want to take the family wherever it went, and the Coupe was stretched and made taller, providing space for two small rear seats. The 2-seat Coupe remained in production, but the 2+2 proved popular, even though the exquisite proportions were effectively ruined, the frontal area enlarged by 5%, and the weight went up by about 100kg (45lb). The stretch was achieved by lengthening the wheelbase by 9in (22.86cm) and the overall length by 2in (5cm). Windscreen rake was steeper and it was 1½in (3.8cm) taller. The doors were enlarged by 8½in (21.59cm). Higher spring rates and stiffer dampers were necessary on account of the additional weight. Speed and acceleration suffered by about 10%, with the Borg-Warner Model 8 automatic transmission.

Whatever the marketing justification, the E-type had now gone the way of the XK150, and changed from one of the finest sporting cars in the world to a slightly dumpy touring car. It was a touring car of great merit still, but the lithe look had gone.

BODY
Coupe; 2-doors; 2+2-seats; weight 1401.6kg (3090lb).

ENGINE
6-cylinders, in line; front; 92.07 x 106mm; compr 9:1; 4325cc; 355.4kW (265bhp) @ 5400rpm; 84.6kW/L (63.1bhp/L); 380Nm (39.1mkp) @ 4000rpm.

ENGINE STRUCTURE
Twin chain-driven ohc; 2-valves per cylinder; aluminium cylinder head; cast iron block; 7-bearing crankshaft; Lucas coil ignition; 3 x 2in SU carburettors, water cooled.

TRANSMISSION
Rear wheel drive; single dry plate clutch; 4-speed manual synchromesh gearbox, automatic 3-speed Borg-Warner; hypoid bevel final drive, limited-slip differential, 2.88:1 (automatic).

CHASSIS DETAILS
Steel monocoque; ifs, wishbones & torsion bars, telescopic dampers; rear sub-frame mounted independent, hubs located by drive shafts & lower transverse links, twin coil spring/damper units; servo-assisted disc brakes front and rear; 63.6L (14 Imp gal) (16.8 US gal) fuel tank; 6.40 tyres, 15 rims.

DIMENSIONS
Wheelbase 267cm (105in); front track 127cm (50in); rear track 127cm (50in); ground clearance 14cm (5.5in); turning circle 11.4m L, 9.1m R (37.5ft L, 30ftR); length 467cm (184in); width 165cm (65in); height 127cm (50in).

PERFORMANCE
Maximum speed 218.6kph (136.2mph); acceleration 0-96kph (60mph) 8.9sec; 42.4kph (26.4mph) @ 1000rpm (auto); standing quarter mile 16.4sec; 3.9kg/kW (5.3kg/bhp); average fuel consumption 15.4L/100km (18.3mpg) auto.

Jaguar XJ13 1966

Although the factory had officially and in all practical ways distanced itself from motor racing, there was a tacit ackowledgement within the company that it might at some point be necessary to return to it. Nobody wanted to be caught napping. A clandestine project was born to harness the still-secret V12 engine, for a prototype racing car, which could be made in small numbers should the need arise.

A V12 had been mooted as a successor to the XK since the middle 1950s, starting as a doubled-up version of the 6-cylinder. Engine designer Claude Baily was given the task of creating a power unit which could continue Jaguar's run of success at Le Mans, if required, and then be developed into one suitable for a saloon car. It was essentially the reverse of the process by which the XK was designed for a road car and, almost by default, adapted for racing. Yet the philosophy was much the same. Jaguar would gain recognition for the engine in a sports car before de-tuning and refining it for the road.

The first serious studies for the XJ 13 (for Experimental Jaguar – it was nothing to do with the

BODY
Sports racing; 2-doors; 2-seats; weight 997.9kg (2200lb).

ENGINE
12-cylinders, in 60deg V, mid; 87 x 70mm; 4991cc; 10.4:1 compr; 331.8kW (445bhp) @ 7000rpm; 110.9kW/L (148.8bhp/L); 517.6Nm (53.4mkp) @ 6300rpm.

ENGINE STRUCTURE
4 overhead chain-driven camshafts; 2-valves per cylinder; aluminium cylinder head and block; 3 carburettors per head, later Lucas mechanical fuel injection; water cooled.

TRANSMISSION
Rear wheel drive; racing clutch; 5-speed ZF transaxle gearbox; transaxle final drive, various ratios, usually 4.2:1.

CHASSIS DETAILS
Aluminium monocoque; front suspension wishbones & coil springs/damper units; rear transverse link located by radius

arms, coil spring/damper units; Dunlop (later Girling) racing disc brakes, outboard at rear; 600M racing tyres, 15in rim front, 700M racing tyres,15in rim rear.

DIMENSIONS
Wheelbase 241cm (95in); front track 142cm (56in); rear track 142cm (56in); length 481cm (189.5in); width 180cm (71in); height 100cm (39.5in).

PERFORMANCE
Maximum speed 286.6kph (178mph); 3kg/kW (2.2kg/bhp).

Jaguar XJ13 1966 (2)

later XJ), almost coincided with the launch of the E-type, but it was not built until 1966 and first ran in 1967. It was a mid-engined car with an aluminium monocoque, broadly following principles laid down by Colin Chapman for the Lotus 25, and its associated sports cars. Like the Lotus 49, which Chapman must have been drawing up at almost the same time, the XJ13's engine was a stressed member, and like the Ford-Cosworth DFV carried the final drive transaxle and rear suspension. The whole lot could be removed as a unit. The front monocoque had E-type suspension attached; the rear bodywork like that of the emerging Can-Am racing cars, lifted off as a unit, and was unstressed.

The four-cam V12 engine had the appearance of two XK cylinder heads, and there were common features such as hemispherical heads and chain-driven camshafts. The inlet ports were between the camshafts and the ultimate power that might have been obtainable from a racing unit was around 700bhp (522kW).

It was not to be. The conditions for Jaguar's return to the race track within the time-scale of the XJ13 never materialised. The solitary prototype was well developed and test-driven but remained secret, Jaguar management almost paralysed by fear that if it leaked out demand for its existing cars would collapse and customers would clamour for the V12 which was far from ready.

David Hobbs set a British track record on the Motor Industry Research Association (MIRA) test track at 161.6mph (260.1kph), reaching 175mph (281.6kph) on the straights.

Its emergence from secrecy proved its undoing. In the course of making a film about the V12 E-type in 1971, a heavily-loaded tyre collapsed on the MIRA banking, and the car was wrecked in the ensuing crash. It was rebuilt two years later almost exactly as it had been, on the original formers, and consigned to the museum.

249

Jaguar 420G 1966-1970

When the Mark X gained the 4.2-litre engine, it also inherited the all-synchromesh gearbox, an alternator replaced the dynamo, and a pre-engaged starter not only helped cold starting but also made the process quieter and more refined. The 4.2 Mark X was the first car to use Varamatic, the trade name for a variable-ratio power steering, which subsequently set the pattern for almost all PAS systems. Jaguar's had been a bit lifeless, particularly the Mark X's, but Varamatic constantly altered the ratio from 4¼turns near the straight-ahead position to 2 turns as it approached full lock, which felt better and improved its accuracy.

Almost alone among Jaguars, the Mark X never suffered from the over-adornment which had been used to distinguish later editions. It was available with a limousine division, anticipating the later use of its floorpan for the magnificent Daimler Limousine, and in 1966 changed its name from Mark X to 420G. This seems to have been prompted by America; the 420 came from the engine size, the G evidently meant Grand and was added to segregate it from the S-class variant known simply as the 420.

BODY
Saloon; 4-doors; 5 -seats; weight 1778kg (3920lb).

ENGINE
6-cylinders, in line; front; 92.07 x 106mm; 4235cc; compr 8:1 (7:1, 9:1 optional); 197.6kW (265bhp) @ 5400rpm; 47kW/L (63.1bhp/L); 380Nm(39.1mkp)@ 4000rpm.

ENGINE STRUCTURE
Two chain-driven ohc; 2 valves per cylinder; 'straight port' aluminium alloy cylinder head, hemispherical combustion chambers; cast iron cylinder block; 3 SU 2ins HD8 carburettors; 7-bearing crankshaft; water cooled.

TRANSMISSION
Rear wheel drive; diaphragm single dry plate clutch; 4-speed all synchromesh manual gearbox, automatic 3-speed Borg-Warner Model 8; hypoid bevel final drive, limited slip differential, 3.54:1.

CHASSIS DETAILS
Steel monocoque; front suspension wishbones, coil springs, telescopic dampers; irs, hubs located by drive shafts & lower transverse links; twin coil spring/damper units; servo-assisted disc brakes, inboard at rear; 90.9L (20 Imp gal) (24 US gal); tyres 205, 14in rim.

DIMENSIONS
Wheelbase 305cm (120ins), front and rear track 147cm (58in); ground clearance 14.4cm (5.75in); turning circle 10.9 L, 11m R(35.75ft L, 36ft R); length 513cm (202in); width 193cm (76cm); height 138cm (54.5in).

PERFORMANCE
Max speed 189.7kph (118.2mph) auto; 34.7kph (21.6mph) @ 1000rpm in top gear; accel 0-96kph (60mph) 10.3sec auto; standing km 17.4sec; 8kg/kW (6.7kg/bhp); average fuel cons 21.1L/100km (13.4mpg)auto.

Jaguar 240 1967-1969

In September 1967 the Mark 2 gave way to the 240 and 340, effectively the old 2.4 and 3.4 at bargain prices. The 240 was probably the better buy, now that Jaguar had addressed its power deficit, enabling it to reach over 100mph by giving it a "straight port" cylinder head like the 4.2. At £1364 including purchase tax it was only £20 more than the first 2.4 of 1956, at the modest sacrifice of replacing the fine leather, with which Jaguars were traditionally furnished, with Ambla leather-like material. It was a perfectly adequate substitute. Rather more of a disappointment was Jaguar's failure to offer power steering even as an option. The steering was both heavy and low-geared, and with the 240's nose-heaviness increased due to bumper-trimming and other savings, parking could be a tiresome business. Laycock de Normanville overdrive was an extra £56, for although the 240 was a bargain, it was by no means an economy option at around 17mpg (16.61L/100km) with the normal gearing. A 4.27:1 axle replaced the 4.55 when overdrive was fitted giving a more leisurely gait. The Mark 2's handling was unimpaired, but inevitably against independently-sprung stable-mates, it felt less smooth.

BODY
Saloon; 4-door; 4-seats; weight 1448.8kg (3194lb).

ENGINE
6-cylinders, in line; front; 83 x 76.5mm; 2483cc; compr 8:1 (7:1 optional); 99.2kW (133bhp) @ 5500rpm; 39.7kW/L (53.2bhp/L); 195.8Nm (20.2mkp)@ 3700rpm.

ENGINE STRUCTURE
Twin chain-driven ohc; 2-valves per cylinder; straight-port aluminium cylinder head; cast iron block; 7-bearing crankshaft; Lucas coil ignition; 2 1¾in SU carburettors, water cooled.

TRANSMISSION
Rear wheel drive; clutch single dry plate; manual gearbox 4-speed synchromesh, overdrive optional, automatic 3-speed Borg-Warner; hypoid bevel final drive, 4.55:1, overdrive 4.27:1.

CHASSIS DETAILS
Monocoque steel body; front suspension wishbones & coil springs; rear trailing link with cantilever semi-elliptic springs and radius arms, telescopic dampers front & rear; servo-assisted disc brakes; Burman recirculating ball steering; 54.6L (12 Imp gal) (14.4US gal) fuel tank; 6.40 tyres, 15in rims.

DIMENSIONS
Wheelbase 273cm (107.4in); front track 140cm (55in); rear track 131cm (51.4in); ground clearance 17.8cm (7in); turning circle 11.5m L, 11.2m R (37.8ft L, 36.6ft R); length 459cm (180.75in); width 169cm (66.5in); height 146cm (57.5in).

PERFORMANCE
Max speed 169kph (105mph); 17.2kph (16.95mph) at 1000rpm in top gear; accel 0-96kph (060mph) 12.5sec; standing quarter mile 18.7sec; 14.6kg/kW (10.9kg/bhp); av fuel cons 16.6L/100km (17mpg).

Jaguar 340 1967-1968

At 12 years old, the Mark 2 approached the end of the road, and the 240 and 340 were effectively special editions to see it through until the model range was rationalised with the arrival of the XJ6 in September 1968. Although the 340 was discontinued promptly, the rather more numerous 240 carried on until April 1969. The price of the 340, with most of the same thrifty features, was £1422 and it was also available with a Borg-Warner Model 35 automatic transmission.

BODY
Saloon; 4-doors; 4-seats; weight 1525kg (3362lb).

ENGINE
6-cylinders, in line; front; 83 x 106mm; 3442cc; compr 8:1 (7:1 optional); 156.6kW (210bhp) @ 5500rpm; max torque 216lb/ft @ 3000rpm; 46.1kW/L (61.8bhp/L); 289.7Nm (29.9mkp) @ 3000rpm.

ENGINE STRUCTURE
2 chain-driven ohc; 2-valves per cylinder; 'B type' aluminium cylinder head, cast iron block; 7-bearing crankshaft; 2 SU 1⅞in HD6 carburettors; water cooled.

TRANSMISSION
Rear wheel drive; single dry plate clutch; 4-speed synchromesh gearbox, overdrive optional, automatic 3-speed Borg-Warner; hypoid bevel final drive, 3.54:1, 3.77:1 overdrive.

CHASSIS DETAILS
Monocoque steel body; ifs, wishbones & coil springs; rear trailing link with cantilever semi-elliptic trailing radius arms; telescopic dampers front & rear; servo-assisted disc brakes; Burman recirculating ball steering; 54.6L (12 Imp gal) (14.4US gal) fuel tank; 6.40 tyres, 15in rims.

DIMENSIONS
Wheelbase 273cm (107.4in); front track 140cm (55in); rear track 131cm (51.4in); ground clearance 15.2cm (6in); turning circle 10.7m L, 11.1m R (35ft L, 36.5ft R); length 459cm (180.75in); width 169cm (66.5in); height 146cm (57.5in).

PERFORMANCE
Max speed 198kph (123mph); 34.4kph (21.4mph) @ 1000rpm in top gear; accel 0-96kph (0-60mph) 11.9sec; standing quarter mile 17.2sec; 9.7kg/kW (7.3kg/bhp); av fuel consump. 12.8-16.6L/100km (17-22mpg).

Far left: Browns Lane. A 1950s picture of the former Daimler factory built under a 1930s plan for "shadow" plants to aid wartime production. Main office block on right by car park. Plant much expanded central to Jaguar production in 1990s.

Jaguar 420 1967-1968

Impatience over the protracted development of the XJ6 explained the haste with which the 420 was brought in. When it was introduced in October 1966 the XJ6 was still two years away, but Jaguar sales were faltering and there was a requirement for a saloon above the S-type, more expensive than the Mark II but below the Mark X in price and size. A face-lift of the S-type looked like the way ahead using the newly modified 4.2-litre engine.

It turned out to be more difficult than expected. Sir William's restyle followed the forward-sloping-nose theme of the Mark X and numerous Italian coachbuilders. It was a fad, but it was not the first time Jaguar followed a fashion where leadership had eluded it, and the 420 duly appeared with four headlights and a traditional grille. There was a matching Daimler Sovereign, which shared the innovation of a padded roll of black Vinyl along the top of the facia. Jaguar never ignored safety, although in some instances such as the spear-shaped steering column boss, it may have appeared so. Now the change from solid wood to a soft surround subtly acknowledged that even a Jaguar driver could have an accident.

BODY
Saloon; 4-doors; 5-seats; weight 1790kg (3947lb).

ENGINE
6-cylinders, in line; front; 92.07 x 106mm; compr 8:1; 4235cc; 182.7kW (245bhp) @ 5500rpm; 43.5kW/L (58.3bhp/L); 379.5Nm (39.1mkp @ 3750rpm.

ENGINE STRUCTURE
2 chain-driven ohc; 2-valves per cylinder; aluminium alloy cylinder head; cast iron block; 7-bearing crankshaft; 2 SU HD8 carburettors; water cooled.

TRANSMISSION
Rear wheel drive; diaphragm single dry plate clutch; 4-speed manual synchromesh gearbox, overdrive optional, automatic 3-speed Borg-Warner Model 8; hypoid bevel final drive 3.54:1, overdrive 3.77:1.

CHASSIS DETAILS
Monocoque steel body; ifs, wishbones & coil springs with telescopic dampers, anti-roll bar, rear sub-frame mounted independent, hubs located by drive shafts & lower transverse links, twin coil spring/damper units; servo-assisted disc brakes inboard at rear; fuel tank capacity 63.6L (14 Imp gal) (16.8US gal); 185 Dunlop SP tyres, 15in rims.

DIMENSIONS
Wheelbase 305cm (120in); front track 147cm (58in); rear track 147cm (58in); ground clearance 17.8cm (7in); turning circle 11.7m L, 12m R (38.5ft L, 39.25 R); length 513cm (202in); width 193cm (76in); height 138cm (54.5in).

PERFORMANCE
Max speed 196kph (122mph); acceleration 0-96kph (60mph) 9.9sec; 32.3kph (20.1mph) @ 1000rpm; standing quarter mile 16.7sec; 9.8kg/kW (7.3kg/bhp); average fuel consumption 18L/100km (15.7mpg).

Variations on a Jaguar

Jaguar, born
of a bespoke
coachbuilder, was
itself a tempting
platform for coachbuilt
creations. Jaguar
chassis were used
by specialist designers
to float ideas, not
all of which were
conspicuous success.
Bertone and Giugiaro
were among those who
submitted designs for
1970s production cars.
One of Bertone's
earlier efforts *(right)*
on the XK150 in 1957
caught the Jaguar
idiom well.

Below: Less successful,
William Towns's knife-
edged creation, like
his later Aston Martin,
were wide of the mark.
Pop-up headlamps
proved a passing fad
and the leaping Jaguar
looks quite out
of place.

Above: Bertone executed a well-proportioned body on a 3.8-litre S-type (above). The 1966 FT-type had a lean-forward grille like the Touring Sunbeam Venezia which the Bertone effort closely resembled. It was difficult to improve on a Lyons original.

(Left and above): Pininfarina's 1978 XJ-S Spyder was fanciful but not wide of the mark. The F-type, abandoned as overweight when Ford took over, had similar proportions.

Jaguar E-Type 4.2 Series II 2-seat roadster 1968-1970

After seven years most of the E-type's foibles were seen off. It no longer consumed large quantities of oil (112 miles to the quart [180km to 2.27 litres] according to *Car & Driver*), and it did not leak rainwater into the boot or on to the drivers' feet. The air duct for cooling the occupants was diverted away from the engine where it picked up too much heat, and other alterations were made without Jaguar, in its circumspect way ever claiming that much had changed.

The "Series 1½" made in small numbers at the end of 1967, was identifiable by its open headlights, even though it kept the small air intake opening of the first cars. The Series 2 proper of October 1968 gained the larger air intake, with two electric fans to handle the new optional air conditioning. Adwest PAS and bolt-on chrome steel wheels became available, and the standard wire wheels were strengthened, following some trouble with broken spokes. Wrap-round bumpers and the headlight changes were largely made at the behest of irksome American regulations. Large flasher units front and rear and the bigger air intake made the car look heavier.

BODY
Coupe; 2-doors; 2-seats; weight 1206kg (2658.7lb).

ENGINE
6-cylinders, in line; front; 87 x 106mm; 3781cc; compr 9:1 (8:1 optional); 197.6kW (265bhp) @ 5500rpm; 348.7Nm (36mkp) @ 4000rpm.

ENGINE STRUCTURE
Twin chain-driven ohc; 2-valves per cylinder; aluminium cylinder head; cast iron block; 7-bearing crankshaft; Lucas coil ignition; 3 x 2in SU carburettors, water cooled.

TRANSMISSION
Rear wheel drive; single dry plate clutch; 4-speed manual gearbox, synchromesh 2,3,4; hypoid bevel final drive, limited-slip differential, ratio 3.31:1, options 4.09:1, 3.77:1, 3.07:1, 3.27:1.

CHASSIS DETAILS
Monocoque steel; ifs, wishbone, torsion bars, telescopic dampers, anti-roll bar, independent rear susp by lower wishbone, upper driveshaft link, radius arms, twin coil spring/damper units, anti-roll bar; servo-assisted discs front & rear; 63.6L (14 Imp gal) (16.8US gal) fuel tank; 185 VR Dunlops x 16 tyres.

DIMENSIONS
Wheelbase 244cm (96in); front track 127cm (50in); rear track 127cm (50in); ground clearance 12.7cm (5in); turning circle 12.3m R (40.4ft), 11.7m L (38.4ft); length 444cm (175in); width 165cm (65in); height 119.4cm (47in).

PERFORMANCE
Maximum speed 243.1kph (151mph); acceleration 0-96kph (60mph) 7.0sec; 36.9kph (23mph) @ 1000rpm; standing quarter mile 14.7sec; 6.1kg/kW (4.6kg/bhp); average fuel consumption 15.8L/100km (17.9mpg).

Jaguar E-Type 4.2 series II coupe 1968-1970

The changes to the roadster were carried through to the Coupe, and included revisions to the interior, where the instrument panel was changed to comply with US federal safety standards. Toggle switches were exchanged for rockers, and some minor controls modified including those for the screen wipers which now numbered two, not three. The cockpit interior was rounded-off and dangerous projections eradicated.

American preoccupation with safety and emission controls slowed Jaguar's new model programme. One development engineer in three was redeployed, at a cost of a quarter of a million pounds (the best part of 2.5 million in 1990s values), to secure the E-type's compliance with 1968 regulations. The brakes were brought up to date with three-piston calipers at the front, and the crash-impact operation of the centre section was shown to be satisfactory, but a good deal remained to be done such as a complete redesign of the doors to meet "anti-burst" rules. The engine used in export cars was extensively modified to comply with exhaust emission laws which extended from California, where they were long overdue, to the rest of America.

BODY
Coupe; 2-doors; 2-seats; weight 1407.1kg (3102lb).

ENGINE
6-cylinders, in line; front; 92.07 x 106mm; 4235cc; compr 9:1; 197.6kW (265bhp) @ 5400rpm; 47.1kW/L (63.1bhp/L); 380Nm (39.1mkp) @ 4000rpm.

ENGINE STRUCTURE
Twin chain-driven ohc; 2-valves per cylinder; aluminium cylinder head; cast iron block; 7-bearing crankshaft; Lucas coil ignition; 2 Stromberg CD, 3 x 2in SU carburettors others, water cooled.

TRANSMISSION
Rear wheel drive; single dry plate clutch; 4-speed synchromesh manual gearbox; hypoid bevel final drive, limited slip differential.

CHASSIS DETAILS
Monocoque steel; front suspension by wishbone, torsion bar, anti-roll bar, telescopic dampers; independent rear suspension, lower wishbone, upper drive shaftlink, radius arms, coil springs, anti-roll bar; front brakes servo-assisted discs, rear servo-assisted inboard discs; 63.6L (14 Imp gal) (16.8US gal) fuel tank; 185 tyres, 15in.

DIMENSIONS
Wheelbase 244cm (96in); front track 127cm (50in); rear track 127cm (50in); ground clearance 14cm (5.5in); turning circle 10.9m L, 11.7m R (35.75ft L, 38.5ft R); length 444cm (175in); width 165cm (65in); height 122cm (48in).

PERFORMANCE
Maximum speed 241.5kph (150mph); acceleration 0-96kph (60mph) 7.1sec; 39.2kph (24.4mph) @ 1000rpm; standing quarter mile 14.9sec; 7.1kg/kW (5.3kg/bhp); average fuel consumption 15.3L/100km (18.5mpg).

Jaguar E-Type 4.2 series II 2+2 1968-1970

The upright windscreen of the 2+2, which ensured its place in history as the first unattractive E-type, came in for change with the Series 2. Jaguar tried to put it right, by altering the rake from an erect 46½ degrees to a shallower 53½ degrees, with the bottom of the screen moved forward. A rather obvious trim adjustment was needed to camouflage the change. It was intended to be an improvement, but the proportions of the 2+2 never really matched the perfection of the original, and the amendments tended to make things worse.

As if the deterioration in the car's appearance was not enough, the emission control measures for US market cars made it appreciably slower. Fuel injection, used by Jaguar in racing, was not sufficiently well developed to be reliable. It was difficult to secure even running at slow speeds, and a solution was reached with special Stromberg carburettors, and complicated cross-over manifolding extending right across the top of the engine to the exhaust. It worked well at the expense of vigour, and although the fuel consumption and initial acceleration of a so-called Federal E-type improved, peak power was reduced to 177bhp (1131.99kW).

BODY
Coupe; 2-doors; 2+2-seats; weight 1401.6kg (3090lb).

ENGINE
6-cylinders, in line; front; 92.07 x 106mm; compr 9:1; 4235cc; 355.4kW (265bhp) @ 5400rpm; 84kW/L (62.6bhp/L); 380Nm (39.1mkp) @ 4000rpm.

ENGINE STRUCTURE
Twin chain-driven ohc; 2-valves per cylinder; aluminium cylinder head; cast iron block; 7-bearing crankshaft; Lucas coil ignition; 3 x 2in SU carburettors (fed 2 Stromberg), water cooled.

TRANSMISSION
Rear wheel drive; single dry plate clutch; 4-speed manual synchromesh gearbox, automatic 3-speed Borg-Warner; hypoid bevel final drive, limited-slip differential, 2.88:1 (automatic).

CHASSIS DETAILS
Steel monocoque; ifs, wishbones & torsion bars, telescopic dampers; rear sub-frame mounted independent, hubs located by drive shafts & lower transverse links, twin coil spring/damper units; servo-assisted disc brakes front and rear; 63.6L (14 Imp gal) (16.8 US gal) fuel tank; 185tyres, 15 rims.

DIMENSIONS
Wheelbase 267cm (105in); front track 127cm (50in); rear track 127cm (50in); ground clearance 14cm (5.5in); turning circle 11.4m L, 9.1m R (37.5ft L, 30ftR); length 467cm (184in); width 165cm (65in); height 127cm (50in).

PERFORMANCE
Federal version: max speed 218.6kph (136.2mph); accel 0-96kph (60mph) 8.9sec; 42.4kph (26.4mph) @ 1000rpm (auto); standing quarter mile 16.4sec; 3.9kg/kW (5.3kg/bhp); average fuel consumption 15.4L/100km (18.3mpg) auto.

Jaguar XJ6 1968-1973

There were few technical innovations or fashion statements in the XJ6, yet it was a keynote car in a number of ways. It rationalised the range which had been in danger of losing its way, with blurred distinctions between models and an air of improvisation as car succeeded car. A new policy was badly needed to introduce economies to the production process. The proliferation of different models threatened the "good value" element of Jaguars which had been as crucial to their success as their speed and luxury.

Most of the XJ6's mechanical elements were based on well-established Jaguar practice. It had the XK engine of which over a quarter of a million had been made, and the E-type independent rear suspension, so it was more in execution than basic design that the new car was able to distinguish itself. It did so with such accomplishment that it became the prototype for every Jaguar up to the 1990s. The XJ6 was the first stage of an approach that was to become familiar throughout the world motor industry, namely a requirement to reduce the number of "platforms", or chassis types in old jargon, to take advantage of new production techniques.

BODY
Saloon; 4 door; 5 seats; weight 1540kg (3395lb).

ENGINE
6-cylinders, in line; front; 92.7 x 106mm; 4235cc; compr 9:1 (8:1, 7:1 optional); 182.7 (245bhp) @ 5500rpm; 43.5kW/L (58.3bhp/L); 379.5Nm (39.1mkp) @ 3750rpm.

ENGINE STRUCTURE
2 chain-driven ohc; 2-valves per cylinder; 'straight port' aluminium alloy cylinder head, hemispherical combustion chambers; cast iron block; 7-bearing crankshaft; 2 SU 2in HD8 carburettors.

TRANSMISSION
Rear wheel drive; single dry plate clutch; 4-speed synchromesh manual gearbox, overdrive optional; automatic 3-speed Borg-Warner Model 8; hypoid bevel final drive 3.77:1 (auto).

CHASSIS DETAILS
Steel monocoque; ifs, semi-trailing double wishbones, coil springs, anti-roll bar, telescopic dampers; rear independent, lower wishbone/upper driveshaft link, radius arms, twin coil springs; servo-assisted disc brakes, inboard at rear; rack and pinion; PAS; 2 fuel tanks total 104.6L (23 Imp gal) (27.6US gal); E70 VR x 15 SP tyres, 6in rims.

DIMENSIONS
Wheelbase 276.5cm (109in); front track 147cm (58in); rear track 149cm (58.6in); ground clearance 15cm; turning circle 11m (36.1ft); length 481.5cm (189.6in); width 177cm (69.6in); height 134.5cm (53in).

PERFORMANCE
Max 199kph (124mph); 34.4kph (21.4mph) @ 1000rpm; 0-96kph (60mph) 8.8sec; stand quarter mile 16.5sec; 8.4kg/kW (6.3kg/bhp); 18.5L/100km (15.3mpg).

Far right: **2.8-litre works car**

Jaguar XJ6 1968-1973 (2)

The process of evolution, which came to be recognised as the best way forward for even the most progressive car maker, was employed to bring in the most significant new Jaguar since the XK120 and the Mark VII.

The key new ingredient was refinement. Jaguars were invariably a good deal quieter than average, their bulk alone often saw to that, but even before the fuel crises of the 1970s, it was expedient to design lighter weight and more economical cars. But modern unitary body construction was reducing their ability to absorb sound and, as luxury car manufacturers, Jaguar became obliged to find new ways of insulating the occupants from engine and road noise. Low-profile tyres made the latter as significant as the former, while wind-roar in the higher speed ranges was subdued by improvements in window-sealing.

There were other issues to be addressed. Safety

and emission regulations grew increasingly important. Luxury cars from lower-priced manufacturers were improving, with Ford introducing independent rear suspension on its new Zephyr Mark III. It was no match for Jaguar's, but it was an indication that having rid itself of competition from above, there were rivals emerging from beneath. Mercedes-Benz was always a strong player in the market and BMW was materialising as another. Rover put a competent American V8 engine into its strongest contender, and there were competitively-priced alternatives to the new Jaguar from Vauxhall and Volvo.

The XJ6 was introduced with a choice of 2.8 or 4.2 litre engines with automatic transmission, air conditioning, and electrically operated windows among the principal options. Out went the 340, and the 420 continued, only as the Daimler Sovereign.

Jaguar XJ6 2.8 1968-1973

The XJ6 body was entirely new. Dimensionally it was closest to the 420, even though its purpose was to effect a replacement for the entire range of Jaguar saloons, and ultimately the E-type as well. Its achievement was to secure the continuity of the Jaguar house style, the turn-in of the rear window line, the graceful body sides slimmer than the Mark X and the well-framed front with its four headlamps echoing the previous range. Once again Sir William Lyons had caught the mood of the time, with the subtle enhancement, even though the most important technical aspect of the car was to be supremely quiet.

This was achieved through carefully designed sub-frames carrying the engine and suspension. The well-established E-type rear suspension was encased in its own "cage" insulated from the body by rubber buffers, and the engine and front suspension followed suit. A cross-beam carried the front suspension in rubber V-blocks, and the engine in rubber-bushed bearings. Its mass helping to damp out unwanted road noise, it established a new industry standard of refinement that lasted for the best part of two decades.

BODY
Saloon; 4-door; 5-seats; weight 1536.8kg (3388lb).

ENGINE
6-cylinders, in line; front; 83 x 86mm; 2791cc; compr 9:1 (7:1, 8:1 optional); 105.9kW (142bhp DIN) @ 5500rpm; 37.9kW/L (50.9bhp/L); 200.7Nm (20.7mkp) @ 4250 rpm.

ENGINE STRUCTURE
2 chain-driven ohc; 2-valves per cylinder; aluminium alloy cylinder head, cast iron cylinder block; 7-bearing crankshaft; 2 SU 2in HD8 carburettors; water cooled.

TRANSMISSION
Rear wheel drive; single dry plate clutch; 4-speed synchromesh manual gearbox, overdrive optional, automatic 3-speed Borg-Warner Model 35; hypoid bevel final drive ratio 4.27:1.

CHASSIS DETAILS
Steel monocoque; ifs, semi-trailing double wishbones, coil springs, telescopic dampers, anti-roll bar; indep rear, lower wishbone/upper driveshaft link, radius arms, twin coil springs; servo-assisted disc brakes, inboard at rear; rack & pinion, PAS; 105L(27.8 Imp gal) (33.4US gal) fuel tank; E70 VR tyres, 15in rims.

DIMENSIONS
Wheelbase 276cm (108.8in); front track 147cm (58in); rear track 149cm (58.6in); ground clearance 15cm (6in); turning circle 11m (36ft); length 481cm (189.5in); width 177cm (69.6in); height 134cm (52.8in).

PERFORMANCE
Maximum speed 187.8kph (117mph); 30kph (18.7mph) @ 1000rpm in top gear; acceleration 0-96kph (0-60mph) 11.3sec; standing km 18.1sec; 14.5kW/kg (10.8kg/bhp); average fuel consumption 12.3-15.7L/100km (16-20mpg).

Jaguar E-Type Series III V12 2-seat roadster 1971-1975

The XJ13 showed that simply doubling-up the XK engine into two banks of twin overhead cam sixes was not a practical proposition. It would have been expensive to make, and too bulky for a road car. But a V12 was now company policy, and once it was recognised under the brilliant tutelage of Walter Hassan, who returned to Jaguar from Coventry-Climax, that a flat-head engine with one overhead camshaft per bank could do a good job at road-car speeds, the die was cast. It was not an adaptation of a racing engine; it was technically and spiritually a road car unit.

A V12 made sense in America, land of the ubiquitous V8, where twelve cylinders exerted romantic appeal. Ferrari and Lamborghini were already in the market with V12s, and America enjoyed a long tradition of smooth-running turbine-like 12-cylinder Lincolns and Cadillacs. The new engine contained some surprises. Its combustion chambers were in the piston crowns and the valves were in-line instead of being inclined like the XK. Yet with aluminium block and heads, it was relatively light, and only 80lb (36.29kg) heavier than the 6-cylinder.

BODY
Sports; 2-doors; 2-seats; weight 1515kg (3340lb).

ENGINE
12-cyl in V; 90 x 70mm; 5343cc; compr 9:1; 205.8kW (276bhp) @ 5850rpm; [optional 8:1 engine 260bhp]; 38.5kW/L (51.7bhp/L); 407.7Nm (42mkp) @ 3600rpm.

ENGINE STRUCTURE
Single chain-driven ohc per bank; 2-valves per cylinder; aluminium alloy cylinder heads and block; 7-bearing crankshaft; 4 Zenith 175 CDSE carburettors; Lucas Opus Mk II electronic ignition; water cooled.

TRANSMISSION
Rwd; single dry plate clutch; 4-speed synchromesh manual gearbox, automatic 3-speed Borg-Warner; Salisbury hypoid bevel final drive, 3.31:1 (3.07:1 auto).

CHASSIS DETAILS
Steel monocoque; ifs, wishbones & torsion bars, telescopic dampers, anti-roll bar, anti-dive geometry; rear, hubs located by drive shafts & lower transverse links; twin coil spring/damper units, anti-roll bar; servo-assisted ventilated disc brakes, inboard at rear; dual fluid circuits; rack & pinion, PAS; 81.8L (18 Imp gal) (21.6 US gal) fuel tank; Dunlop SP Sport E70 VRs, 15in rims.

DIMENSIONS
Wheelbase 266.7cm (105in); front track 138.7cm(54.5in), rear 134.6cm (53in); ground clearance 15cm (5.9in); turning circle 11m (36ft); length 468.4cm (184.5in); width 167.8cm (66.25in); height 122.6cm (48.4in).

PERFORMANCE
Max speed 241kph (150mph); 34kph (21.2mph) @ 1000rpm; accel 0-96kph (62mph) 6.4sec; standing quarter mile 14.5sec; 7.4kg/kW (5.5kg/bhp); average fuel consumption 16-22L/100km (12.8-17.7mpg).

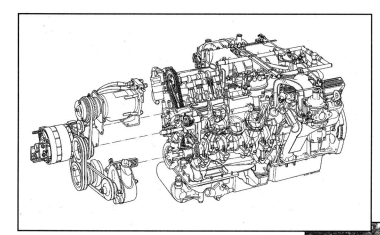

Above: Complexity
of first V12, which doubled-
up two twin ohc XK engines,
led to single-cam design.
Belt drives at front powered
air conditioning compressor,
alternator, and power
steering pump. Distributor
on top of engine had
its own internal shaft
and gear drive.
Top right: View from front,
with belt drives dismantled,
shows 60 degree cylinder
angle.

Jaguar E-Type Series III V12 2-seat roadster US-spec 1972-1975

The V12 came out with carburettors because the fuel injection system was not ready in time. It had electronic ignition, and was installed in a stretched E-type, essentially an adaptation of the decade-old design. United States emission regulations imposed Zenith-Stromberg carburettors which cost the car 22bhp (16.4kW), and knocked a full second off the 0-60mph (96.5kph) time. Some 66kg (145.6lb) was added to the weight, and top speed was 11mph (17.7kph) slower.

Yet the American E-type needed all the revisions. The front tubular outriggers were redesigned to accommodate the larger and stronger engine. Anti-dive front suspension like the XJ6's was included; there were ventilated discs at the front and the problematical inboard rear discs were provided with a scoop for cooling airflow. Stronger bulkheads and enlargement of the centre section gave space for small rear seats, and the larger wheels and tyres were accommodated in wider wheelarches. A mesh grille gave the front a Ferrari-like aspect. The real misfortune of the V12 had nothing to do with its conception or design; the world was about to undergo the first oil crisis of the 1970s.

BODY
Sports; 2-doors; 2-seats; weight 1515kg (3340lb).

ENGINE
12-cyl in V; 90 x 70mm; 5343cc; compr 9:1 (opt 8:1); 186.4kW (250bhp) @ 5850rpm; 31.9kW/L (42.7bhp/L); 407.7Nm (42mkp) @ 3600rpm.

ENGINE STRUCTURE
Single chain-driven ohc per bank; 2-valves per cylinder; aluminium alloy cylinder heads and block; 7-bearing crankshaft; 4 Zenith 175 CDSE carburettors; Lucas Opus Mk II electronic ignition; water cooled.

TRANSMISSION
Rwd; single dry plate clutch; 4-speed synchromesh manual gearbox, automatic 3-speed Borg-Warner; Salisbury hypoid bevel final drive, 3.54:1.

CHASSIS DETAILS
Steel monocoque; ifs, wishbones & torsion bars, telescopic dampers, anti-roll bar, anti-dive geometry; rear, hubs located by drive shafts/lower transverse links; twin coil spring/damper units, anti-roll bar; servo-assisted ventilated disc brakes, inboard at rear; dual fluid circuits; rack & pinion; PAS; 81.8L (18 Imp gal) (21.6 US gal) fuel tank; Dunlop SP Sport E70 VRs, 15in rims.

DIMENSIONS
Wheelbase 266.7cm (105in); front track 138.7cm(54.5in), rear 134.6cm (53in); ground clearance 15cm (5.9in); turning circle 11m (36ft); length 468.4cm (184.5in); width 167.8cm (66.25in); height 122.6cm (48.4in).

PERFORMANCE
UK: Max speed 241kph (150mph); 36.1kph (22.5mph) @ 1000rpm; accel 0-96kph (62mph) 7.4sec; standing km 14.5sec; 7.4kg/kW (5.5kg/bhp); average fuel consumption 16-22L/ 100km (12.8-17.7mpg).

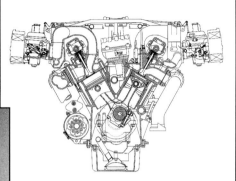

Left: Walter Hassan, one of post-war Britain's outstanding engine designers, was responsible for the Formula 1 Coventry-Climax engines and with Harry Mundy the Jaguar V12 *(above)*. The flat-head single ohc design was later modified to accommodate the Michael May combustion chambers.

Jaguar E-Type Series III V12 2+2 1972-1975

The heavy fuel consumption of the V12 E-type proved a burden, but even that might not have proved fatal if the rest of the car had been up to the mark. The engine was magnificent, but the suspension was now barely good enough. The ride was still agreeable and the equilibrium between handling and roadholding still satisfactory. Critics complained that the steering was lifeless compared to newer rivals, the accommodation was cramped for such a large car, the air conditioning was fine, but the ordinary heating and ventilation system (never a Jaguar forte) was plainly inadequate.

The duplicity of the original E-type's 150mph (241.4kph) road test speeds was now revealed, for even with the extra power of the V12 the new car fell far short. The Dunlop radial-ply tyres with which the first examples were shod squealed embarrassingly and there were doubts about quality. Probably for the first time since the foundation of Jaguar serious concern was expressed about its workmanship and the reliability of components. It was a lamentable time in the United States where the unfortunate Lucas Prince of Darkness reputation took a long time to eradicate.

BODY
Sports; 2-doors; 2-seats; weight 1511kg (3331lb).

ENGINE
12-cyl in V; 90 x 70mm; 5343cc; compr 9:1; 205.8kW (276bhp) @ 5850rpm; [optional 8:1 engine 260bhp]; 38.5kW/L (51.7bhp/L); 407.7Nm (42mkp) @ 3600rpm.

ENGINE STRUCTURE
Single chain-driven ohc per bank; 2-valves per cylinder; aluminium alloy cylinder heads and block; 7-bearing crankshaft; 4 Zenith 175 CDSE carburettors; Lucas Opus Mk II electronic ignition; water cooled.

TRANSMISSION
Rwd; single dry plate clutch; 4-speed synchromesh manual gearbox, automatic 3-speed Borg-Warner; Salisbury hypoid bevel final drive, 3.31:1 (3.07:1 auto).

CHASSIS DETAILS
Steel monocoque; ifs, wishbones & torsion bars, telescopic dampers, anti-roll bar, anti-dive geometry; rear, hubs located by drive shafts/lower transverse links; twin coil spring/damper units, anti-roll bar; servo-assisted ventilated disc brakes, inboard at rear; dual fluid circuits; rack & pinion; PAS; 81.8L (18 Imp gal) (21.6 US gal) fuel tank; Dunlop SP Sport E70 VRs, 15in rims.

DIMENSIONS
Wheelbase 266.7cm (105in); front track 138.7cm(54.5in), rear 134.6cm (53in); ground clearance 15cm (5.9in); turning circle 11m (36ft); length 468.4cm (184.5in); width 167.8cm (66.25in); height 122.6cm (48.4in).

PERFORMANCE
Maximum speed 241kph (150mph); 34kph (21.2mph) @ 1000rpm; accel 0-96kph (62mph) 6.4sec; standing km 14.5sec; 7.3kg/kW (5.5kg/bhp); av erage fuel consumption 16-22L/100km (12.8-17.7mpg).

Above: Harry
Mundy (above)
co-designer of the
V12 engine of the
Series III E-type
seen (right) with
one of the Royal
Air Force's then-
new Jaguar tactical
support aircraft.

Jaguar XJ12 1972-1973

Barely a year after the V12 was installed in the E-type, the XJ12 saloon was announced, to the accompaniment of a strike at the Browns Lane plant. Jaguar was less a victim of the labour unrest that plagued the British motor industry than many others, but the trade unions took the opportunity of the launch to create disruption. It was soon over, and a 25-year chapter of Jaguar history opened with a car that will always be regarded as the epitome of the luxury car.

It was not the first 12-cylinder production car by any means, but it may well be one of the last. It was about to be overtaken by the first oil crisis which signalled the end of the so-called gas-guzzler. With hindsight a fuel-extravagant V12 was probably not a good idea in the 1970s, but it was an era of conspicuous consumption. Improvident exploitation of the world's resources was not yet an issue; oil crises and concern for the environment were still no more than clouds on the horizon. The XJ12 was regarded as a masterpiece although not for long. Within a twelve-month the Yom Kippur war and the Arab oil embargo would ring the alarm bells that echoed throughout its career.

BODY
Saloon; 4-doors; 4/5-seats; weight 1935kg (4265lb).

ENGINE
12-cylinders, in 60deg V; front; 90 x 70mm; 5343cc; compr 9:1; 200.6kW (269bhp DIN)@ 6000rpm; 37.5kW/L (50.3bhp/L); 405Nm (41.8mkp) @ 3500rpm.

ENGINE STRUCTURE
Twin chain-driven ohc; 2-valves per cylinder; aluminium cylinder head; cast iron block; 7-bearing crankshaft; Lucas coil ignition; 4 Stromberg carburettors, water cooled.

TRANSMISSION
Rear wheel drive; automatic gearbox 3-speed Borg-Warner; hypoid bevel limited-slip differential final drive,3.31:1.

CHASSIS DETAILS
Steel monocoque; ifs, semi-trailing double wishbones, coil springs, telescopic dampers; anti-roll bar; rear independent, lower wishbone/upper driveshaft link, radius arms, twin coil springs; servo-assisted disc brakes, rear inboard; 2 braking circuits; rack & pinion steering; PAS; 91L (20 Imp gal) (24 US gal) fuel tank; E70 VR-15 SP tyres, 6in rims.

DIMENSIONS
Wheelbase 286.5cm (112.5in); front track 147cm (58in); rear track 149cm (58.6in); ground clearance 15cm (5.9in); turning circle 11m (36ft); length 492cm (193.6in); width 177cm (69.6in); height 177cm (52.8in).

PERFORMANCE
Maximum speed 223.8kph (139mph); 36.7kph (22.9mph) @ 1000rpm; acceleration 0-96kph (60mph) 7.4sec; standing km 15.7sec; 9.6kg/kW (7.2kg/bhp); average fuel consumption 24.78L/100km (11.4mpg).

Scorpion light tank

When Jaguar acquired Daimler in 1960, replacements for its armoured cars were already in hand. A tracked vehicle was considered, which would be light enough for air transportation, and fast enough to be used for reconnaisance. The result was the Scorpion, the world's first aluminium armoured fighting vehicle. It needed 200bhp (around 150kW) from an engine narrow enough to fit alongside the driver. Vehicle width was restricted to 7ft (213cm) to fit inside an aircraft, and after considering a General Motors 4-cylinder two-stroke and a Perkins 5.8-litre diesel, a low-stressed 4.2-litre XK engine proved a resounding success. It was quiet, reliable, and was the required 12% of the total vehicle weight.

Versions ranged from the Scorpion light tank armed with cannon or machine gun, a personnel carrier capable of carrying five assault troops, to the Samaritan armoured ambulance. The Samson had a heavy-duty winch for recovery and engineering work, and the Scimitar was designed for counter-insurgency patrols. Battle honours included the Gulf War and peace-keeping duty in Bosnia.

BODY
Armoured, with up to 8 seats; weight 81700.6kg (18016lb); main armament 7.62mm GP machine gun.

ENGINE
6-cylinders; front; 92.07 x 106mm; 4235cc; compr 7.75:1; 145.4kW (195bhp) @ 5000rpm; 282Nm (34.6mkp) @ 3500rpm.

ENGINE STRUCTURE
2 chain-driven ohc; 2-valves per cylinder; aluminium cylinder head, cast iron block; 7-bearing crankshaft; Solex twin-choke carburettor; water cooled

TRANSMISSION
Merrit-Wilson TN15X semi-automatic, hot-shift epicyclic 7-speed (forward and reverse) hydraulically-operated gearbox, centrifugal clutch; 3.667 final drive to front sprockets.

CHASSIS DETAILS
E74S Alcan aluminium alloy hull, forged front and welded panels;

suspension trailing arm, transverse torsion bar; hydraulic lever-arm dampers; 3-pot caliper disc brakes; steering in unit with final drive, triple differential; FOT Hycatrol flexible self-sealing and flame-resistant fuel tank 386.4L (85 Imp gal) (102 US gal); 432mm wide manganese and steel tracks with rubber pads.

DIMENSIONS
(Spartan APC)
Length 488.2cm (192.2in); width 223.5cm (88in); height 226.1cm (89in)to top of machine gun; vertical obstacle 49.5cm (19.5in); turn radii vary with gear ratio: 167.6cm (66in) 1st gear, 33.2m (109ft)7th gear.

PERFORMANCE
Max speed 50mph+; 0-30mph 16sec; fuel consumption 62.8L/100km (4.5mpg) @ 30mph; range 350miles approx on road; max gradient 31deg (60%); 561.9kg/kW (419kg/bhp).

Left: XK engine to right of driver. 17/21st Lancers' Scorpion tank took lap record for fastest tracked vehicle on the Nürburgring.

Jaguar XJ6 Series II 1973-1979

Second thoughts on the XJ6 enhanced its appearance; a smaller radiator grille was prompted by bumpers raised to American regulation height. Heating and ventilation, never a Jaguar asset, were improved by extensive modifications to the bulkhead. At long last the old water-valve-controlled heater gave way to an air-blending one, providing a prompt response to temperature change demand. Heater output was increased and a new air-conditioning unit, with flaps and valves operated automatically, made it a match for rivals in export markets. The interior improvements included changes to switchgear and facia.

By 1975 the need for fuel economy was acknowledged, with a new engine variant using the traditional 83mm x 106mm bore and stroke, giving the same 3442cc swept volume of the original XK. It was not the old cylinder block however, but an adaptation of the 4.2-litre with offset bores and "straight-port" head. To emphasise the thrifty nature of the 3.4 it was offered with cloth-trimmed upholstery at £4794 against the leather-trimmed 4.2's £5136. Price differences between UK manual and automatic versions were abolished.

Spec for 4.2-litre *(see text)*

BODY
Saloon; 4-doors; 4/5-seats; 1790kg (3946lb).

ENGINE
6-cylinders, in line; front; 92.04 x 106mm; 4235cc; compr 7.8:1; 124.5kW (167bhp DIN) @ 4500rpm; 29.4kw/L (39.4bhp/L); 20.7mkg @ 4250rpm; 312.7Nm (32.2mkp) @ 3000rpm. (9:1 compr engine 135.7kW (182bhp) @ 4500rpm).

ENGINE STRUCTURE
2 chain-driven ohc; 2-valves per cylinder; aluminium alloy cylinder head; 7-bearing crank; 2 SU HS8 carburettors; water cooled.

TRANSMISSION
Rear wheel drive; clutch sdp; 4-speed synchromesh gearbox, overdrive optional, automatic 3-speed Borg-Warner; hypoid bevel final drive, ratio 3.07:1or 3.31:1.

CHASSIS DETAILS
Steel monocoque; ifs, wishbones & coil springs, telescopic dampers, anti-roll bar; rear sub-frame mounted independent, hubs located by drive shafts & lower transverse links, twin coil spring/damper units; servo-assisted disc brakes, inboard rear; 91L (20 Imp gal) (24 US gal); E70VR tyres, 15in rims.

DIMENSIONS
Wheelbase 276cm (108.8in); front track 147cm (58in); rear track 149cm (58.6in); ground clearance 15cm (5.9in); turning circle 11m (36ft); length 484cm (190.7in) [US 495cm (194.8cm)]; width 177cm (69.7in); height 137cm (54.1in).

PERFORMANCE
Max speed 187kph (116mph); 44kph (27.4mph) @ 1000rpm in top gear overdrive; accel 0-96kph (0-60mph)8.7sec; standing km 17.7sec; 14.4kg/kW (10.7kg/bhp); av fuel cons 12.3-15.7L/100km (18-23mpg).

Jaguar XJ6 and XJ12 Series II LWB 1973-1979

The first XJ saloon with the wheelbase extended by 4in (10.16cm) was a Daimler Vanden Plas Double-Six, the alternative version of the V12 with a high-quality hand-finished interior applied by the Vanden Plas coachworks at Kingsbury, North London. This specially luxurious version, with vinyl roof and extra-deep-gloss paintwork, was introduced in September 1972.

Rear-seat XJ legroom was hitherto scarcely adequate, and a month later the LWB option was extended to all 6- and 12-cylinder saloons. The decision to stretch the XJ was a reaction to competition from roomy Mercedes-Benz and Rover models, and in due course it became standard for subsequent versions of the XJ, even though this first edition added some 176lb (80kg) to its weight and slowed the 0-100mph (160.9kph) time by 1.0sec. The cars were known as XJ6L and XJ12L and the Daimler as the Sovereign LWB. Handling seemed unaffected. Of more concern as the 1970s wore on were continuing doubts about quality. Under the British Leyland regime inspection procedures were less exacting, and both detail and engineering standards deteriorated.

BODY
Saloon; 4-doors; 5-seats; weight 1870kg (4122lb).

ENGINE
12-cylinders, in 60 deg V; front; 90 x 70mm, 5343cc; compr 9:1; 179kW (240bhp DIN) @ 5400rpm; 33.5kW/L (44.9bhp/L); 407.8Nm (42.1mkp) @ 3500rpm.

ENGINE STRUCTURE
Twin chain-driven ohc; 2-valves per cylinder; aluminium cylinder head; cast iron block; 7-bearing crankshaft; Lucas coil ignition; 4 Stromberg carburettors, water cooled.

TRANSMISSION
Rear wheel drive; automatic gearbox 3-speed Borg-Warner; hypoid bevel limited-slip differential final drive, 3.31:1.

CHASSIS DETAILS
Steel monocoque; ifs, semi-trailing double wishbones, coil springs, telescopic dampers; anti-roll bar; rear independent, lower wishbone/upper driveshaft link, radius arms, twin coil springs; servo-assisted disc brakes, rear inboard; 2 braking circuits; rack & pinion steering; PAS; 91L (20 Imp gal) (24 US gal) fuel tank; E70 VR-15 SP tyres, 6in rims.

DIMENSIONS
Wheelbase 286.5cm (113in), front track 147cm (57.9in), rear track 148cm (58.3in), ground clearance 18cm (7in), turning circle 11m (36ft), length 494.5cm (194.7in), width 177cm (69.7in), height 137.5cm (54.1in).

PERFORMANCE
Maximum speed 225kph (140mph); 36.7kph (22.9mph) @ 1000rpm; acceleration 0-100kph (62mph) 7.9sec; 5.7-10.6kg/kW (7.6-7.9kg/bhp); average fuel consumption 18.8-25.6L/100km (11-15mpg).

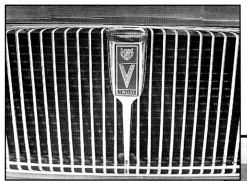

Jaguar XJ6 2-door Coupe 1973-1977

There was something of a hiatus between the announcement of what became a Jaguar classic, the 2-door XJ, and the start of serious production. When it was introduced to the press in the summer of 1973, Jaguar explained that the examples shown were protoypes, and no more would be made until the following year. In the event it was the spring of 1975 before any went on sale, and the model remained in production for only two years. A total of 6505 XJ6Cs and 1873 XJ12Cs were made before it was discontinued, pending introduction of the XJ-S.

Part of the delay was due to difficulties in engineering a pillarless 2-door. Reinforcement was built into the rear quarters, because the roof and B-post (the central pillar), played a key role in the car's strength. There were difficulties with the rear-most side window, which tended to be drawn out into the slipstream at a critical point of low pressure, creating wind-noise. The fact of the matter was that the management took a short-term view, regarding the coupe as something of a distraction from its preoccupation with saloons, and did not accord it a very high priority.

BODY
Coupe; 2-doors; 5-seats; weight 1750kg (3858lb).

ENGINE
6-cylinders, in line; front; 92.04 x 106mm; 4235cc; compr 7.8:1; 124.5kW (167bhp DIN) @ 4500rpm; 29.4kw/L (39.4bhp/L); 20.7mkg @ 4250rpm; 312.7Nm (32.2mkp) @ 3000rpm. (9:1 compr engine 135.7kW (182bhp) @ 4500rpm).

ENGINE STRUCTURE
2 chain-driven ohc; 2-valves per cylinder; aluminium alloy cylinder head; 7-bearing crank; 2 SU HS8 carburettors; water cooled.

TRANSMISSION
Rear wheel drive; clutch sdp; 4-speed synchromesh gearbox, overdrive optional, automatic 3-speed Borg-Warner; hypoid bevel final drive, ratio 3.07:1or 3.31:1.

CHASSIS DETAILS
Steel monocoque; ifs, wishbones & coil springs, telescopic dampers, anti-roll bar; rear sub-frame mounted independent, hubs located by drive shafts & lower transverse links, twin coil spring/damper units; servo-assisted disc brakes, inboard rear; 91L (20 Imp gal) (24 US gal); E70VR tyres, 15in rims.

DIMENSIONS
Wheelbase 276.5cm (108.9in); front track 147cm (58in); rear track 149cm (58.6in); ground clearance 15cm (5.9in); turning circle 11m (36ft); length 484.5cm (190.7in) [US 495cm (194.8cm)]; width 177cm (69.7in); height 137cm (54.1in).

PERFORMANCE
Maximum speed 187kph (116mph); 44kph (27.4mph) @ 1000rpm in top gear overdrive; accel 0-96kph (0-60mph)8.7sec; standing km 17.7sec; 14.1kg/kW (10.5kg/bhp); average fuel consumption 12.3-15.7L/100km (18-23mpg).

Jaguar XJ12 2-door Coupe 1973-1977

The 2-door Jaguar was never officially known as a Coupe but the "C" suffix ensured its adoption. The roof was covered in smart black vinyl, a fashionable adornment which also served to disguise the thickness of the C-post (the rear pillar), necessary to meet roll-over safety regulations as well as ensure body stiffness comparable with the 4-door car. The result was one of the best-looking of all the XJ series. Mounted on what would come to be known as the short wheelbase, the proportions of the car were striking and the vinyl gave it the "hardtop convertible" appearance not only popular in America where it was created, but anywhere elegant cars were appreciated.

A 2-door car is seldom as practical as a 4-door, and access to the rear seats of the coupe Jaguar was not easy. Despite the bolstering of the C-post, the 2-door cars were some 50lb (22.6kg) lighter than their 4-door counterparts, although the Series II cars, like almost every Jaguar, did put on weight over the 'series I' on account of the increasing burden of safety regulations, heavier bumpers, and equipment such as electric windows fitted as standard.

BODY
Coupe; 2-doors; 5-seats; weight 1835kg (4045.4lb).

ENGINE
12-cylinders, in 60 deg V; front; 90 x 70mm, 5343cc; compr 9:1; 179kW (240bhp DIN) @ 5750rpm; 33.5kW/L (44.9bhp/L); 407.8Nm (42.1mkp) @ 3500rpm.

ENGINE STRUCTURE
Twin chain-driven ohc; 2-valves per cylinder; aluminium cylinder head; cast iron block; 7-bearing crankshaft; Lucas coil ignition; fuel injection; water cooled.

TRANSMISSION
Rear wheel drive; automatic gearbox 3-speed Borg-Warner; hypoid bevel limited-slip differential final drive,3.31:1.

CHASSIS DETAILS
Steel monocoque; ifs, semi-trailing double wishbones, coil springs, telescopic dampers; anti-roll bar; rear independent, lower wishbone/upper driveshaft link, radius arms, twin coil springs; servo-assisted disc brakes, rear inboard; 2 braking circuits; rack & pinion steering; PAS; 91L (20 Imp gal) (24 US gal) fuel tank; E70 VR-15 SP tyres, 6in rims.

DIMENSIONS
Wheelbase 276.5cm (108.9in), front track 147cm (57.9in), rear track 148cm (58.3in), ground clearance 18cm (7in), turning circle 11m (36ft), length 484.5cm (190.8in), width 177cm (69.7in), height 137.5cm (54.1in).

PERFORMANCE
Maximum speed 216.7kph (135mph); 36.7kph (22.9mph) @ 1000rpm; acceleration 0-100kph (62mph) 8.6sec; 10.3kg/kW (7.6bhp/bhp); average fuel consumption 17.7-23.5L/100km (12-16mpg).

Jaguar E-type SCCA 1974

Although the works carefully distanced itself from racing in Europe throughout the 1960s, a Jaguar development engineer, Peter Taylor, successfully ran a V12 E-type in British amateur racing. The Sports Car Club of America (SCCA) ran championships for production sports cars, for which a V12 E-type was developed by Huffaker Engineering Inc of San Raphael, California. Another was evolved by Group 44 Inc in Washington, both with encouragement from British Leyland Inc, but independent of each other and the Jaguar factory. The teams won regional titles, and the Group 44 car won the national SCCA championship.

Its moving spirit was Bob Tullius, already devoted to British sports cars through MG, Austin-Healey, and Triumph. He persuaded British Leyland Inc to support a racing version of Walter Hassan's inspired one-cam-per-bank V12. Quaker State Oil sponsored the car against Porsche and Chevrolet Corvette opposition, and it won the SCCA B production category, which allowed only limited modifications. The racing was so essentially amateur that each team built only one car.

BODY
Sports; 2-doors; 2-seats; 1211kg (2670lb).

ENGINE
12-cylinders; in 60 deg V; front; 90 x 70mm; 5343cc; 343kW (460bhp) @ 7000rpm; 64.2kW/L (86.1bhp/L).

ENGINE STRUCTURE
One chain-driven ohc per bank; 2-valves per cylinder; aluminium alloy cylinder head; cast iron block; 7-bearing crankshaft; 4 horizontal Zenith carburettors.

TRANSMISSION
Rear wheel drive; 5-speed.

CHASSIS DETAILS
Steel monocoque; ifs, wishbones & torsion bars, telescopic dampers, anti-roll bar, anti-dive geometry; rear, hubs located by drive shafts & lower transverse links; twin coil spring/damper units, anti-roll bar; servo-assisted ventilated disc brakes, inboard at rear; dual fluid circuits; rack & pinion; PAS; 81.8L (18 Imp gal) (21.6 US gal) fuel tank.

DIMENSIONS
Wheelbase 266.7cm (105in); front track 138.7cm(54.5in), rear 134.6cm (53in); ground clearance 15cm (5.9in); turning circle 11m (36ft); length 468.4cm (184.5in); width 167.8cm (66.25in); height 122.6cm (48.4in).

Right: Joe Huffaker's E-type was similar to that of Bob Tullius except for paintwork and rollover hoop.

Jaguar XJ12 Series II fuel injection 1975-1979

Fuel injection, fitted at first to the XJ12C, sprayed into the inlet manifold of the V12 engine and not directly into the cylinders. By 1975 the price of oil had trebled and the V12's fuel consumption was becoming something of an issue. Exhaust emission regulations were being imposed in America, and since it seemed only a matter of time before they would be adopted in Europe, the days of carburettors were numbered.

The system, originated at Bendix, was developed by Bosch then adopted jointly by Lucas and Jaguar to redress the loss of power caused by restrictive emission control equipment, and improve fuel consumption. Jaguar had used fuel injection in racing, but making it work as reliably as carburettors was a formidable task. It restored the engine's 285DIN bhp (212.53kW) at 5750rpm, a slightly lower speed than with carburettors, and the rear axle ratio was raised to 3.07:1 from 3.31:1. Performance was slightly down, largely owing to the inevitable increase in weight, but fuel consumption was much better. Alas it was all relative. *Autocar's* 1975 road test cheerfully recorded an improvement from 11.4mpg (24.7L/100km) to 13.8mpg (20.47L/100km).

BODY
Saloon; 4-doors (2-doors); 5-seats; 1920kg (4232.8lb).

ENGINE
12-cylinders, in 60deg V; 90 x 70mm, 5343cc; compr 9:1; 212.5kW (285bhp) @ 5750rpm; 39.8kW/L (53.3bhp/L); 399Nm (41.1mkp) @ 4200rpm.

ENGINE STRUCTURE
One chain-driven ohc per bank; 2-valves per cylinder; aluminium alloy block and heads; 7-bearing crankshaft; Bosch-Bendix-Lucas D-Jetronic fuel injection.

TRANSMISSION
Rear wheel drive; automatic gearbox 3-speed Borg-Warner; hypoid bevel limited-slip differential final drive, 3.31:1.

CHASSIS DETAILS
Steel monocoque; ifs, semi-trailing double wishbones, coil springs, telescopic dampers; anti-roll bar; rear independent, lower wishbone/upper driveshaft link, radius arms, twin coil springs; servo-assisted disc brakes, rear inboard; 2 braking circuits; rack & pinion steering; PAS; 91L (20 Imp gal) (24 US gal) fuel tank; E70 VR-15 SP tyres, 6in rims.

DIMENSIONS
Wheelbase 286.5cm (112.8in); front track 147cm (57.9in); rear track 148cm (58.3in); ground clearance 18cm (7in); turning circle 11m (36ft); length 494.5cm (194.7in); width 177cm (68.7in); height 137.5cm (54.1in).

PERFORMANCE
Max speed 225kph (140.2mph); 36.7kph (22.9mph) @ 1000rpm; accel 0-96kph (60mph) 7.9sec; 9kg/kW (6.7kg/bhp); average fuel consumption 18.8-25.6L/100km (11-15mpg).
10:1 compression & digital fi gave 223.5kW (299.8bhp); US emission controls limited output to 181.7kW (243.6bhp).

Cars with 10:1
compression and digital
fuel injection gave
223.5kW (299.8bhp)
but US market emission
control equipment
limited output to
181.7kW (243.6bhp).

Jaguar XJ-S 1975-1981

The gestation period for new models, protracted enough already for Jaguar, grew even longer under British Leyland. The XJ-S was scarcely a replacement for the E-type as it had been in its heyday, but it was a logical enough successor to the rather over-weight, somewhat ponderous E-type of the 1970s. The basis for the car already existed in the platform of the short wheelbase XJ12. It was only necessary to reposition the rear bulkhead, provide a sleek fixed-head coupe body, and there was a new model. Jaguar had done it before with the XK120, an abbreviated version of the Mark V saloon chassis, so the XJ-S was based on the 108.8in (276.35cm) wheelbase XJ6, shortened some 6.8in (17.27cm) by moving the entire rear suspension forwards.

At the front, the integral chassis bracing for the engine mountings survived, along with a sub-frame carrying the brakes and suspension. Everywhere there were insulated mountings to maintain the air of refinement for which Jaguars were becoming noted. Moulded sound-damping panels were introduced, even the coiled petrol feed pipe was enclosed in a foam tube,

BODY
Coupe; 2-doors; 2+2-seats; weight 1750kg (3936lb).

ENGINE
12-cylinders, in 60deg V; front; 5343cc; compr 9:1; 212.5kW (285bhp)@ 5757rpm; 39.8 kW/L; 399Nm (41.1mkp)@ 4500rpm.

ENGINE STRUCTURE
One ohc per bank; 2-valves per cylinder; aluminium alloy cylinder head; 7-bearing crankshaft; D-Jetronic ind fuel injection; water cooled.

TRANSMISSION
Rear wheel drive; single dry plate clutch; 5-speed synchromesh gearbox, (1977) automatic 3-speed Borg-Warner; hypoid bevel final drive, limited-slip differential 3.54:1.

CHASSIS DETAILS
Steel monocoque; front suspension with semi-trailing wishbones & coil springs, telescopic dampers, anti-roll bar;

rear sub-frame mounted independent, hubs located by drive shafts & lower transverse links, twin coil/spring damper units, anti-roll bar; servo-assisted ventilated disc brakes, inboard at rear; 91L (20 Imp gal) (24 US gal); 205/70VR tyres, 6in rims.

DIMENSIONS
Wheelbase 259cm (102in); front track 149cm (58.6in); rear track 149cm (58.6in); ground clearance 14cm (5.5in); turning circle 11.5m (37.7ft); length 488cm (192.3in); width 179cm (70.6in); height 121cm (47.8in).

PERFORMANCE
Maximum speed 241kph (150mph); 40kph (24.9mph) @ 1000rpm; (8.1kg/kW (6.1kg/bhp); acceleration 0-97kph (60mph) 6.8sec; average fuel consumption 13.2-26.2L/100km (10.8-21.4mpg), auto 14.3-24.8L/100km (11.4-19.8mpg).

so that the occupants would not hear the sound of fuel gushing through. It was perhaps just as well; it must have made a noise like the bath running out. The 12-cylinder engine had a voracious thirst.

New safety regulations were pending, ensuring that the XJ-S had crumple zones fore and aft, and the fuel tanks were no longer contained in the rear wings like the XJ6 but in a safer tank forward of the deep boot. Safety rules looked likely to outlaw open cars. The entire world industry thought so, and shelved open-car plans wholesale. Accordingly an open XJ-S did not look like an option. The regulations were rescinded in 1974, but by then the design was frozen, and an open-topped version frozen out.

The XJ-S body shape arrived at by Jaguar's own aerodynamicist Malcolm Sayer was controversial. It was the first Jaguar on which Sir William Lyons's astute word was not final, and perhaps the first which failed to win almost universal acclaim. It deferred to fashion on a number of counts including the concave rear window and rectangular headlamps. It had the old SS Jaguar proportions of a large engine compartment, and small, low-roofed cabin, yet it somehow never made the grade as beautiful.

The XJ-S was announced with the V12 engine. There was a choice of manual gearshift or a Borg-Warner Model 12 automatic which most customers went for. The XJ-S was never going to be a sports car in the style of the E-type, although it had some sporting pretensions such as a Powr-Lok limited slip diff as standard. Californian cars' exhaust recirculation reduced the power output to 244bhp (181.9kW).

Jaguar XJ12C Gp2 ETC Broadspeed 1976

British Leyland seemed to believe that all it had to do was turn on a tap at Jaguar and competition victories would flow. It held a famous press conference in London, at which it announced not simply participation in the European Touring Car Championship, but its firm intention of winning it. After all, if an amateur outfit in America could do so well, a works-supported operation in Britain should brook no opposition in particular from BMW, which had gained much useful publicity from winning races. Humility was never a strong suit at Leyland and its hopes were quickly dashed.

Preparation of the cars was entrusted to Ralph Broad, who had a fine track record with Minis and Triumphs, but the XJ12C turned out to be too large, too heavy, and too complicated ever to make a race winner. A saloon had been the choice of the marketing department. Had the XJ-S been adopted instead the story might have been different. As it was, the cars suffered from fundamental problems such as oil surge, and even when dry-sump lubrication was allowed, it was too late to make them reliable and the team was withdrawn in 1977.

BODY
Coupe; 2-doors; 2-seats; weight 1450.2kg (3197lb).

ENGINE
12-cylinders, in 60 deg V; front; 90.6 x 70mm; compr 12:1; 5416cc; 417.6kW (560bhp) @ 8000; 77kW/L (103.4bhp/L).

ENGINE STRUCTURE
One chain-driven ohc per bank; 2-valves per cylinder; Cosworth pistons; aluminium cylinder heads; 7-bearing crankshaft; Lucas mechanical fuel injection; wet sump lubrication.

TRANSMISSION
Rear wheel drive; 4-speed close-ratio gearbox; AP clutch.

CHASSIS DETAILS
Modified XJ12C coupe rolling chassis; steel & GRP body panels; Armstrong dampers; AP cast-iron brake discs, outboard front, inboard rear; 122.8L (27 Imp gal) (32.4 US gal) fuel tank; Dunlop tyres.

DIMENSIONS
Wheelbase 287cm (113in); front track 147.3cm (58in); rear track 147.3cm (58in).

PERFORMANCE
Maximum speed 273kph (170mph); 3.5kg/kW (2.6kg/bhp).

Right: Ralph Broad never lost faith in the XJ12, and firmly believed that it would have been a winner in 1978. The team was unlucky not to win the 1977 TT at Silverstone, and Leyland lost patience with it.

Jaguar XJ6 3.4 Series III 1979-1986

It was a tribute to the merit of the original XJ6 that it lasted over ten years with only two minor facelifts, and could still be called upon for a third incarnation lasting another seven. The stretch of 1973 was perhaps the biggest change, most of the others being the result of safety and emission control legislation. Its real replacement, the XJ40, had been under active development since 1972, but it was still a long way off. Nobody could have foreseen that it would be 1986 before it would appear with the major replacement of the XK engine known as the AJ6.

The series III came into being in March 1979, with only a sleeker roofline and detail changes to the windows to show that some £7 million had been spent in retooling and improving it. Pininfarina was consulted on refining the appearance, the first time Jaguar had gone outside the company for advice on styling. The effect was agreeable. The subtle improvements gave more headroom and lowered the waistline. The 3.4 was introduced with cloth upholstery at £12,750, to provide a low-priced entry into Jaguar ownership and retain the reputation for good value in an inflationary market.

BODY

Saloon; 4-doors; 5-seats; weight 1765kg (3891lb).

ENGINE

6-cylinders, in line; front; 83 x 106 mm; compr 8.4:1; 3442cc; 120kW (160.9bhp) @ 5000rpm; 35.2kW/L (46.8bhp/L); 255Nm (26.3mkp) @ 4000rpm.

ENGINE STRUCTURE

Valves in 70deg V; 2-valves per cylinder; 2 chain-driven ohc; straight port aluminium alloy cylinder head, hemispherical combustion chambers; 7-bearing crankshaft; 2 horizontal SW HIF7 carburettors; water cooled.

TRANSMISSION

Rear wheel drive; 5-speed gearbox, or Borg-Warner auto; [type] final drive, 3.54:1.

CHASSIS DETAIL

Steel monocoque; ifs, semi-trailing double wishbones, coil springs, anti-roll bar; rear independent, lower wishbone/ upper driveshaft link, radius arms, twin coil springs, telescopic dampers; servo ventilated disc brakes front & rear; rack and pinion steering; 91L (20 Imp gal) (24 US gal) fuel tank; ER70 VR 15 tyres, 6in rim width.

DIMENSIONS

Wheelbase 284.5cm (112in); front track 148cm (58.3in), rear track 149.5cm (58.9in); ground clearance 18cm (7in); turning circle 11.7m (38.4ft); length 496cm (195.3in); width 177cm (69.9in); height 137.5cm (54.1in).

PERFORMANCE

Maximum speed 188 kph (auto 185)(117, 115.2mph); accel 0-96kph (60mph) 11.1sec; 14.7kg/kW (11kg/bhp); standing km 17.2sec, 17.6 auto; average fuel consumption 9.8-20.3 L/ 100km (13.9-28.8mpg), auto 11.2-19.1L/100km (14.8-25.2mpg).

Jaguar XJ6 4.2 Series III 1979-1986

Fuel injection was the major change to the 4.2-litre XJ6, together with the OPUS electronic ignition, already fitted to North American cars. The result was a welcome improvement in consumption, although even at touring speeds most owners still failed to reach 20mpg (14.1l/100km); disheartening as petrol prices led the inflationary spiral. An anomaly of the new range was that the carburettor 3.4-litre car returned about the same fuel consumption as the 4.2 and was slower.

Higher gearing was brought in to try and achieve better economy, and a fine balance was achieved, without acceleration being affected. *Motor* reported, "Acceleration from rest to 70mph (112.6kph) is virtually unchanged (from a Series II 4.2) and from then on is significantly better." The car's exemplary handling, ride, and roadholding enabled it to match opposition from Mercedes-Benz, even though "some traditional shortcomings remain." One of these was the sluggish performance of the Borg-Warner automatic which led *Motor* to conclude that many owners might specify Jaguar's new five-speed manual inherited from Rover's splendid (and in some respects rival) SD1.

BODY
Saloon; 4-doors; 5-seats; weight 1830kg (4034.4lb).

ENGINE
6-cylinders, in line; front; 92.07 x 106 mm; 4235cc; compr 8.7:1; 153kW (205.1bhp) @ 5000rpm; 36.4kW/L (48.4bhp/L); 314 Nm (32.4mkp) @ 1500-4500rpm.

ENGINE STRUCTURE
Valves in 70deg V; X valves per cylinder; 2 chain-driven ohc; straight port aluminium alloy cylinder head, hemispherical combustion chambers; 7-bearing crankshaft; L-Jetronic injection; water cooled.

TRANSMISSION
Rear wheel drive; 5-speed gearbox, or Borg-Warner auto; final drive, 3.31:1 or 3.54:1.

CHASSIS DETAIL
Steel monocoque; ifs, semi-trailing double wishbones, coil springs, anti-roll bar; rear independent, lower wishbone/upper driveshaft link, radius arms, twin coil springs, telescopic dampers; servo ventilated disc brakes front & rear; rack and pinion steering; 91L (20 Imp gal) (24 US gal) fuel tank; ER70 VR 15 tyres, 6in rim width.

DIMENSIONS
Wheelbase 284.5cm (112in); front track 148cm (58.3in), rear track 149.5cm (58.9in), ground clearance 18cm (7in),turning circle 11.7m, length 496cm (195.3in), width 177cm (69.9in), height 137.5cm (54.1in).

PERFORMANCE
Maximum speed 200 kph (195 auto) (124.6mph, 121.5 auto), acceleration 0-96kph (60mph) 10sec; 12kg/kW (8.9kg/bhp); average fuel consumption 9.9-21.3 L/100km (13.3-28.5mpg), automatic 10-19.5L/100km (14.5-28.2mpg).

Jaguar XJ12 5.3 Series III 1979-1992

The V12 was still Jaguar's flagship, but its fuel consumption was no longer acceptable, and Harry Mundy, responsible along with Walter Hassan for its development, recruited a young Swiss engineer Michael May to design a new cylinder head. May evolved a double combustion chamber in which the incoming charge swirled into a "fireball" round the spark plug. The aim was clean firing and lean-burn to meet the demands of exhaust emission and lower consumption.

The V12's original combustion chamber was in the piston crown. May's new one was machined into the cylinder head and came in with flat-topped pistons, more powerful electronic ignition, and reprogrammed Lucas digital fuel injection. The results were encouraging, although with official fuel consumption figures of 15mpg (18.8L/100km) instead of 12.5mpg (22.6L/100km) on the urban cycle, and 21.5mpg (13.1L/100km) instead of 18.2mpg (15.5L/100km), it was still not exactly frugal. With the May "Fireball" head the new V12 was known as HE for High Efficiency, and proceeded further up-market with alloy wheels, and a host of hitherto optional items included.

BODY
Saloon; 4-doors; 5-seats; weight 1925.5kg (4245lb).

ENGINE
12-cylinders, in 60deg V; front; 90 x 70mm; 5434cc; compr 9:1; 212.5kW (284.9bhp)@ 5750rpm; 39.1kW/L (52.4bhp/L); 399Nm (41.1mkp) @ 4200rpm.
With digital inj; compr 10:1; 223.5kW (299.7bhp)@ 5400rpm; 41.8kW/L (55.2bhp/L); 436Nm (44.9mkp)@ 3900rpm.

ENGINE STRUCTURE
2-valves per cyl; twin chain-driven ohc; aluminium alloy cylinder heads and block; 7-bearing crankshaft; electronic fuel injection; water cooled.

TRANSMISSION
Rear wheel drive; automatic 3-speed gearbox; hypoid bevel final drive, limited-slip differential, 3.07:1 or 3.31:1.

CHASSIS DETAILS
Steel monocoque; front suspension by wishbones & coil springs, telescopic dampers, anti-roll bar, rear independent, hubs located by drive shafts & lower transverse links, twin coil spring/damper units; servo-assisted ventilated disc brakes, inboard at rear; 91L(20 Imp gal) (24 US gal) fuel tank; 205/70VR15 tyres, 6in rims.

DIMENSIONS
Wheelbase 287cm (112.8in); front track 148cm (58.3in); rear track 150cm (58.9in); ground clearance 18cm (7in); turning circle 11.7m (38.4ft); length 496cm (195.3in); width 177cm (69.7in); height 137cm (54in).

PERFORMANCE
Max speed 235.6kph (146mph); 37kph (23mph) @ 1000rpm; accel 0-96kph (60mph) 7.6sec; 9.1kg/kW (6.8kg/bhp); average fuel consumption 14.6-25.9L/100km (10.9-19.3mpg).

Series III V12 cars
evolved. XJ12 ran
from 1979-1981;
XJ12 HE from 1981-
1983; Sovereign HE
from 1983-1989; and
Sovereign V12 from
1989-1992.

Jaguar XJ-S SCCA Trans-Am Group 44 1976

After the Group 44 E-type won the Sports Car Club of America's amateur championships, Bob Tullius turned his attention to the 1976 Trans-Am races in the United States and Canada. New rules brought in B Production cars with essentially standard suspension, and in the XJ-S Jaguar's case with the rubber sound-deadening insulation removed. Brakes remained a problem, in particular with the cooling of the inboard units at the rear, even with ventilated discs. The team tried the water-cooling arrangement, developed for the British Broadspeed cars, without success. Six Weber carburettors were used after fuel injection was found unraceworthy. Tullius won the 1977 Category 1 title from a Porsche 911SC, revised rules in 1978 favoured the Chevrolet Corvette, but Group 44 raised the car's power to 560bhp (417.6kW) at around 8,000rpm by developing the camshaft and cylinder head. It procured a lightweight body shell and won seven races against the Corvette's three, finishing the season with a flourish which brought Jaguar the manufacturers' title. Jaguar was trying to stay aloof from racing, but the enthusiasm of its customers gradually drove it back to the track.

BODY
Sports coupe; 2-doors; 2-seats; weight 1428.9kg (3150lb).

ENGINE
12-cylinders, in 60deg V; front; 90 x 70mm; 5343cc; 391.5kW (525bhp) @ 7500; 73.3kW/L (98.3bhp/L).

ENGINE STRUCTURE
One chain-driven ohc per bank; 2-valves per cylinder; aluminium alloy cylinder head; cast iron block; 7-bearing crank; 6 Weber double-choke carburettors; dry sump lubrication.

TRANSMISSION
Rear wheel drive; 4-speed gearbox; AP racing clutch.

CHASSIS DETAILS
Modified XJ-S coupe rolling chassis; steel & GRP body panels; Koni dampers; twin caliper AP brakes, outboard front, inboard rear; 145.5L (32 Imp gal) (38.4US gal); Minilite wheels 10 x 15in, Goodyear tyres.

DIMENSIONS
Wheelbase 259.1cm (102in); front track 154.9cm (61in); rear track 152.4cm (60in).

Jaguar XJ-S SCCA Trans-Am Group 44 1981

British Leyland went into decline in the United States, but Jaguar, now independent, supported Group 44's XJ-S in the 1981 Trans-Am. Under revised rules a "silhouette" design preserved the car's appearance, allowing fundamental modifications underneath. It had a tubular frame clad in body panels that were a mixture of lightweight acid-dipped steel and aluminium. Some suspension components were standard XJ-S, while the engine was moved 8in (20.32cm) rearwards.

The dry-sump V12 could now run reliably at 8000rpm with titanium valves, stronger valve springs, and improved valve cooling. The SCCA bargained a weight penalty of 200lb (90.7kg) in exchange for non-standard Weber carburettors and independent rear suspension. Tullius won three races, and the car performed with credit, although not reliably enough to accumulate enough points to win the series. The title went by a narrow margin to a Chevrolet Corvette which only won two races. In three years of Trans-Am Tullius took part in 29 races, winning 15 to gain the Sir William Lyons International Jaguar trophy, and inaugurate a new era of Jaguar in competition.

BODY
Sports coupe; 2-doors; 2-seats; weight 1161.2kg (2560lb).

ENGINE
12-cylinders, in 60 deg V]; front; 90 x 70mm; 5343cc; 425kW (570bhp) @ 8000rpm; 79.5kW/L (106.7bhp/L).

ENGINE STRUCTURE
One chain-driven ohc per bank; 2-valves per cylinder; aluminium alloy cylinder head; cast iron block; 7-bearing crank; 6 Weber double-choke carburettors; dry sump lubrication.

TRANSMISSION
Rear wheel drive; 4-speed gearbox; AP racing clutch.

CHASSIS DETAILS
Steel tube spaceframe with modified XJ-S suspension, dipped steel panels; aluminium doors, bonnet, boot lid; Koni dampers; independent rear suspension; AP cast iron brake discs outboard front, inboard rear; 122.7L (27 Imp gal); (32.4US gal) fuel tank; Goodyear tyres, 10in rims.

DIMENSIONS
Wheelbase 259.1cm (102in); front track 157.5cm (62in); rear track 152.4cm (60in).

PERFORMANCE
2.7kg/kW (2kg/bhp).

Jaguar XJ-S TWR-Motul 1982

Encouraged by the success in America, as soon as Jaguar regained its independence it again contemplated racing, but did so cautiously remembering the Broadspeed debacle. There was no question of reorganising a works competition department. Motor racing had moved on since the 1950s, required specialist knowledge, and a major redeployment of engineering would have been unrealistic. John Egan (later Sir John), who had taken Jaguar back into private hands, saw an opportunity to enhance the firm in the eyes of shareholders, the world, and ultimately a purchaser.

Tom Walkinshaw had a fine track record with Rover, Ford, Mazda, and BMW, and approached Jaguar with a proposal to engage in the European Touring Car Championship of 1982. His study of the regulations prompted a search for a car homologated with the widest possible tyres, independent suspension, and although the XJ-S was heavy it filled the bill. Fuel injection gave the car a strong advantage due to restrictions on altering the engine manifolding. It won its first race before the end of the season, and narrowly missed winning the entire championship in 1983.

BODY
Coupe; 2-doors; 2+2-seats; weight 1750kg (3936lb).

ENGINE
12-cylinders, in 60deg V; front; 5343cc; compr 9:1; 212.5kW (285bhp)@ 5757rpm; 39.8 kW/L (53.3bhp/L); 399Nm (40.7mkp) @ 4500rpm.

ENGINE STRUCTURE
2 chain-driven ohc; 2-valves per cylinder; aluminium alloy cylinder head, pent-roof combustion chambers; aluminium block; 7-bearing crankshaft; D-Jetronic ind fuel injection; water cooled.

TRANSMISSION
Rear wheel drive; single dry plate clutch; 4-5-speed manual synchromesh gearbox.

CHASSIS DETAILS
Steel monocoque; front susp semi-trailing wishbones & coil springs, telescopic dampers, anti-roll bar; rear sub-frame mounted independent, hubs located by drive shafts & lower transverse links, twin coil/spring damper units, anti-roll bar; servo-assisted ventilated disc brakes at front, servo-assisted inboard disc brakes rear; 205/70VR tyres, 6in rims.

DIMENSIONS
Wheelbase 259cm (102in); front track 149cm (58.6in); rear track 149cm (58.6in); ground clearance 14cm (5.5in); length 488cm (192.3in); width 179cm (70.6in); height 121cm (47.8in).

PERFORMANCE
8.2kg/kW (6.1kg/bhp).

Facing page: John Egan *(top left)* **understood how racing affected Jaguar's share price, and supported Tom Walkinshaw with the ETC XJS.**

XJRs explained

Jaguar's XJR racing programme began and ended in America but its main successes were in Europe. Its three World Sports Car Championship titles (two with V12-powered cars), and two Le Mans victories (bringing Jaguar's tally to seven), were achieved by the Oxfordshire Tom Walkinshaw Racing (TWR) team, breaking Porsche's long domination of endurance racing. Jaguar's success began in 1982, when Bob Tullius raced his XJR-5 at Elkhart Lake, and ended in January 1993 when TWR's last XJR-12D retired from the Daytona 24-Hours when in the lead.

In America TWR Inc based in Valparaiso won its first race at Daytona in 1988, repeating the success the following year, each a prelude to major victories at Le Mans. Major US titles eluded it as first Nissan then Toyota gained the initiative with turbocharged GTP cars. Jaguar titles XJR-1, 2, 3 and 4 belonged to the cars of Bob Tullius, who created Group 44 in collaboration with Mike Dale, Jaguar's chief executive in America. They were respectively Group 44's E-type roadster of 1975, the XJ-S Trans-Am car of 1976, the XJ-S Trans-Am car of 1977 and the final XJ-S prepared

for Trans-Am in 1981.

They all had V12 engines, so Tullius arrived in GTP racing via highly developed road cars, just as Tom Walkinshaw did in Group C three years later. The Group 44 team was supported by Jaguar Cars North America both financially and in engineering expertise. Jaguar Cars Limited in Coventry controlled TWR's programmes, collecting sponsorship money and paying TWR on a fee basis. TWR was responsible for engineering, designing, building and developing the non-Group 44 XJRs.

In 1983 Tullius won four GTP races outright, and started 1984 with a one-two success in the second Miami Grand Prix. He brought two cars to Le Mans in 1984 and again in 1985, which were good flag-waving exercises, although disappointing in terms of results.

Craggy, irascible perfectionists both, Tullius and Walkinshaw were too alike to survive as Jaguar siblings. Walkinshaw's team was successful right away in the United States, winning the Sun Bank Daytona 24-Hour race on its first appearance in January 1988. Tullius persisted in driving and managing well into his fifties,

XJRs explained

while Walkinshaw had the tide running in his direction, after winning the 1987 Sportscar World Championship.

Tullius raced his XJR-7 against Walkinshaw's new XJR-9 at Daytona in 1988 despite losing Jaguar's support. His car was presented immaculately in white with dual-green striping around the skirt. Its successor which he proposed to call XJR-8 made a surprise appearance at the 1992 Monterey Historic Weekend, with revised rounded and aerodynamic bodywork, and would have created a stir in the IMSA paddocks.

Tom Walkinshaw campaigned a V12 XJ-S in the European Touring Car Championship for three years, winning the Drivers' Championship in 1984. He engaged Tony Southgate to design the XJR-6 prior to Jaguar's firm commitment, and the car was competitive at Mosport, Canada, in August 1985.

The first victory at Silverstone, in May 1986, was something of a false dawn because the Jaguar did not win again that year. Looking a little strange as Gallahers' mauve and white Silk Cut livery replaced British racing green, the XJR-6 next came close to success at Spa where Thierry Boutsen, in Walter Brun's Porsche,

fended off Derek Warwick to win the 1000 kilometre race by less than a second. The Jaguar was consistently well-placed all season however and if Warwick could have finished second instead of third in the final race at Fuji in Japan, it would have been enough for two titles, the Teams' Championship for Silk Cut Jaguar and the Drivers' Championship for him.

Statistically the XJR-8 was the most successful, winning eight of its ten events. It was raced only in 1987, and virtually swept the board enabling Silk Cut Jaguar to win the Teams' Championship, and Raul Boesel, with four victories, the Drivers' Championship.

Despite a strenuous effort by TWR to win the Le Mans 24-Hours, preparing three cars, two retired and one lost time with a gearbox fault allowing Porsche to claim its twelfth success.

The breakthrough came in 1988, when TWR Inc swept to victory at Daytona with the new XJR-9, followed by an impressive victory by the Silk Cut team at Le Mans. The American-based team, directed by Tony Dowe and engineered by Ian Reed, continued to campaign the XJRs in the IMSA Camel GT series until

XJRs explained

Daytona 1993, and would win the big 24-Hour race again in 1990 with the XJR-12.

Peter Sauber's team, backed by Mercedes-Benz, looked increasingly threatening in the World Championship. It started 1988 with a rather lucky win at Jerez but came on strongly after Le Mans with the twin-turbo C9 model. It won at Brno in Czechoslovakia with worrying ease, then three times more, showing that the Jaguar V12 had met its match in short-distance sprint events. In 1989 race distances were reduced to 480 kilometres putting more emphasis on sheer speed.

Silk Cut Jaguar won the Teams' Championship for the second time, though not with ease, and Martin Brundle won the Drivers' Championship. In July 1988 TWR ran an experimental 48-valve V-12 engine at Brands Hatch in the quest for extra power, but the dual camshafts and valve gear added 15kg at the top of the V12, making the car feel unbalanced. Although the 7-litre engine developed 798bhp, and could have yielded 830bhp, it would not have managed sufficient fuel economy so was set aside.

A second series of XJRs was put in hand for 1989. Tony Southgate designed a new chassis to accept small, light aluminium V6 engines, more compact than the V12s. With twin turbochargers they developed 650bhp at 3.0-litre capacity for IMSA (XJR-10), with restrictors demanded by the regulations, and 750bhp for Group C (XJR-11).

The XJR-10 was more successful in America than the XJR-11 was in the World Championship. The 11 was not sufficiently developed or reliable in its first season and, after a frustrating and embarrassing weekend at Spa, Walkinshaw dispatched the old V12s to Mexico just to get an agreeable result.

The Mercedes C11s were giant-killers, and the XJR-11 enjoyed just one success. It saved Jaguar's reputation at Silverstone in May 1990, following the disqualification of one Mercedes and a rare breakdown of the other, by scoring a splendid one-two victory.

Right: Glories relived. Banner-waving British fans greet the parade finish of the victorious Jaguars at Le Mans 1988.

XJRs explained

A month later Silk Cut Jaguars scored a superb first and second at Le Mans, an achievement that crowned the entire programme. The winning car was engineered and prepared by TWR Inc in Valparaiso and was referred to within the team as "the American car". It was driven by John Nielsen and Price Cobb, and Brundle transferred to it when his own XJR-12 broke down.

Attention was now focused on 1991, and this time Silk Cut Jaguar had its rivals on the run. Ross Brawn was engaged as technical director to prepare a Formula 1-like two-seater, using a Jaguar version of the Ford HB engine.

At Suzuka, at Monza and at Silverstone, the XJR-14s were four seconds per lap quicker than the Peugeot 905s and Mercedes C291s, a substantial margin. Despite a couple of mechanical hiccups, the Silk Cut team virtually secured the title by mid-season, which was just as well, because Peugeot struck top form in the second half.

The XJR-14s were not sent to Le Mans, and TWR prepared XJR-12s at the 1000kg weight insisted upon by FISA, which was intent on driving the turbos out of contention. TWR increased the engine size to 7.4-litres, giving the cars swift acceleration out of the new chicanes, but the drivers had to use the throttle pedal with great care in view of the fuel consumption restrictions.

The quad-rotor Mazdas were given a surprisingly lenient weight limit of 830kg, and the advantage of 170kg made them highly competitive. The Sauber Mercedes C11s dominated much of the race but broke down, allowing Mazda victory followed by the trio of Silk Cut Jaguars, reliable but outpaced.

Jaguar won its third world championship, Teo Fabi was champion driver, but the Gallaher's Silk Cut contract had come to an end. Jaguar itself was not in a happy state financially, so the Group C programme was closed down. The XJR-14 was painted in Bud Light colours and raced by TWR Inc in the IMSA Championship in 1992. Davy Jones scored a couple of runaway wins but the team's record was patchy.

The final appearance of the XJR-12 was at the Rolex Daytona 24-Hours on January 30-31 1993.

XJRs explained

Two of the three Jaguars went out early, one with a broken oil seal and another, a new car with some experimental features, with a handling problem. The third kept going and was an hour in the lead on Sunday afternoon when it dropped a valve and ruined the engine.

Walkinshaw intended to run a team at Le Mans in June 1994, but the Automobile Club de l'Ouest seemed determined to hand the race to Peugeot, and would allow the Jaguars to run only with 34mm inlet air restrictors, and a theoretical output of less than 600bhp. Walkinshaw did not see this as a realistic proposal, and concentrated instead on the preparation of three XJ220s for the Grand Touring category. *MLC*

TWR JAGUAR TEAM

Results in Percentages

YEAR	MODEL	STARTS	FINISHES	TOP 3	WINS
1985	XJR-6	8	3 (35%)	2 (25%)	0 (0%)
1986	XJR-6	20	11 (55%)	6 (30%)	1 (5%)
1987	XJR-8	22	16 (73%)	13 (59%)	8 (36%)
1988	XJR-9	27	17 (63%)	13 (48%)	6 (22%)
1989	XJR-9/ XJR-11	21	10 (48%)	1 (5%)	0 (0%)
1990	XJR-11/ XJR-12	22	14 (64%)	8 (36%)	2 (9%)
1991	XJR-14 / XJR-12	17	14 (82%)	11 (65%)	3 (18%)

Jaguar XJR-5 Group 44 IMSA 1983

Company head John Egan knew that he had to add value to Jaguar beyond the confines of Europe. Companies once took part in racing in order to sell cars; Egan took part in racing in order to sell the company. So when Bob Tullius came up with a plan to race Jaguars under International Motor Sports Association (IMSA) regulations, with the long-term aim of competing at Le Mans, he found a willing ear. Once again the key ingredient was to be the magnificent V12 engine.

The XJR-5 was raced in the IMSA Grand Touring Prototype (GTP) category which specified a minimum weight according to engine type. Support for Group 44 was covert; Jaguar had done things in racing this way before and it was adept at it. BMW and Chevrolet were the real adversaries. Tullius's fifth racing Jaguar, the XJR-5, had a monocoque front section and daringly used the long V12 engine as a stressed member of a chassis designed by Lee Dykstra. The car was beautiful but heavy, gained six wins and fourteen second places, but no championships. It went to Le Mans twice, finishing 13th in 1985, the first Jaguar to complete the 24-Hour classic for 22 years. Jaguar was back in racing.

BODY
Sports racing; 2-doors; nominal 2-seats; scrutineering weight 900kg (1984lb) (IMSA minimum for 6.0-litre, 4-valve engines).

ENGINE
12-cylinders, in 60 deg V; mid; 6.0-litre rated at 650bhp initially.

ENGINE STRUCTURE
One chain-driven ohc per bank; 2-valves per cylinder; aluminium cylinder head; cast iron block; 7-bearing crankshaft; 6 Weber carburettors, later Lucas-Micos engine management system, water cooled.

TRANSMISSION
Rear wheel drive; Borg & Beck racing triple plate clutch (later AP); 5-speed Hewland VG 5-200 manual gearbox; transaxle final drive.

CHASSIS DETAILS
Aluminium honeycomb & steel semi-monocoque, fibreglass body panels; suspension upper & lower wishbones, coil spring/damper units front & rear; Lockheed racing ventilated disc brakes (later AP) front & rear; rack and pinion PAS; 122.7L (27 Imp gal) (32.4US gal) fuel tank; Goodyear racing tyres 23.5 x 11.5-16 front, 27 x 14-16 rear.

DIMENSIONS
Wheelbase 276cm (108.5in); front track 168cm (66in); rear track 157cm (62in); length 475cm (187in); width 198cm (78in); height 104cm (41in).

RACES

First race: Road America (Elkhart Lake). 22.08.1982
Last race: Columbus, Ohio. 6.10.1985
Number of races: 57   **Victories:** 6
Road Atlanta Bob Tullius/Bill Adam 10.04.1983
Lime Rock Bob Tullius/Bill Adam 30.05.1983
Mosport Park Bob Tullius/Bill Adam 14.08.1983
Pocono Bob Tullius/Doc Bundy 11.09.1983

IMSA Championship 1983

Bob Tullius scored 121 points.
Runner-up to Al Holbert (March-Porsche), 201 points.
Miami GP Brian Redman/Doc Bundy 26.02.1984
           Bob Tullius/Pat Bedard. 2nd
Road Atlanta Brian Redman/Hurley Haywood 14.04.1985
           Bob Tullius/Chip Robinson 2nd

Le Mans appearances

1984

John Watson/Claude Ballot-Lena/Tony Adamowicz:
7th after 14 hours, retired due to tyre failure.
Bob Tullius/Brian Redman/Doc Bundy:
6th after 14 hours, retired due to gearbox failure.

1985

Hurley Haywood/Brian Redman/Bill Adam:
15th after 9 hours, retired due to driveshaft failure.
Bob Tullius/Chip Robinson/Claude Ballot-Lena:
13th overall, 1st in GTP.

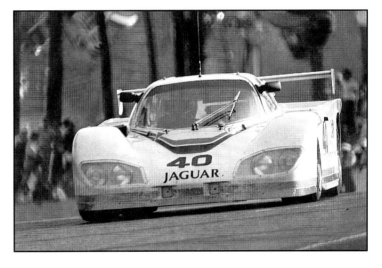

Jaguar XJR-6 Group C TWR

An achievement of the American Group 44 team was to demonstrate that a Jaguar need not be built in Coventry. Indeed it need not even be built in England yet it could still be every inch a Jaguar. The Americans had taken a brave stab at Le Mans, leading at one stage, showing it was possible to make a Jaguar capable of winning outright. Jaguar Cars was about to refloat itself on the stock market, so a return to Le Mans was opportune. Before the end of the year a design was put in hand for Tom Walkinshaw Racing (TWR), by Tony Southgate. In 1985 Group 44 again took part at Le Mans, but it was not until the autumn that the XJR-6 (Walkinshaw took over the "XJR" terminology – Group 44 had to leap-frog it for XJR-7) ran in its first race. It had a carbon-fibre monocoque, Kevlar and carbon bodywork, and its dry-sump V12 enabled Southgate to provide it with a better ground-effect shape than Porsche, BMW, or Mercedes-Benz. The engine was 6.0-litres to begin with producing 650bhp (484.7kW), later enlarged to 6.2-litres and 690bhp (514.54kW). The first full season in 1986 was a success, with a clear win in the Silverstone 1000kms, despite a gallant failure at Le Mans.

BODY
Group C sports racing; 2-doors; nominal 2-seats; 890kg (1962lb).

ENGINE
12-cylinders, in 60 deg V; mid; 92 x 78mm; 6222cc; (increased to 94 x 78mm, 6496cc); 484.7kW (650bhp) @ 8000rpm; 77.9kW/L (104.5bhp/L).

ENGINE STRUCTURE
One chain-driven ohc per bank; 2-valves per cylinder; aluminium cylinder head; cast iron block; 7-bearing crankshaft; dry sump engine, Lucas Micos engine management system; water cooled.

TRANSMISSION
Rear wheel drive; AP racing triple plate; 5-speed March manual gearbox; transaxle final drive.

CHASSIS DETAILS
Composite & glass-fibre monocoque with carbon-fibre reinforced glass-fibre bodywork; front suspension, fabricated wishbones actuating push-rods to centrally-mounted spring/damper units, rear magnesium-alloy uprights & steel coil springs, Koni dampers housed within wheels; ventilated disc brakes front & rear; rack and pinion PAS; 100L(22Imp gal) (26.4US gal) fuel tank; Dunlop racing tyres.

DIMENSIONS
Wheelbase 278cm (109.5in); front and rear track 150cm (59in); length 480cm (189in); width 200cm (78.75in); height 110cm (43.3in).

PERFORMANCE
Maximum speed dependent on gearing.

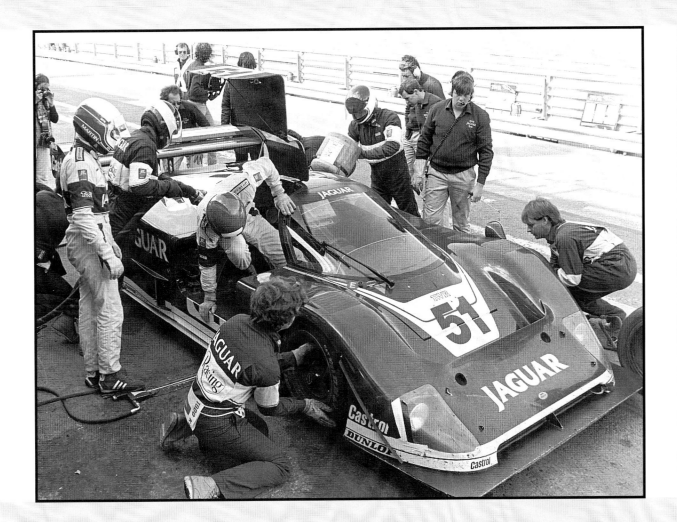

Jaguar XJR-6 Group C TWR (2)

Southgate chose carbon fibre and Kevlar composite materials for the monocoque and bodywork to maximise torsional rigidity and keep the weight as low as possible. The body design was tested in the Imperial College wind tunnel and the XJR-6 featured covers which hid the rear wheels. Their function was to maximise the aerodynamic ground-effect from the twin venturis underneath, which was more than Porsche could achieve with a flat boxer-engine layout. The XJR-6 never raced with the 6.0-litre engine. It was built by Tom Walkinshaw Racing, Kidlington, Oxfordshire, for Sports Car World Championship, Group C.

RACES
First race: Mosport, Canada, 11.08.1986.
Last race: Fuji, Japan, 5.10.1986.
Number of races: 14   **Victories:** 1

Silverstone 1000kms Eddie Cheever/Derek Warwick 5.5.1986

1986 Sports Car World Championship:
Teams' Championship: Silk Cut Jaguar third with 47 points.

Drivers' Championship: Derek Warwick third with 81 points.

Le Mans appearances
1986
Brian Redman/Hurley Haywood/Hans Heyer (52): 5th after 3 hours, ran out of fuel.
Gianfranco Brancantelli/Win Percy/Armin Hahne (53): 4th after 9 hours, retired with broken driveshaft.
Derek Warwick/Eddie Cheever/Jean-Louis Schlesser (51):
2nd after 16 hours, retired with body and mechanical damage due to tyre failure.

Jaguar XJR-7

A development of the XJR-5, the XJR-7 featured higher downforce with lower drag, a smaller frontal area and improved cooling for the side radiators. Although similar in appearance to the 5, the XJR-7 was entirely new forward of the 6-litre Jaguar V12 engine. The honeycomb aluminium monocoque was lined with Kevlar for extra stiffness, with machined aluminium surfaces underneath the monocoque, and around the sills. Composite materials were used for the one-piece fuel tank cover and seat, and pedal box. The car's weight increased to 2,080lb (943kg).

XJR-7 was built by Group 44 Inc, Winchester, Virginia for IMSA, and was designed by Lee Dykstra.

RACES
First race: Daytona 3-Hours, 1.12.1985.
Last race: Daytona 24-Hours, 3.2.1988.
Number of races: 28   **Victories:** 3

Daytona 3-Hours Bob Tullius/Chip Robinson 26.10.1986
Riverside   Hurley Haywood/John Morton 26.4.1987
Palm Beach   Hurley Haywood/John Morton 21.6.1987

Le Mans appearances
None

BODY
Sports racing; 2-doors; nominal 2-seats; scrutineering weight 900kg (1984lb) (IMSA minimum for 6.0-litre, 4-valve engines).

ENGINE
12-cylinders, in 60 deg V; mid; 6.0-litre (650bhp), increased to 6.5-litre rated at 690bhp by 1986.

ENGINE STRUCTURE
One chain-driven ohc per bank; 2-valves per cylinder; aluminium cylinder head; cast iron block; 7-bearing crankshaft; Lucas-Micos engine management system, water cooled.

TRANSMISSION
Rear wheel drive; Borg & Beck racing triple plate clutch (later AP); 5-speed Hewland VGC manual gearbox; transaxle final drive.

CHASSIS DETAILS
Aluminium honeycomb & steel semi-monocoque, fibreglass body panels; suspension upper & lower wishbones, coil spring/damper units front & rear; Lockheed racing ventilated disc brakes (later AP) front & rear; rack and pinion PAS; 122.7L (27 Imp gal) (32.4US gal) fuel tank; Goodyear racing tyres 23.5 x 11.5-16 front, 27 x 14-16 rear.

DIMENSIONS
Wheelbase 276cm (108.5in); front track 168cm (66in); rear track 157cm (62in); length 475cm (187in); width 198cm (78in); height 104cm (41in).

Jaguar XJR-8, 8LM

The XJR-8 and 8LM (Le Mans) were evolutions of the XJR-6, using the same monocoques and concentrating on detail improvements for reliability and weight. Capacity of the V12 engines increased to 6,995cc (94 x 84mm), rated at 720bhp. The scrutineering weight was reduced to 850kg. Sixty-four modifications included inclining the V12 engines higher at the rear to reduce driveshaft angles, redesigning the starter motor, fuel pumps on quick-release board, minor bodywork changes, tyre temperature sensors.

 XJR-8 was built by TWR, Kidlington, Oxfordshire for Group C, and was designed by Tony Southgate.

 Pictured on right is a cutaway showing the 1995 XJR-6 from which the 8 evolved.

RACES
First race: Jarama, 22 March 1987.
Last race: Fuji, 27 September 1987.
Number of races: 10   **Victories:** 8

Jarama 360kms	Jan Lammers/John Watson	22.03.1987
Jerez 1000kms	Raul Boesel/Eddie Cheever	29.03.1987
Monza 1000kms	Jan Lammers/John Watson	12.04.1987
Silverstone 1000kms	Raul Boesel/Eddie Cheever	10.05.1987
Brands Hatch 1000kms	Raul Boesel/John Nielsen	26.07.1987
Nurburgring 1000kms	Raul Boesel/Eddie Cheever	23.08.1987
Spa 1000kms	Raul Boesel/Martin Brundle/Johnny Dumfries	6.09.1987
Fuji 1000kms	Jan Lammers/John Watson	27.09.1987

World Champion Team: Silk Cut Jaguar.
World Champion Driver: Raul Boesel
Le Mans appearances
1987
Eddie Cheever/Raul Boesel/Jan Lammers (4):
2nd after 18 hours, gearbox breakage, finished 5th.
Jan Lammers/John Watson/Win Percy (5):
4th after 11 hours, Percy crashed due to tyre failure.
Martin Brundle/John Nielsen/(res. Amin Hahne)(6):
2nd after 16 hours, retired with valve spring failure.

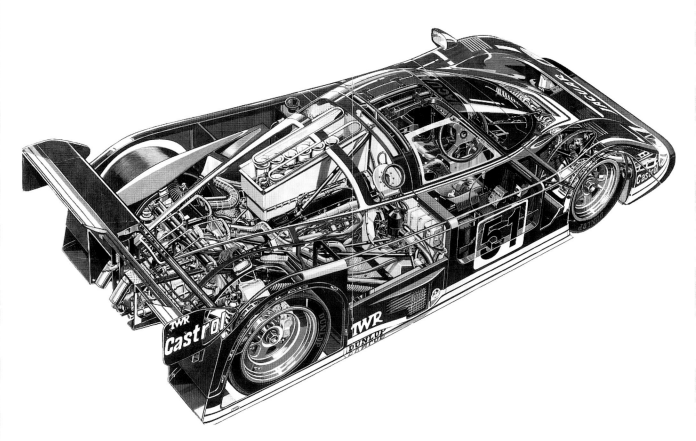

Jaguar XJR-9 and 9LM

The XJR-9 and 9LM were evolutions of the XJR-8, doing double service as a World Sports Prototype Championship (WSPC) and International Motor Sports Association (IMSA) car. The main difference was a 120-litre (26.3gal) fuel tank for IMSA and a 100 litre (22gal) one for the WSPC. A fuel efficiency ingredient in WSPC rules, and a certain volatility in the IMSA regulations resulted in Jaguar driver John Nielsen narrowly losing to Geoffrey Brabham in a Nissan. For the first time, the same car of one make and one racing organisation was competitive on both sides of the Atlantic, missing one title by a whisker in the last race and winning the other convincingly in 6 rounds out of 10 including a parade finish at the magic Le Mans.

Various changes were made for the V12's dual need to suit the IMSA and Group C regulations. 17in diameter wheels were fitted front and rear to satisfy the IMSA regulation and this necessitated a new design for the rear suspension, still with dampers and springs within the wheel rim. The incline on the engine was reduced, a benefit of the smaller wheels (previously 19in at the rear).

BODY
Group C sports racing; 2-doors; nominal 2-seats; weight 850kg (1873.91lb) WSP OR 900kg (1984.14lb) IMSA.

ENGINE
One chain-driven ohc per bank; 2-valves per cylinder; aluminium cylinder head; cast iron block; 7-bearing crankshaft; Lucas-Micos engine management system, water cooled.

TRANSMISSION
Rear wheel drive; clutch AP racing triple plate; 5-speed TWR/March manual gearbox; transaxle final drive.

CHASSIS DETAILS
Carbon fibre & Kevlar monocoque in composite of carbon fibre & Kevlar; front suspension, wishbones, pushrods to spring/damper units mounted horizontally in centre; rear magnesium uprights, titanium coil springs & damper units mounted within wheel; ventilated disc brakes front & rear; rack and pinion PAS; 120L (26.3 Imp gal) (31.6 US gal)IMSA, 100L (22 Imp gal) (26.4 US gal) WSPC fuel tank; Dunlop racing tyres, 17in rims front, 19in rims rear, 19in (WSP) or 17in (IMSA) rims.

DIMENSIONS
Wheelbase 278cm (109.5in); front track 150cm (59in); rear track 150cm (59in); length 480cm (189in); width 200cm (78.75in); height 110cm (43.3in).

Jaguar XJR-9 and 9LM (2)

In Group C the 7.0-litre engine was retained, though rated at 750bhp, and at Brands Hatch (July 1988) a 48-valve engine was run as an experiment. For IMSA, the regulations required a 6.0-litre engine developing 650bhp.

RACES

First race: Daytona 24-Hours, 30/31.01.1988.
Last race: Mexico, 29.10.1989
Number of races: 40 (16 in Group C, 24 in IMSA).
Victories: 9 (6 in Group C, 3 in IMSA)

Daytona 24-Hours Nielsen/Brundle/Price Cobb 30/31.01.1988
Jarama 360kms Brundle/Cheever 13.03.1988
Monza 1000kms Brundle/Cheever 10.04.1988
Silverstone 1000kms Brundle/Cheever 8.05.1988
Le Mans 24-Hours Lammers/Dumfries/Wallace 11/7.06.1988
Brands Hatch 1000kms Brundle/Nielsen/Wallace 24.07.1988
Fuji 1000kms Martin Brundle/Eddie Cheever 9.10.1988
World Champion Team: Silk Cut Jaguar.
World Champion Driver: Martin Brundle
Del Mar Martin Brundle/Jan Lammers 23.10.1988
Tampa Price Cobb 1.10.1990

Le Mans appearances
1988
Jan Lammers/Johnny Dumfries/Andy Wallace (2): 1st overall.
Derek Daly/Larry Perkins/Kevin Kogan (22): 4th overall.
Price Cobb/Davy Jones/Danny Sullivan (21): 16th overall.
Martin Brundle/John Nielsen (1):
3rd at 19 hours, retired with cylinder head gasket failure.
John Watson/Raul Boesel/Henri Pescarolo (3):
7th at 8 hours, retired with transmission failure.
1989
Jan Lammers/Patrick Tambay/Andrew Gilbert-Scott (1): 4th overall. Alain Ferte/Michael Ferte/Eliseo Salazar (4): 8th overall.
John Nielsen/Andy Wallace/Price Cobb (2):
4th at 13 hours retired with cylinder head gasket failure.
Davy Jones/Derek Daly (3): leading at 3 hours, engine failed.

Jaguar XJR-10

Realising that the Jaguar V12 cars were ageing and becoming uncompetitive in sprint events, Tom Walkinshaw initiated the XJR-10 and XJR-11 programmes in 1988. Tony Southgate designed entirely new cars to accept turbocharged V6 engines, 3.0-litre capacity for IMSA, and 3.5-litre capacity for the Group C Sportscar World Championship.

Walkinshaw also bought the rights to the Austin Rover Metro 6R4 competition car, powered by a 3.0-litre V6 engine, some features of which were incorporated in the JaguarSport JRV-6 engine designed and developed at Kidlington by a team of TWR engineers led by Allan Scott.

The all-aluminium 90-degree V6 was considerably smaller and lighter than the production-based V12, allowing the XJR-10 to be more compact and have the benefit of larger venturi tunnels. XJR-10 needed ballast to reach the IMSA scrutineering weight of 2,100lb (953kg). The engine had twin overhead camshafts, belt driven, and four valves per cylinder, with Bosch fuel injection and Zytek management. Twin Garrett turbochargers were installed. The IMSA engine developed 650bhp, the larger capacity Group C engine 750bhp.

The engine bore the rear suspension loads and, as with the 12-cylinder cars, Southgate located the rear suspension outboard, within the 18in wheel rims, to maximise the space available for the venturi tunnels. Minor changes were made to the suspensions before the 1990 season to suit the Goodyear Eagle tyres and the track was widened.

Neither the XJR-10 nor the XJR-16 which followed was raced in endurance events at Daytona or Sebring, the design intended for shorter distances.

Engine: TWR/JaguarSport V6 3.0-litre twin-turbo, 650bhp.
Transmission: TWR 5-speed. **Tyres:** Goodyear.

RACES

First race: Lime Rock 29 May 1989. **Last race:** Lime Rock 27.05.1991. **Number of races:** 26   **Victories:** 6

Portland	Price Cobb/Jan Lammers	30.07.1989
Del Mar	Jan Lammers	22.10.1989
Lime Rock	Price Cobb/John Nielsen	28.05.1990
Portland	Davy Jones	29.07.1990
West Palm Beach	Davy Jones	03.03.1991
Miami GP	Raul Boesel	07.04.1991

Jaguar **XJR-11**

The Jaguar XJR-11 first raced nearly two months after the IMSA specification XJR-10, though very similar in design. The debut was delayed until after Le Mans, priority given to the V12 outing. The XJR-11 was a more nimble car than the V12, and claimed pole position on its first appearance at Brands Hatch, but was far from reliable in the first season.

For the 1990 season, changes were made to the suspensions to suit Goodyear tyres, and Bosch Motronic engine management replaced Zytek (though not on the IMSA XJR-10s). With greatly improved reliability, the XJR-11 finished 1st and 2nd at Silverstone in May 1991, maintaining Jaguar's unbeaten record at the home circuit.

XJR-11 was built by TWR, Kidlington, Oxfordshire for Group C, and designed by Tony Southgate, developed for 1989 by Ross Brawn.

The engine was aluminium with a forged steel crankshaft, titanium and steel connecting rods and forged titanium pistons. XJR-11 was not as lucky as XJR-10, coming up against the Sauber Mercedes team in 1989, and a change in the regulations which ruled out turbochargers for 1991, restraining its development. It became essentially an interim design, yet won one race, scored two second places, and three thirds.

Engine: TWR/JaguarSport V6 3.5-litre twin-turbo, 750bhp.
Transmission: TWR 5-speed.
Tyres: Goodyear.

RACES
First race: Brands Hatch, 23.07.1989.
Last race: Mexico City, 7.10.1990.
Number of races: 13. Victories: 1.

Silverstone 480kms Martin Brundle/Alain Ferte 20.05.1990
2nd Lan Lammers/Andy Wallace.

Right: 1990 driver line-up Silk Cut Jaguar team. Back row Martin Brundle *(left)* and Alain Ferte *(right)*, in front Jan Lammers (left) and Andy Wallace.

Jaguar XJR-12 and 12LM 1990

The old V12 was reinstated for long-distance racing in 1990. Two races mattered more than anything, the 24-hour events at Daytona and Le Mans. Jan Lammers and Andy Wallace, of the 1988 Le Mans-winning team, took command at Daytona driving their XJR-9, and they were followed home by Martin Brundle, Price Cobb, and John Neilsen in a similar car.

The XJR-12 finished first and second at Le Mans; not quite the parade lap of 1988 but a win nonetheless and Jaguar's seventh in the 24-Hour classic. In 1991 Walkinshaw felt that he had achieved one of Jaguar's best Le Mans performances ever when the team finished second, third, and fourth beaten only by freak fuel consumption regulations which weighed down the Jaguars and the Mercedes-Benzes at 1,000kg against a Nissan's 830kg. The crowning achievement of 1991 was victory of the XJR-14 powered by the Ford HB grand prix V8 in the WSPC series with three 1-2 victories. The Silk Cut sponsorship came to an end, and with it six highly successful seasons of works racing Jaguars.

BODY
FIA/IMSA sports racing; 2-doors; nominal 2-seats; 850kg (1873.9lb) WSP/ 900kg (1984.1lb) IMSA.

ENGINE
12-cylinders, in 60 deg V; mid; 7-litres (750bhp) and 7.4-litres for Le Mans in 1991 (750bhp). IMSA specification, 6.0-litres rated at 650bhp. **Transmission:** TWR 5-speed. **Tyres:** Goodyear racing, 17in rims front, 19in (WSP) ir 17in (IMSA) rear.

DIMENSIONS
Wheelbase 278cm (109.5in); front track 150cm (59in); rear track 150cm (59in); length 480cm (189in); width 200cm (78.75in); height 110cm (43.3in).

PERFORMANCE
Speed dependent on gearing.

RACES
First race: Daytona 24-Hours, 3/4.02.1990.
Last race: Daytona 24-Hours, 30/31.01.1993.
Number of races: 10 (IMSA 8, Group C 2) **Victories:** 3

Daytona 24-Hours: 3/4.02.1990
Jan Lammers/Davy Jones/Andy Wallace.
2nd Martin Brundle/John Nielsen/Price Cobb.
Le Mans 24-Hours: 16/17.6.1990
John Nielson/Price Cobb/Martin Brundle.
2nd Jan Lammers/Andy Wallace/Franz Konrad.
Daytona 24-Hours: 1/2.2.1992
1st GTP, 2nd o/a Jones/Brabham/ Goodyear/Pruett.

Le Mans appearances
1990
John Nielsen/Price Cobb/Martin Brundle (3): 1st overall.

Jan Lammers/Andy Wallace/Franz Konrad (2): 2nd overall.

Davy Jones/Michel Ferte/Eliseo Salazar (4):
11th after 20 hours, retired with engine failure.

Martin Brundle/AlainFerte/David Leslie (1):
5th after 15 hours, retired with water pump failure.

1991
Davy Jones/Raul Boesel/Michel Ferte (35): 2nd overall.

Teo Fabi/Bob Wollek/Kenny Acheson (34): 3rd overall.

Derek Warwick/John Nielsen/Andy Wallace (33): 4th
overall. David Leslie/Mauro Martini/Jeff Krosnoff (36)
(Suntec entry):
18th at 17 hours, retired with input shaft failure.

Jaguar XJR-14

The XJR-14 was Jaguar's third fresh XJR design and the first by Ross Brawn, now TWR's technical director. It was virtually a two-seat Grand Prix car, as Brawn described it, powered by the successful Ford HB V8 Grand Prix engine, adapted with a Bosch 1.8 Motronic engine management system and redesignated JaguarSport. It was prepared for the FIA's new Sports Car World Championship, introduced in 1991 for 3.5-litre cars.

The XJR-14 used composite materials for the chassis and bodywork, produced by TWR's associated ASTEC company. Two features were unusual, the torsion bar front suspension, and the centre positioning for the gearshift. The torsion bar suspension was a space-saver, located in a transverse box above the driver's legs, but the rear suspension was more conventional in being located inboard, above the gearbox, with pushrod actuation of the springs and dampers.

TWR designed the 6-speed gearbox, which was again unusual in locating the gears ahead of the differential.

Aerodynamic efficiency was crucial and Brawn made full use of the regulations by having a two-tier rear wing, the lower blade virtually an extension of the bodywork. Radiators were mounted in the sidepods, and instead of doors, the XJR-14 had detachable side windows. So compact was the interior that only jockey-size drivers were comfortable in the cockpit.

The XJR-14 had carbon brake discs and was far removed from the popular impression of a sports car. It needed ballast to reach the minimum weight of 750kg and was never considered for Le Mans or Daytona. The wheels were 17in diameter at the front, 18in diameter at the rear, and Goodyear supplied the tyres. Castrol supplied lubricants for all XJRs built by Tom Walkinshaw Racing.

XJR-14 was built by TWR Kidlington, Oxfordshire, for 1991 Sportscar World Championship, Group C, IMSA in 1992, and designed by Ross Brawn.

Engine: Ford HB origin JaguarSport V8, 3.5-litres rated at circa 650-700bhp, depending on fuel specification. **Transmission:** TWR 6-speed. **Tyres:** Goodyear.

RACES

First race: Suzuka, 14.04.1991.
Last race: Del Mar, 11.10.1992.
Number of races: 18 (7 in Gp C, 11 in IMSA).
Victories: 3 in Gp C, 2 in IMSA.

Monza 430kms 5.5.1991:
Martin Brundle/Derek Warwick
2nd Teo Fabi/Martin Brundle.
Silverstone 430kms Teo Fabi/Derek Warwick
19.05.1991
Nurburgring 430kms, 18.08.1991:
David Brabham/Derek Warwick
2nd Teo Fabi/David Brabham.
World Champion Team: Silk Cut Jaguar.
World Champion Driver: Teo Fabi
Road Atlanta Davy Jones, 26.04. 1992
Mid-Ohio Davy Jones, 31.05.1992

Jaguar XJR-15 1990

Two mid-engined supercars, XJR-15 and XJ220, emerging from roughly the same organisation at about the same time, was surprising to say the least. XJR-15 began as an attempt by Tom Walkinshaw and JaguarSport to fashion a road car from XJR-9, V12 racer and 1988 Le Mans winner. Called XJR-9R (for Road), work started on it in 1989, and in its early stages it was little more than a jury-rigged racing car chassis with road car bodywork.

    This was impractical, and new bodywork was devised by Peter Stevens the former Lotus designer, with more glass, a small rear wing, and proper doors. Speculative buying of classic cars, with its attendant spiralling prices, was still rife when a limited run of XJR-15 was proposed. But Jaguar was about to produce XJ220, so in November 1990 the main thrust of XJR-15 was switched to racing. The racing car's chassis tub remained, and the body was made in glass reinforced plastic and carbon fibre. Unlike the XJ220 which changed to the V6 engine, the XJR-15 kept the V12 of 6.0-litres and 450bhp (335.6kW), and was virtually a racing car with road car ground clearance.

BODY
Mid-engined sports racer; 2-doors; 2-seats; weight 1050kg (2315lb).

ENGINE
12-cylinders in 60 deg V; mid; 90 x 78.5mm; compr 11:1; 5993cc; 335.6kW (450bhp) @ 6250rpm; 55.9kW/L (75.1bhp/L); 570Nm (58.8mkp) @ 4500rpm.

ENGINE STRUCTURE
2-valves per cylinder; twin chain driven camshafts; aluminium alloy cylinder head and block; Lucas/Zytec fuel inj; 7-bearing crankshaft; water cooled.

TRANSMISSION
Rear wheel drive; AP racing triple plate clutch; 6-speed TWR gearbox; transaxle final drive.

CHASSIS DETAILS
Glass reinforced plastic & carbon fibre monocoque; ifs, wishbones actuating pushrods to spring/damper units mounted horizontally in centre of car, rear alloy uprights, coil springs & damper units mounted within wheel; ventilated disc brakes front & rear; Goodyear or Bridgestone tyres,9.5in rim front, 13in rims.

DIMENSIONS
Wheelbase 278cm (109.5in); track 150cm (59in); length 480cm (189in); width 190cm (74.8in); height 110cm (43.3in).

PERFORMANCE
Maximum speed 297kph (185mph); acceleration 0-96kph (60mph) 2.0sec (est); 3.1kg/kW (2.3kg/bhp).

Right: **the Jaguar XJR-15 being admired at Silverstone.**

Jaguar XJR-15 Intercontinental Challenge 1991

Priced at £500,000 the XJR-15 was, above all, to be a prestige product. It was powered by a 6.0-litre version of Jaguar's V12 rated at over 450 horsepower with Zytek electronic injection and management. TWR's six-speed gearbox, developed for Le Mans but not adopted, was specified for the series of 50 cars built, though with the option of an FF Developments all-synchromesh five-speed.

Taking part in a specially-run racing series was effectively a condition of owning one of the 30 XJR-15s made. At a million dollars a time, JaguarSport delivered a fully prepared car to the starting grids at Monaco, Silverstone, and Spa for supporting races at each grand prix. Another million dollars awaited the prize winners, although owners could not expect much in the way of a return, especially those engaging professional drivers.

Although it was greeted with some scepticism, the series was popular and well supported. Derek Warwick, of the works team of XJR-14s, won the first round in Monaco leading from pole position. David Brabham was second, Davy Jones third, and Juan Fangio II fourth. The drivers' good behaviour over 16 laps of Monte Carlo contrasted with the "demolition derby" at Silverstone, in which 11 of the 16 competing cars were damaged. Fangio won with Bob Wollek second. Armin Hahne won the final round at Spa, in which the drivers were not told the race distance. Tom Walkinshaw, who was in charge of proceedings, concealed it to ensure a competitive event with fewer damaged cars.

The XJR-15s were celebrated for having insufficient downforce at the rear and needed delicate handling at racing speeds. Towards the end of the run a special series of four cars was made with a high back wing and 7.0-litre engines. These were much improved and all exported to Japan. They were built by JaguarSport, Broadstone, Oxfordshire, for the Intercontinental Challenge, and designed by Eddie Hinckley, Dave Fullerton, and Peter Stevens of TWR.

Engine: Jaguar V12, 6.0-litres, over 450bhp. **Transmission:** TWR 6-speed, or FF 5-speed (synchro). **Tyres:** Bridgestone.

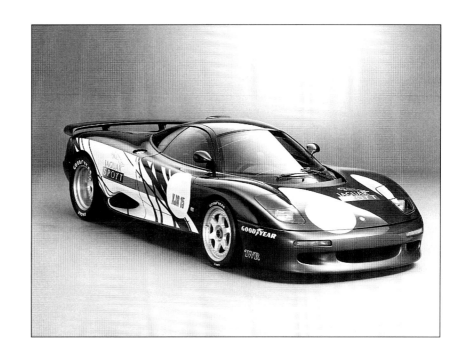

RACES

First race: Monaco, 11 May 1991.
Last Race: Spa, 25 August 1991.
Number of races: 3.   **Victories:** 3

Monaco	Derek Warwick	11.051991
Silverstone	Juan Fangio II	14.07.1991
Spa	Armin Hahne	25.08.1991.

Jaguar XJR-16, XJR-17

An evolution of the XJR-10, the 16 was developed by chief designer Ross Brawn and by TWR Inc. to suit the bumpy track conditions of many American circuits. It was developed in secrecy and was appreciably quicker than the powerful NPTI Nissan team cars, winning its debut race at Road Atlanta. Davy Jones achieved four victories in the XJR-16, which was in service for less than one full season.

XJR-16 was built by TWR, Kidlington, Oxfordshire, for IMSA, and designed by Tony Southgate, developed by Ian Reed and Dave Rendall, TWR Inc.

Engine: TWR/JaguarSport V6 3.0-litre, rated at 650bhp.
Transmission: TWR 5-speed.
Tyres: Goodyear.

RACES
First race: Road Atlanta, 28 April 1991.
Last Race: Del Mar, 13 October 1991.
Number of races: 10. **Victories:** 4.

Road Atlanta	Davy Jones	28.04.1991
Mid-Ohio ·	Davy Jones	02.06.1991
Laguna Seca	Davy Jones	21.7.1991
Road America	Davy Jones	25.08.1991

The Jaguar XJR-17 was developed late in 1991 for the IMSA Camel Light category, respectively with the 3.0- or 3.5-litre V6 engines. However the turbochargers were removed and this evolution of the XJR-16 became a more conventional machine. The 17 was tested once, at Silverstone in January 1992, but all sales negotiations failed and it was never raced by TWR. It once appeared at a Castle Combe club meeting, driven by Brian Chatfield.

XJR-17 was built by TWR, Kidlington, Oxfordshire, and designed by TWR Racing, developed from XJR-16. It never raced.

Jaguar XJ-S 5.3 HE 1981-1985

The May fireball head came not a moment too soon. XJ-S annual sales fell from over 4,000 in the 1970s to a calamitous 1100 in 1980. The 1981 disclosure of the lean-burn HE stemmed the decline of a car that started badly, but recovered to become something of a Jaguar classic. Recovery was on the way but not yet. Jaguar Cars had first to be liberated from British Leyland corporatism, before reliability could be dealt with, and the XJ-S brought up to scratch. It needed 6½in wheel rims, and gained an elegant interior, with wood veneer on facia and door cappings. For all its marketing expertise, British Leyland neglected one of the strongest weapons in its armoury, British quality.

The HE engine was necessary to ease the fuel consumption burden. *Motor* in October 1981 offered faint praise: "It is now possible to achieve an astounding 22mpg (12.84L/100km) at an average speed over 650 miles (1046km) of 62mph (100kph)." This must have been a great comfort. Obligatory American calaytic converters cancelled out the advantage, and it was quite easy to reduce a Federal XJ-S to single figure mpg (under 10mpg; less than 28.25l/100km).

BODY
Sports coupe; 2-doors; 4-seats; weight 1770kg (3902lb).

ENGINE
12-cylinders, in 60 deg V; front; 90 x 70mm; 5343cc; compr 12.5:1; 220kW (295bhp) @ 5500rpm; 41.2 kW/L (55.2bhp/L); 432 Nm (44mkp)@ 3000rpm.

ENGINE STRUCTURE
One ohc per bank; 2-valves per cylinder; aluminium alloy cylinder head and block; 7-bearing crankshaft; D-Jetronic ind fuel injection; water cooled.

TRANSMISSION
Rear wheel drive; automatic gearbox; final drive, limited slip differential, 2.88:1.

CHASSIS DETAILS
Steel monocoque; front suspension, wishbones, helical springs, telescopic dampers; rear suspension trailing arms, swinging half-axle and coaxial dampers; servo ventilated disc brakes; rack and pinion steering; 91L (20 Imp gal) (24 US gal) fuel tank; 215 70 VR15 tyres, 6.5in rims.

DIMENSIONS
Wheelbase 259cm (102in); front track 147.5cm (58in); rear track 149cm (58.6in); ground clearance 14cm (5.5in); turning circle 11.5m (37.7ft); length 484cm (187in); width 179cm (70.5in); height 127cm (50in).

PERFORMANCE
Maximum speed 240kph (149.5mph); 43.5kph (27.1mph) @ 1000rpm; acceleration 0-96kph 60mph 8sec; 8.1kg/kW (5.9kg/bhp); average fuel consumption 10-18L/100km (15.7-28.3mpg).

V12 XJS coupes continued in production until 1993.

Above: Crucial
to the demand
for fuel economy,
the May cylinder
head gave
a swirl to the
ingoing charge.

Jaguar XJ-S 3.6 1983-1991

The AJ6 (Advanced Jaguar 6-cylinder) was probably overdue, even though when it came it was less than perfect. The old XK was heavy and slow-revving, having been designed when long strokes were still custom and practice in the UK. It was not as reliable or as hard-wearing as modern engines, nor as quiet, it needed more attention and was not as easy to equip with emission controls and electronics. Above all it was made expensively on old machinery and that, in the end, was its downfall. One approach was a 6-cylinder one-bank version of the V12 with the same bore spacing, valves, camshaft, and May combustion chambers, but only a 2.9-litre went into production.

The 3.6-litre AJ6 was a straight six like the old XK, with two chain-driven overhead camshafts, a 4-valve head and cylinder dimensions near-square. The block was no longer iron but aluminium, although not made in the elegant die-casting way visualised by Harry Mundy, now power units chief in succession to Walter Hassan. It had shrink-fit dry liners, closed-off at the cylinder head which had two inlet valves angled at 24 degrees, and two slightly smaller exhausts at 23 degrees.

BODY

Coupe; 2-doors; 4-seats; weight 1660kg (3660lb).

ENGINE

6-cylinders, in line; front; 91 x 92mm; 3590cc; compr. 9.6:1; 167.8kW (225bhp) @ 5000rpm; 46.7kW/L (62.7bhp/L); 332.5Nm (34.3mkp) @ 4000rpm

ENGINE STRUCTURE

2 chain-driven overhead camshafts; 4-valves per cylinder; aluminium alloy cylinder head, pent-roof combustion chambers; aluminium alloy; 7-bearing crankshaft; D-Jetronic fuel injection; water cooled.

TRANSMISSION

Rear wheel drive; Getrag 5-spd synchromesh gearbox; limited slip diff, final drive 3.54:1.

CHASSIS DETAILS

Steel monocoque; front suspension with semi-trailing wishbones & coil springs, telescopic dampers, anti-roll bar; rear sub-frame mounted independent, hubs located by drive shafts & lower transverse links, twin coil/spring damper units, anti-roll bar; servo-assisted ventilated disc brakes, inboard at rear; 91L (20 Imp gal) (24 US gal); 205/70VR tyres, 6in rims.

DIMENSIONS

Wheelbase 259cm (102in); front track 148cm (58in); rear track 149cm (58.5in); ground clearance 14cm (5.5in); turning circle 12m (39.4ft); length 476.5cm (187.6in); width 179.5cm (71.5in); height 126cm (50in).

PERFORMANCE

Maximum speed 233kph (141mph); 46.8kph (29.2mph) @ 1000rpm; acceleration 0-96kph (60mph) 7.4sec; standing km 15.9sec; 9.9kg/kW (7.4kg/bhp) average fuel consumption 16L/100km (17.6mpg).

Right: 1988-89 model.

Jaguar XJ-S 3.6 cabriolet 1983-1987

Jaguar was never quick to make changes. The XJ-S was not yet ready to have the top removed entirely, since omitting the roof would tend to make the XJ6-based monocoque sag in the middle. A great deal of engineering work and a lot of time was needed to produce an open car, even one with some of the roof still in place. The compromise arrangement recalled the roof bracing of the late-lamented Triumph Stag. The framework was kept in place but there were removable close-fitting panels, resulting in a pleasingly-proportioned car from which Malcolm Sayer's well-intentioned, but ill-judged "flying buttresses" were at last eliminated.

More significantly the XJ-S was available for the first time with a 6-cylinder engine, the AJ6 being tried out first in a low-production-volume model where its weaknesses would be exposed, but not to too many customers. It was a sensible move which almost certainly saved the model's life. It is difficult to see how it could have survived with only the 12-cylinder. The delightfully smooth and perfectly adequate 3.6 was offered with the option of a Getrag manual gearbox.

BODY
Cabriolet; 2-doors; 2-seats; weight 1660.2kg (3660lb).

ENGINE
6-cylinders, in line; front; 91 x 92mm; 3590cc; compr. 9.6:1; 167.8kW (225bhp) @ 5000rpm; 46.7kW/L (62.7bhp/L); 332.5Nm (34.3mkp) @ 4000rpm

ENGINE STRUCTURE
2 chain-driven overhead camshafts; 4-valves per cylinder; aluminium alloy cylinder head, pent-roof combustion chambers; aluminium alloy; 7-bearing crankshaft; D-Jetronic fuel injection; water cooled.

TRANSMISSION
Rear wheel drive; Getrag 5-spd synchromesh gearbox; limited slip diff, final drive 3.54:1.

CHASSIS DETAILS
Steel monocoque; front suspension with semi-trailing wishbones & coil springs, telescopic dampers, anti-roll bar; rear sub-frame mounted independent, hubs located by drive shafts & lower transverse links, twin coil/spring damper units, anti-roll bar; servo-assisted ventilated disc brakes, inboard at rear; 91L (20 Imp gal) (24 US gal); 205/70VR tyres, 6in rims.

DIMENSIONS
Wheelbase 259cm (102in); front track 149cm (58.6in); rear track 149cm (58.6in); ground clearance 14cm (5.5in); turning circle12m (39.4ft); length 476.5cm (187.6in); width 179cm (70.6in); height 121cm (47.8in).

PERFORMANCE
Maximum speed 227kph (141mph); 46.8kph (29.2mph)@ 1000rpm; acceleration 0-97kph (60mph) 7.4 sec; standing km 15.9sec; 9.9/kW (7.4kg/bhp); average fuel consumption 16.05l/100km (17.6mpg).

Jaguar XJ-S TWR-Motul Spa 24 Hours-winning car 1984

Walkinshaw's resourceful team employed valve springs from the Ford-Cosworth DFV engine on the racing V12. In its first season red-hot valves practically melted so many valve springs, not just when the engine was running but through heat-soak when it stopped, that only the best would do. Cooling remained a problem which resulted in a number of oil and water coolers being incorporated. Cosworth also supplied special pistons for 1984, when the car developed a water-cooling system for the brakes, that had defeated the Broadspeed team in 1976.

Tom Walkinshaw Racing, now officially supported by Jaguar, finished 3rd in the European Touring Car Championship in 1982, came 2nd in 1983 by the narrowest of margins (it beat BMW by 5 wins to 4 until the last 3 rounds) so a three-car team contested 1984. It won at Monza, Donington, took the first 3 places at Pergusa and Brno, came 1st and 2nd at Mugello and Salzburgring, but its best victory was the 24 Hours of Spa, which put Jaguar firmly back into long-distance endurance racing. Walkinshaw won the title with Hans Heyer of Germany 2nd also in a Jaguar.

BODY
Coupe; 2-doors; 2+2-seats; weight 1750kg (3936lb).

ENGINE
12-cylinders, in 60deg V; front; 5343cc; compr 9:1; 212.5kW (285bhp)@ 5757rpm; 39.8 kW/L (53.3bhp/L); 399Nm (40.7mkp) @ 4500rpm.

ENGINE STRUCTURE
2 chain-driven ohc; 2-valves per cylinder; aluminium alloy cylinder head, pent-roof combustion chambers; aluminium block; 7-bearing crankshaft; D-Jetronic ind fuel injection; water cooled.

TRANSMISSION
Rear wheel drive; single dry plate clutch; 4-5-speed manual synchromesh gearbox.

CHASSIS DETAILS
Steel monocoque; front susp semi-trailing wishbones & coil springs, telescopic dampers, anti-roll bar; rear sub-frame mounted independent, hubs located by drive shafts & lower transverse links, twin coil/spring damper units, anti-roll bar; servo-assisted ventilated disc brakes at front, servo-assisted inboard disc brakes rear; 205/70VR tyres, 6in rims.

DIMENSIONS
Wheelbase 259cm (102in); front track 149cm (58.6in); rear track 149cm (58.6in); ground clearance 14cm (5.5in); length 488cm (192.3in); width 179cm (70.6in); height 121cm (47.8in).

PERFORMANCE
8.2kg/kW (6.1kg/bhp).

Jaguar XJ-S 5.3 cabriolet 1985-1988

Delays in delivering Cabriolets were blamed on the circuitous route they took during production. Bodyshells were built without the roof and rear deck, then taken from Castle Bromwich to Park Sheet Metal at Exhall where the buttresses were removed, the floor reinforced, and the central roll-over bar welded in place. The shell was returned to Castle Bromwich where it was painted, then moved once again to Browns Lane to be assembled with the engine and transmission, suspension and wheels, and fully trimmed. Next was yet another journey, to Aston Martin Tickford at Bedworth, where the rear hood and Targa top panels were made, before it went back to Browns Lane for checks and road test prior to delivery. The lines were a little severe, but there was at last a Jaguar with a partial soft-top once again in the catalogue.

Sales of the XJ-S were on the turn. Improved reliability was the principal reason for an increase to 4808 in 1983 and 6028 in 1984. In 1985 sales received a further boost with the V12 Cabriolet for which the production process was streamlined, and the HE badge dropped in favour of a "V12".

BODY
Cabriolet; 2-doors; 2-seats; weight 1800kg (3968lb).

ENGINE
12-cylinders in 60 deg V; 90 x 70mm; 5343cc; compr 12.5:1; 217kW (291bhp) @ 5500rpm; 40.6kW/L (54.5bhp/L); 432Nm (44.6mkp) @ 3250rpm.

ENGINE STRUCTURE
One ohc per bank; aluminium alloy cylinder head and block; 7-bearing crankshaft; Lucas-Bosch digital fuel injection; water cooled.

TRANSMISSION
Rear wheel drive; single dry plate clutch; automatic gearbox 3-speed GM Turbo-Hydra-Matic 400; hypoid bevel final drive, limited-slip differential, 2.88:1.

CHASSIS DETAILS
Monocoque steel body; front suspension semi-trailing wishbones & coil springs, telescopic dampers, anti-roll bar; rear sub-frame mounted independent, hubs located by drive shafts & lower transverse links, twin coil spring/damper units, anti-roll bar; servo-assisted ventilated disc brakes at front, inboard at rear; 91L (20 Imp gal) (24US gal) fuel tank; 215/70VR15 tyres, 6.5in rims.

DIMENSIONS
Wheelbase 259cm (102in); front track 149cm (58.6in); rear track 150.1cm (59.1in); ground clearance 14cm (5.5in); turning circle 12m (39.4ft); length 476.5cm (187.6in); width 179cm (70.6in); height 121cm (47.8in).

PERFORMANCE
Maximum speed 241kph (150mph); 43kph (26.8mph) @1000rpm; accel 0-96kph (60mph) 7.6sec; 8.4kg/kW (6.3kg/bhp); average fuel consumption 10-18L/100km (15.7-28.25mpg).

Above: F R W (Lofty) England was perhaps second only to Sir William Lyons in creating Jaguar's reputation. As service manager, he interpreted Lyons's style of discreet, understated quality to the extended Jaguar empire.

Jaguar XJ6 2.9 (XJ40) 1986-1990

By the time the XJ40 reached the market, only three world-class luxury-car volume manufacturers remained; Mercedes-Benz, BMW, and Jaguar. Of these Jaguar was the smallest, but growing, and earning respect which five years before would have been unthinkable. Yet the XJ40 launch was nearly spoiled by British Leyland indecision and political meddling. The car took 15 years to emerge and suffered badly from under-investment. Fortunately the lasting influence of FRW (Lofty) England who initiated it in 1972, Jim Randle the director of vehicle engineering who developed it, and John Egan who took over in 1980 with a £78 million production programme, brought it to fruition.

Shown in the second week of the 1986 Paris Salon, the XJ40 was unmistakably a Jaguar, the lowest-priced single-cam 2.9-litre at £16,400 with tweed upholstery and figured walnut, causing concern at Ford and Rover. Technical improvements included new rear suspension, yet it did bear the marks of low rank; four headlamps instead of glass-fronted pairs, a single coachline, no chrome bodyside moulding, steel wheels, and black instead of chrome window frames.

BODY
Saloon; 4-doors; 5-seats; weight 1720kg (3792lb).

ENGINE
6-cylinders, in line; front; 91 x 74.8, 2919cc; compr 12.6:1; 123kW (165bhp) @ 5600rpm; 42.1kW/L (56.5bhp/L); 239Nm (24.6mkp) @ 4000rpm.

ENGINE STRUCTURE
AJ6 one chain-driven ohc; 2-valves per cylinder; aluminium alloy cylinder head and block; 7-bearing crankshaft; Bosch LH-Jetronic fuel inj; water cooled.

TRANSMISSION
Rear wheel drive, 5-speed synchromesh gearbox or 4-speed auto ZF 4 HP 22; limited slip differential, 3.77:1 (4.09:1 auto).

CHASSIS DETAILS
Steel unitary bodyshell; ifs, wishbones, telescopic dampers; rear suspension, lower wishbone, semi-trailing arms, telescopic dampers; servo-assisted ventilated disc brakes; 89L (19.6 Imp gal) (23.5 US gal) fuel tank; 220/65 VR 390 tyres, 7in rims.

DIMENSIONS
Wheelbase 287cm (113in), front & rear track 150cm (59in), ground clearance 17.5-12cm (4.7-6.9in), turning circle 12.9m (42.3ft), length 499cm (196.5in), width 180cm (70.9in), height 138/136cm (53.5-54.3in).

PERFORMANCE
Maximum speed 193kph (120.2mph), 190kph (119.7mph) auto; 42.8kph (27mph) @ 1000rpm; accel 0-96kph (62mph) 9.6sec, 10.8sec auto; 14kg/kW (10.4kg/bhp); average fuel consumption 7.3-14.5L/100km (19.5-38.7mpg), 7.8-18.3L/100km (15.4-36.2mpg) auto.

Jaguar XJ220 1988

The mid-engined Jaguar XJ220 might still have been a secret of the 1988 motor show, had not Sir John Egan leaked it himself at the opening of the firm's Whitley Engineering Centre the previous May. Yet spectacular though it was, replicating the mid-engined racing car that not only won the 1988 Le Mans, but also clinched the drivers' and constructors' endurance world championships the previous week in Japan, it could also be regarded as a morale-booster for Jaguar's share price. The stock market, no less than the customers, wanted to see Jaguars match the sophistication and reliability of BMWs and Mercedes-Benzes.

The XJ220 began in 1985 as an off-duty project for a group of engineers under Jim Randle, the director of product engineering. It was designed to meet racing regulations but they changed while it was under way, and Tom Walkinshaw Racing (TWR) met them instead. In many essentials the XJ220 was an up-date of the XJ13, with a 48-valve 6.2-litre 4-cam V12 engine. An aluminium monocoque, with an underbody venturi giving over 2500lbs (1134kg) of downthrust, was developed secretly with Alcan using bonding as well

BODY
Mid-engined coupe; 2-doors; 2-seats; 1564kg (3448lb).

ENGINE
12-cylinders, in 60deg V; compr 10.0:1; 92 x 78mm; 6222cc; 373kW (over 500bhp) @ 7000rpm; 59.9kW/L (80.4bhp/L); over 542Nm (55.9mkp) @ 5000rpm.

ENGINE STRUCTURE
2 chain-driven ohc per bank; 4-valves per cylinder; aluminium alloy heads and block; Zyteck electronic distributor-less ignition and sequential multi-point fuel injection.

TRANSMISSION
4wd, permanent; AP racing twin-plate clutch; 5-speed manual; epicyclic centre differential, hydraulic joints, front centre & rear differentials with viscous couplings; torque split 69% rear, 31% front; final drive ratios 2.88:1 rear, 2.76:1 front, transfer ratio 0.958.

CHASSIS DETAILS
Bonded aluminium chassis with aluminium body panels; front suspension double wishbones with pushrod & rocker-operated spring/damper units, anti-roll bar; rear independent, rocker-operated twin spring damper units; rack and pinion; servo-assisted ventilated disc brakes with ABS front & rear; Pirelli P-Zero 295/40ZR17 tyres.

DIMENSIONS
Wheelbase 284cm (112in); front track 165cm (65in); rear track 165cm (65in); length 514cm (202.4in); width 220cm (86.7in); height 124cm (48.7in).

PERFORMANCE
Maximum speed estimated 322kph (200mph); acceleration 0-96kph (60mph) 3.5sec, 0-160.5kph (0-100mph) 8.0sec, 0-199kph (0-124mph) 12.0sec; 4.1kg/kW (3.1kg/bhp).

Jaguar XJ220 1988 (2)

as rivetting. The possibility of racing and the example of the Porsche 959 prompted the use of four wheel drive, a quill shaft running through the centre of the engine vee distributing torque 31% front and 69% rear. FF Developments supplied Ferguson viscous couplings for the front and rear differentials.

The XJ220 challenged the 959 and the Ferrari F40 for the title of world's fastest production car, with a top speed of around 220mph (354kph).

The XJ220 might have sold for £250,000 if any had been produced beyond the prototype. Randle, who inspired Jaguar to move from a 1960s ideology to a 1980s ideology, hoped that it might repeat the success of the XK120 and attract enough clients to make production a prospect. He also wanted to show that while Coventry may have become something of an outpost of the European motor industry, it still had a mind of its own.

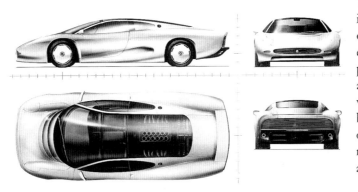

Jaguar XJ-S V12 convertible 1988-1995

Jaguar's new convertible, with both 6- and 12-cylinder engines, proved worth the wait. In terms of accommodation per foot length, though, it might have been regarded as something of a failure. Two seats in a car getting on for 16ft (488cm) long was extravagant and it was two more years before it gained two small extra seats in the rear. Jaguar went to a lot of trouble to make the Convertible, enabling the Cabriolet with its rather clumsy production procedures to be discontinued. A third of the body panels were changed, and even though it looked a little like the cabriolet, the hull was re-engineered to ensure it would not droop with the doors open. The shell was strengthened inside the transmission tunnel and around the bulkheads, and steel tubes built into the door sills and windscreen frame.

The strengthening added 100kg (220lb) over the coupe, and it was 60kg (132.27kb) more than the cabriolet. Driving the convertible up and down kerbs might just make the frame flex, but working in conjunction with the experienced Karmann of West Germany, Jaguar engineers did a good job. The hood did not fold flat under a metal cover, like a BMW's,

BODY
Convertible; 2-doors; 2-seats; weight 1900kg (4189lb) [1993 intro 1985kg (3276lb)].

ENGINE
12-cylinders, in 60 deg V; 90 x 70mm; 5343cc [5994cc]; compr 11.5:1; 213kW (285.6bhp) @ 5150rpm [227kW (304bhp) @ 5350rpm]; 39.9kW/L (53.4bhp/L) [37.9kW/L (50.7bhp/L); 420Nm (42.8mkp) @ 2800rpm [481Nm (49.6mkp) @ 2850rpm].

ENGINE STRUCTURE
One chain-driven ohc per bank; 2-valves per cyl; aluminium alloy cyl head and block; 7-bearing crankshaft; Lucas-Bosch electronic indirect fuel injection.

TRANSMISSION
Rear wheel drive; auto 3-spd GM 400 gearbox; hypoid bevel final drive, limited-slip differential, 2.88:1.

CHASSIS DETAILS
Steel monocoque; front suspension semi-trailing wishbones & coil springs, telescopic dampers, anti-roll bar; indep rear sub-frame, driveshafts & lower transverse links, twin coil springs; servo-assisted ventilated disc brakes; Teves ABS; 82L (18 Imp gal) (21.6US gal) fuel tank; tyres 235/60VR 15 or 215/70 VR 15, 6.5in rims.

DIMENSIONS
Wheelbase 259cm (102in); ground clearance 14cm (5.5in); turning circle 13-13.7m (42.7-45ft); front track 149cm (58.6in); rear track 150cm (59in); length 476.5cm (187.6in); width 179.5cm (74.1in); height 125cm (49.4in).

PERFORMANCE
Max speed 241kph (150mph); 42kph (26.2mph) @ 1000rpm; 0-96kph (60mph) 8sec; 8.3kg/kW (6.7kg/bhp) [8.7kg/kW (6.5kg/bhp)]; av fuel cons 10.6-18.6L/100km (15.2-26.7mpg).

361

a refinement one could have wished for. It sat upright, like a pram's, spoiling the car's smooth lines. It was not as quiet as a BMW's either, but it was padded and lined to give the air conditioning a chance.

Security from determined burglars could never be guaranteed with a soft-top, but Jaguar tried, with a radio which could be removed and carried in a tastefully designed shoulder-bag. The boot was lockable, deep, and although the large spare wheel took up a good deal of it, enough remained to accommodate luggage sufficient for a Grand Tour.

Jaguar said the XJ-S Convertible would do 150mph, yet it was a car in which one did not feel compelled to

hurry. Indeed, only the very wealthy could afford to, since making use of the swift acceleration and high speed brought the mpg perilously close to extravagance. At a steady 75mph it did 22.5mpg (12.6L/100km), but sank to 15mpg (18.8L/100km) in city driving.

The XJ-S Convertible was a good way of generating profit, and was as spectacular a car as anything from traditional sources such as Stuttgart, Milan, Detroit, or even Maranello. At £36,000, not a lot in world terms, it had what was one of the world's smoothest 12-cylinder engines, a spectacular appearance, a rich interior, and a ride that soaked up bumps as successfully as any metal-spring system in existence.

Jaguar XJ6 3.6 1986-1989 (XJ40)

The XJ40 range had a choice of engines, a 2.9 and a 3.6-litre, and three models – the XJ6, Jaguar Sovereign and Daimler which was 3.6-litres with automatic transmission only. Standard transmission was a Getrag 5-speed manual and there was a no-cost option of a ZF 4-speed automatic. Sovereign standard fittings included cruise control, anti-lock brakes, air-conditioning, better cosmetics and the sumptuous leather-and-burr-walnut interior at which the British excelled and everyone else tried to copy.

The rear suspension was the result of much experiment. The brakes were moved from inboard, where they had been since the first E-type, to outboard, increasing the theoretical disadvantage of unsprung weight. For all practical purposes however this was undetectable and rather more serviceable. The discs no longer overheated the differential or oil seals. The independent suspension had an arrangement which made the springing compliant in the sense that the wheels could move slightly rearwards on bump and rebound, reducing road-transmitted noise to one of the industry's lowest. Anti-dive and anti-squat technology

BODY
Saloon; 4-doors; 4/5-seats; weight 1770kg (3902lb).

ENGINE
6-cylinders, in line; 91 x 92mm; 3590cc; compr 9.6:1; 165kW (221bhp)@ 5000rpm; 46kW/L (61.6bhp/L); 337 Nm (34.7mkp) @ 4000rpm.

ENGINE STRUCTURE
2 chain-driven ohc; 4-valves per cyl; aluminium alloy cylinder head and block; Lucas-Bosch digital fuel injection; 7-bearing crank.

TRANSMISSION
Rear wheel drive; single dry plate clutch; 5-speed Getrag manual gearbox, automatic 4-speed ZF; hypoid bevel final drive, 3.54:1.

CHASSIS DETAILS
Steel monocoque; front suspension wishbones & coil springs, telescopic dampers, anti-roll bar; rear independent, lower wishbones & driveshafts acting as upper links, coil spring/damper

units, optional self-levelling; servo-assisted ventilated disc brakes, ABS optional; rack and pinion; 89L (19.6 Imp gal) (23.5 US gal) fuel tank; 225/65VR390 TD or 205/70VR15 tyres, 7in rims.

DIMENSIONS
Wheelbase 287cm (113in); front track 150cm (59.1in); rear track 150cm (59.1in); ground clearance 17.5-12cm (6.9-4.7in); turning circle 12.4-12.9m (40.7-42.3ft); length 499cm (196.4in); width 180cm (70.7in); height 138cm (54.3in).

PERFORMANCE
Maximum speed 219kph (136.4mph); 47.5-47kph (29.2-29.6mpg) @ 1000rpm; acceleration 0-96kph (60mph) 7.4sec (manual); 10.7kg/kW (8kg/bhp); average fuel consumption 7.9-15.2L/100km (18.6-35.8mpg).

Jaguar XJ6 4.0 1989-1994 (XJ40)

made the XJ40 one of the best-handling and riding saloon cars in the world.

One of its design requirements was a reduction in construction costs. The bodyshell weight was reduced from 380kg (837.7lb) for the Series 3, to 295kg (650.3lb), which presented a challenge to designers who believed in using body mass to reduce noise and vibration. This was achieved instead by increased stiffness and fewer body parts, 425 against the Series 3's 558, and a new strong one-piece body side.

The 3.6-litre AJ6 engine was not an immediate success. It was insufficiently refined, and although it accounted for 90% of Jaguar sales, by 1989 was superseded by a 3980cc unit with a forged steel crankshaft. The stroke was increased by 10mm, new pistons fitted, and the compression reduced by a single point to 9.5:1. The camshaft profiles were changed and Lucas digital ignition and fuel injection introduced. The ZF 4HP 24E automatic had sport and economy throttle response patterns.

BODY
Saloon; 4-doors; 4/5-seats; weight 1800kg (4145lb).

ENGINE
6-cylinders, in line; 91 x 102mm; 3980cc; compr 9.5:1; 166kW (223bhp) @ 4750rpm; 41.7kW/L (55.9bhp/L); 377 Nm (38.9mkp) @ 3650rpm.

ENGINE STRUCTURE
2 chain-driven ohc; 4-valves per cyl; aluminium alloy cylinder head and block; Lucas-Bosch digital fuel injection; 7-bearing crank.

TRANSMISSION
Rear wheel drive; single dry plate clutch; 5-speed Getrag manual gearbox, automatic 4-speed ZF; hypoid bevel final drive, 3.58:1.

CHASSIS DETAILS
Steel monocoque; front suspension wishbones, coil springs, telescopic dampers, anti-roll bar; rear independent, lower wishbones & driveshafts acting as upper links, coil spring/damper units, optional self-levelling; servo-assisted ventilated disc brakes, ABS optional; rack and pinion; 89L (19.6 Imp gal) (23.5 US gal) fuel tank; 225/65VR390 TD or 205/70VR15 tyres, 7in rims.

DIMENSIONS
Wheelbase 287cm (113in); front track 150cm (59.1in); rear track 150cm (59.1in); ground clearance 17.5-12cm (6.9-4.7in); turning circle 12.4-12.9m (40.7-42.3ft); length 499cm (196.4in); width 180cm (70.7in); height 138cm (54.3in).

PERFORMANCE
Maximum speed 222-225kph (138-140mph); 47kph (29.3mph) @ 1000rpm; acceleration 0-96kph (60mph) 7.6sec (manual); 11.3kg/kW (8.1kg/bhp); average fuel consumption 8-16.3L/100km (17.3-35.3mpg).

Jaguar Sovereign V12 1989-1992

There were no resources at Jaguar to engineer the 12-cylinder engine into the XJ40, and it remained in the catalogue in the Series 3 body style until 1992. Introduced in 1979, this was essentially a Series 2 modified on advice from Pininfarina, and Jaguar engineers described its revised V12 engine as the strongest they had ever made. Certainly most of its problems were by now ironed out, with the exception of its fuel consumption, which remained a handicap right through to its withdrawal finally from the X300 range in 1997.

BODY
Saloon; 4-doors; 5-seats; weight 1920kg (4233lb).

ENGINE
12-cylinders in 60deg V; front; 90 x 70mm; 5343cc; compr 12.5:1; 217kW (291bhp)@ 5250rpm; 40.6kW/L (55.4bhp/L); 389Nm (40.1mkp) @ 3000rpm.

ENGINE STRUCTURE
One chain-driven ohc per bank; 2-valves per cylinder; aluminium alloy cylinder head and block; 7-bearing crankshaft; Lucas-Bosch digital injection.

TRANSMISSION
Rear wheel drive; automatic GM 400 3-speed gearbox; limited slip diff, 2.88:1.

CHASSIS DETAILS
Steel monocoque; front suspension wishbone, torsion bar, telescopic dampers; rear suspension trailing arms, telescopic dampers; servo-assisted ventilated disc brakes;

rack and pinion, PAS; 91.0L (20 Imp gal) (24US gal) fuel tank; 215/70 tyres, 6in rim.

DIMENSIONS
Wheelbase 286.5cm (112.8in); front track 148cm (58.3in); rear track 149.5cm (58.9in); ground clearance 13cm (5.1in); turning circle 13.4m (44ft); length 496cm (195.3in); width 177cm (69.7in); height 137cm (54in).

PERFORMANCE
Maximum speed 235kph (146.1mph); 43.2kph (27mph)@ 1000rpm; acceleration 0-96kph (60mph) 8.1sec; 8.7kg/6.5kW (kg/bhp); average fuel consumption 8.73L/100km (13.9-25.9mpg), 10.6-18.8L/100km (auto) (15-26.7mpg).

Sovereign nomenclature:
XJ12 SIII 1979-1981
XJ12 SIII 1981-1983
Sovereign HE 1983-1989
Sovereign V12 1989-1992

Two roles for V12.
Left: in Forward
Engineering's rebuild
of Norman Buckley's
XK-engined Miss
Windermere. Both
were record-breakers.
Right: XJ12 Sovereign.

Jaguar production XJ220 1989-1992

Jaguar maintained that the XJ220 was no more than a design study until December 1989, when it revealed plans to put it into production in limited numbers by JaguarSport Ltd, owned jointly by Jaguar and Tom Walkinshaw Racing. Representing the first tangible evidence of Jaguar's ownership by Ford, it provided Detroit with something it longed to have for 25 years. Ford tried to buy Ferrari, and spent £3,000,000 at 1966 prices to break a six-year Ferrari monopoly of Le Mans. Now Ford had a Le Mans winner in the stable again.

In 1989 the speculative classic car boom was at its height, the Porsche 959 and the Ferrari F 40 were commanding huge premiums as collectors' items. A production run of 220 cars was undertaken, with provision to go to 350 if there was a demand. In place of the V12 engine, the production XJ220 had a road-going version of the V6 turbo used in XJR-10 and XJR-11, and rear-wheel drive only. The price had gone up too, to £290,000. Alas the classic car bubble burst, speculative prices collapsed, the 350 "firm orders" Jaguar had evaporated, some in acrimony over deposits paid, and only 280 XJ220s were ever made.

BODY
Mid-engined coupe; 2-doors; 2-seats; 1350kg (2976lb).

ENGINE
6-cylinder in 90 deg V; mid, longitudinal; 94 x 84mm; 3498cc; 404kW (542bhp) @ 6500rpm; 115.5kW/L (154.8bhp/L); 641Nm (66.1mkp) @ 5000rpm.

ENGINE STRUCTURE
2 belt-driven ohc per bank; 4-valves per cylinder; aluminium alloy cylinder heads and block; electronic engine management; 4-bearing crankshaft; 2 Garrett turbochargers with intercoolers.

TRANSMISSION
Rear wheel drive; AP racing twin plate clutch; 5-speed synchromesh manual gearbox; transaxle; limited-slip viscous coupling differential, 2.88:1.

CHASSIS DETAILS
Bonded & riveted aluminium body/chassis unit with aluminium body panels; front suspension double wishbones with pushrod & rocker-operated spring/damper units, anti-roll bar; rear double wishbones with toe-control links, twin rocker-operated spring/damper units, anti-roll bar; servo-assisted ventilated disc brakes with ABS front & rear; rack and pinion PAS; tyres front 245/40ZR17, rear 345/35ZR18, 9in front and 14in rear rims.

DIMENSIONS
Wheelbase 264cm (104in); front and rear track 165cm (65in); length 485cm (191in); width 201cm (79in); height 114cm (45in).

PERFORMANCE
Max speed over 322kph (200mph); accel 0-96kph (60mph) 4sec; 3.3kg/kW (2.5kg/bhp).

Above: William
Hayden grasped
the nettle of under-
investment at
Jaguar. First
Ford-appointed
managing director,
he prepared Jaguar
for the 1990s.

Jaguar XJR 3.6 1988-1989

It said a good deal for its springing that a large Jaguar could be made to feel so spry. Fine tuning of the suspension made it agile and sprightly, a sporting saloon in the idiom of the SS Jaguar of the 1930s, and better than might be expected of a car its size and weight.

The R package included some appliqué; metallic paint, six-speaker audio, and inlaid walnut veneer, although contrasting piping on the leather seats, and a cream leather-covered steering wheel were perhaps less dignified. Yet if the cosmetics suggested *nouvelle richesse*, there was some good old-fashioned virtue in how the car handled. The penalty for examplary roadholding could be harshness and road noise, but the XJR 3.6 was so quiet to start with, that a few extra grunts and vibrations only just brought it level with most of its rivals. It could be guided with flicks of the wrist rather than armsful of steering lock.

At £8,000 on top of the standard 3.6, the limited-edition XJR was aimed at Jaguar enthusiasts, encouraged by the success of the racing team under Tom Walkinshaw whose JaguarSport firm, jointly owned with Jaguar, developed the car. Walkinshaw identified

BODY
Saloon; 4-doors; 4/5-seats; weight 1770kg (3902lb).

ENGINE
6-cylinders, in line; 91 x 92mm; 3590cc; compr 9.6:1; 165kW (221bhp)@ 5000rpm; 46kW/L (61.6bhp/L); 337 Nm (34.8mkp) @ 4000rpm.

ENGINE STRUCTURE
2 chain-driven ohc; 4-valves per cyl; aluminium alloy cylinder head and block; Lucas-Bosch digital fuel injection; 7-bearing crank.

TRANSMISSION
Rear wheel drive; single dry plate clutch; 5-speed Getrag manual gearbox, automatic 4-speed ZF; hypoid bevel final drive, 3.54:1.

CHASSIS DETAILS
Steel monocoque; front suspension wishbones & coil springs, telescopic dampers, anti-roll bar; rear independent, lower wishbones & driveshafts acting as upper links, coil spring/damper units, optional self-levelling; servo-assisted ventilated disc brakes, ABS optional; rack and pinion; 89L (19.6 Imp gal) (23.5US gal) fuel tank; Pirelli P600 225/55 ZR tyres.

DIMENSIONS
Wheelbase 287cm (113in); front track 150cm (59.1in); rear track 150cm (59.1in); ground clearance 17.5-12cm (6.9-4.7in); turning circle 12.4-12.9m (40.7-42.3ft); length 499cm (196.4in); width 180cm (70.7in); height 138cm (54.3in).

PERFORMANCE
Maximum speed 216.7kph (135mph); 47.5-47kph (29.2-29.6mpg) @ 1000rpm; acceleration 0-96kph (60mph) 8.3sec (manual); 10.7kg/kW (8kg/bhp); average fuel consumption 14.1L/100km (20mpg).

XJR 4.0 1989-1994

Jaguar XJR 3.6 1988-1989 (2)

the flaws, so far as keen drivers were concerned, in the saloon Jaguar's behaviour, such as languid steering and suspension biased towards comfort rather than speed. Responsiveness was one of the XJR's best features, making cornering more accurate at a small cost in steering effort.

The penalties included a tiresome tendency to ride the contours of the road, dive down cambers, and rumble the fat tyres over rough roads as though on cobblestones.

Yet to drivers accustomed to thoroughbred sports cars, this was real delight, and even if the ostentation seemed a little overdone, the XJR held the promise of Jaguar saloons with crisper handling to come.

In 1989 the 3.6-litre engine was replaced by a 4.2-litre 91 x 102mm 3980cc, with 9.5:1 compr, 166kW (223bhp) @ 4750 rpm, and 377Nm (38.9mkp) @ 3650rpm.

Poles apart with common cause. Quietly spoken academic, Jaguar chief engineer Jim Randle *(far left)* wanted Jaguar to win through just as much as gritty, determined Tom Walkinshaw *(left)*.

Jaguar XJR-S 6.0-litre 1989-1993

The XJR-S was immensely powerful, and with its fat tyres and bulging wheel-arches, looked imposing. It was only in rare circumstances that this 6.0-litre version of the XJ-S Coupe could be driven fast enough to exploit its road-holding and muscular traction. The gains in engine power were achieved by changes to the engine management system, induction manifolding, and free-flowing exhaust.

At low speeds it was near-silent and silken-smooth, a match as its joint creator Tom Walkinshaw claimed, for any Porsche or Ferrari. Indeed it was quieter and smoother than most Porsches and all Ferraris, and at £45,500, less than half the price of many. Its closest rival was probably the refined and stylish BMW 850i. High-speed driving classes run by the British School of Motoring (BSM)'s High Performance Course, costing between £200 and £750, were a wise precaution for customers. Yet the car's achievement was not so much its surge of speed, but the way this was blended with the tranquillity of a limousine. Air-conditioning, RDS stereo, and electrically adjustable lumbar seat supports added to its luxury.

BODY
Coupe; 2-doors; 2+2-seats; weight 1800kg (3968lb).

ENGINE
12-cylinders in 60deg V; 90 x 78.5mm); 5993cc; compr 11.2:1; 248kW (332.6bhp) @ 5250rpm; 41.4kW/L (63.3bhp/L); 495Nm (51mkp)@ 3650rpm; 318bhp (Jaguar Sport modified).

ENGINE STRUCTURE
2 ohc per bank; 2-valves per cyl; aluminium alloy cyl heads and block; 7-bearing crankshaft; Lucas-Bosch digital fuel injection.

TRANSMISSION
Rear wheel drive; 3-speed GM 400 automatic gearbox; hypoid bevel final drive, limited-slip differential, 2.88:1.

CHASSIS DETAILS
Steel monocoque; front suspension wishbones & coil springs, telescopic dampers, anti-roll bar; rear independent sub-frame, driveshafts & lower transverse links, twin coil spring/ damper units, anti-roll bar; servo-assisted ventilated disc brakes with ABS front and rear; 89L (19.6 Imp gal) (23.5US gal); tyres 225/250 ZR 16 front, 245/ 55 ZR 16 rear, 8in rims.

DIMENSIONS
Wheelbase 259cm (102in); front track 150cm (59.1in); rear track 152cm (59.7in); ground clearance 12-13.5cm (4.7-5.3in); length 476cm (187.6in); width 188cm (74.1in); height 125cm (49.4in).

PERFORMANCE
Max speed 254kph (159mph); 42kph (26.2mph) @ 1000rpm; 0-96kph (60mph) 7sec; 7.3kg/kW (5.4kg/bhp); av fuel cons 12-21.3L/100km (13.3-23.5mpg).

There was an XJR-S 5.3 of 299bhp from 1988-1989. In 1991 the 6.0-litre's power was increased from 318 to 332.6bhp.

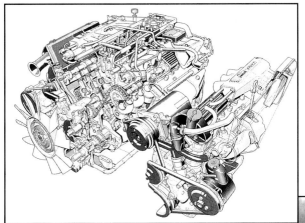

Jaguar XJS 4.0 1991-1996

The revisions to the XJS coupe of June 1994 were the last before the launch of XK8. Its engine was the revised AJ16 which was 7 per cent more powerful and many more percent more refined. New cam profiles, different pistons, valve gear, and sequential fuel injection provided the gains. It was not before time. The AJ6 had required constant development since its introduction in 1986. The XK had been developed over the years too, but its evolution was aspirational; the AJ's was necessary. It was a sturdy engine, but lost out on refinement against rivals from BMW and Mercedes.

The changes made the XJS a shade quicker. By the 1990s gains in performance were hard to come by and were probably less necessary than they had been in the 1960s. The 4.0-litre's 0-60mph (96kph) time was clipped by a mere 0.2sec, and the top speed increment was 8mph (12.8kph). The V12 remained in production with chrome surrounds and black grille. The 4.0-litre car was more practical, with door mirrors, headlamp bezels, and grille in body colour. Prices for the 6-cylinder were unchanged, but the V12 coupe was now £50,500, and the Convertible £58,800.

BODY
Coupe/convertible; 2-doors; 2+2-seats; 1705kg (3759lb)coupe, 1830kg (4034lb) convertible.

ENGINE
AJ6: 6-cylinders, in line; front; 91 x 102cc; 3980cc; compr. 9.5:1; 166kW (223bhp) @ 4750rpm; 41.7kW/L (56bhp/L); 377Nm (38.9mkp) @ 3650rpm.

ENGINE STRUCTURE
DOHC, chain-driven; 4-valves per cyl in 46 deg V; aluminium alloy cyl head & block; 7-bearing crankshaft; Lucas electronic ign.

TRANSMISSION
Rear wheel drive; sdp clutch; 5-speed Getrag synchro, auto 4-speed ZF; hypoid bevel final drive, limited-slip diff, 3.54:1.

CHASSIS DETAILS
Steel monocoque; ifs, twin wishbones, coil springs, anti-roll bar; indep rear susp, lower transverse wishbones, driveshafts as upper links, radius arms, twin coil springs; telescopic (sports) dampers; anti-dive geometry, electronic ABS; hydraulic power-assisted 4-wheel disc brakes, ventilated at front; rack and pinion PAS; 89L (19.6 Imp gal) (23.5 US gal) fuel tank; 235/60 VR or 230/65 ZR 16 tyres, 6.5-7in rims.

DIMENSIONS
Wheelbase 259cm (102in); front track 149cm (58.6in); rear track 150cm (59.2in); turning circle 427cm (13ft); ground clearance 12-13.5cm (4.7-5.3in); length 476cm (187.6in); width 188cm (74.1in); height 125cm (49.4in).

PERFORMANCE
Max speed 227kph (141mph), auto 225kph (140mph); 45kph (28mph) @ 1000rpm; 0-96kph (60mph)7.5sec, auto & convertible 8.4sec; 10.3kg/kW (7.6kg/bhp) coupe, 11kg/kW (8.2bhp/L) convertible; 8.1-16.7L/100km (16.9-34.9mpg).

Jaguar XJ Majestic LWB 4.0 1992

Announced at the motor show in 1992, the Majestic stretched the XJ6 yet again. Available in 3.2 and 4.0-litre versions, it was followed by a 5.3 V12. The elongation by 125mm (5in) was carried out by the Coventry firm of Project Aerospace, providing a taller roof, wider doors, additional side glass, and a larger rear window. The car was returned to Browns Lane Special Vehicle Operation for painting and trimming.

Jaguar asserted that its 1993 cars had 1,500 new or revised components. Unusual familiarity with a 1992 car would have been needed to notice that the rear seat reading lamp was moved to the back of the front seat instead of the rear headrests, and the driver's door switchpack had a veneered surround. The optional airbag became standard, and door pockets and armrests were restyled. The ZF automatic transmission was recalibrated to make gearshifts smoother, and the power steering was lighter. The XJ6 3.2 was now competitively priced at £26,800 with fabric seats instead of tweed. *The Sunday Times* reflected that they might have been sackcloth in view of the sorry market position Jaguar occupied at the time.

BODY
Saloon; 4-doors; 5-seats; weight 1825kg (4023.4lb).

ENGINE
6-cylinders, in line; front; 91 x 102; 3980cc; compr 9.5:1; 166kW (226.6bhp) @ 4750rpm; 41.7kW/L (56.9bhp/L); 377Nm (38.9mkp) @ 3650rpm.

ENGINE STRUCTURE
AJ6, inclined valves in 46deg V; 4-valves per cylinder; twin chain-driven camshafts; aluminium alloy cylinder head and block; 7-bearing crankshaft; Lucas-Bosch electronic fuel injection.

TRANSMISSION
Rear wheel drive; 5-speed gearbox or automatic ZF 4HP22 4-speed; limited slip diff; final drive 3.58:1, 4.09:1 auto.

CHASSIS DETAILS
Steel construction with subframes; front suspension wishbones, coil springs, telescopic dampers; rear suspension, lower wishbone, semi-trailing arms, telescopic dampers; servo-assisted disc brakes; rack and pinion PAS; 86.5L (19 Imp gal) (22.8 US gal) fuel tank; 225/65 ZR 15 tyres, 7in rims.

DIMENSIONS
Wheelbase 299.5cm (118in); front and rear track 150cm (59in); ground clearance 12-17.5cm (4.7-6.9in); turning circle 12.4-12.9m (40.7-42.3ft); length 512cm (201.6in); width 179.5cm (70.7in); height 143cm (56.3in).

PERFORMANCE
Maximum speed 222kph (138mph) auto; 47kph (29mph)@ 1000rpm; acceleration 0-96kph (62mph) 7.6sec, 9.5-10.1sec auto; 11kg/kW (8.1kg/bhp); average fuel consumption 8.9-16.3L/ 100km (17.3-31.7mpg).

Jaguar XJS Lynx Eventer 1993

Lynx Engineering of St Leonards, Sussex, made a clever estate car conversion to the XJS called the Eventer, displaying one at the Geneva motor show in 1990 in a controversial link-up with a scion of the Gucci family. Paolo Gucci's conspicuous extravagance included semi-precious stones round the gearshift. The regular XJS Eventer cost £14,900 on top of the standard coupe's £34,200. Paolo Gucci added what Lynx regarded as Italian designer flair, raising the price to £100,000 for each of the 20 cars planned, although none was ever sold. The show car was stripped of Gucci identity by company lawyers.

All was not what it seemed in the world of *haute couture*. Aldo Gucci, last surviving son of founder Guccio Gucci had recently died, and the family fall-out which followed resulted in the withdrawal of the Gucci connection since Paolo was not entitled to use his name to endorse a product. The so-called Gucci XJS's accessories included a matching Burwood attache case, two suitcases, an umbrella with a Jaguar head handle, a leather-bound log book, two silver pens, hallmarked silver ignition keys, and crocodile-skin armrests, but not in real crocodile. Chris Keith-Lucas of Lynx was worried wildlife protestors might take it out on the car.

Paolo Gucci supplied his own hallmark, a certificate apparently authenticating the design lest two tone paintwork, mock-croc, and the specially woven motif in the carpet was not enough. Lynx was not in the mainstream of car manufacturing but it had a fine reputation for proficient engineering, building accurate replica C and D-type Jaguars or rebuilding real ones. Its XK-SS roadsters were almost indistinguishable from the genuine article; the company gave them a secret code to ensure they were never passed off as real Jaguars.

Lynx made the Eventer estate car or shooting brake conversion on the Jaguar XJS for more than ten years. It had great style, handled like a regular XJS, with a hatchback tail which opened on to a long rather shallow luggage space. The rear seats folded flat, increasing the length of the loading area to 78in (198cm) (you could sleep on it) but the height was limited. The conversion cost £19,500 on top of the price of an XJS.

Jaguar XJ220C Le Mans GT class winner 1993

Although overall victory was beyond Jaguar's reach, David Brabham, John Nielsen, and David Coulthard won the GT class that brought true sports car racing back to Le Mans in 1993. Three XJ220Cs ran against Porsche, Lotus, Ferrari, and Venturi. The winning car completed 306 laps, despite over-heating, leaking fuel, and a challenge to its legality. The Le Mans authorities claimed the cars should have catalytic converters even though no others were so obliged. The Jaguars were built to comply with IMSA rules which did compel emission control equipment, and had efficient ground-effect ducts giving them an edge on the opposition. The Automobile Club de l'Ouest (ACO) maintained it was right yet never asked for its trophy back.

The production "C-type" XJ220 had a stripped-out interior, and composite body panels instead of aluminium. XJ220s also raced in the American Fast Masters series, prepared by Walkinshaw's US operation, with trebled spring rates, and adjustments to roll bars, dampers, and ride height. A data acquisition system in the boot monitored dynamic forces, enabling chassis fine-tuning to be done without reference to a driver.

BODY
Mid-engined coupe; 2-doors; 2-seats.

ENGINE
6-cylinder in 90 deg V; mid, longitudinal; 94 x 84mm; 3498cc; 641Nm (66.1mkp) @ 5000rpm.

ENGINE STRUCTURE
2 belt-driven ohc per bank; 4-valves per cylinder; aluminium alloy cylinder heads and block; electronic engine management; 4-bearing crankshaft; 2 Garrett turbochargers with intercoolers.

TRANSMISSION
Rear wheel drive; AP racing twin plate clutch; 5-speed synchromesh manual gearbox; transaxle; limited-slip viscous coupling differential, 2.88:1.

CHASSIS DETAILS
Bonded & riveted aluminium body/chassis unit with composite and aluminium body panels; front suspension double wishbones with pushrod & rocker-operated spring/damper units, anti-roll bar; rear double wishbones with toe-control links, twin rocker-operated spring/damper units, anti-roll bar; servo-assisted ventilated disc brakes with ABS front & rear; rack and pinion PAS; tyres front 245/40ZR17, rear 345/35ZR18, 9in front and 14in rear rims.

DIMENSIONS
Wheelbase 264cm (104in); front and rear track 165cm (65in); length 485cm (191in); width 201cm (79in); height 114cm (45in).

Jaguar XJ12 (XJ40) 1993-1994

It was 1993 before Jaguar equipped the latest XJ6 with the V12 engine. It was believed at first that a V12 would not fit, because in Leyland times Jaguar engineers deliberately made the engine bay too narrow for the Rover V8 that Leyland threatened to impose on them. Welcomed as the best saloon car in the world, the XJ12 cost £46,600 as shown at the Amsterdam motor show at the beginning of 1993. The Series III 5.3 V12 went out of production in March 1992 so a year passed without a V12 saloon in production. Distinctive features included a gold grille with black vanes. A revised 6-litre engine provided increased power and better torque, with a modest improvement (about 0.5mpg) in fuel consumption. Top speed went up by 16mph (25.75kph) and the 0-60mph (96kph) time was cut by 2sec after changes to the combustion chamber, and additions of electronic ignition and low-loss catalytic converter. The 4-speed automatic gearbox came from GM, not Ford, since they did not have a suitable one to satisfy Jaguar. Companion Daimler Double Sixes had softer springing and even more luxury for an extra £5100. It was the V12's last hurrah, and production stopped in 1997.

BODY
Saloon; 4-doors; 5-seats; weight 1985kg (4376lb).

ENGINE
12-cylinders, in 60deg V; front; 90.0 x.78.5mm, 5994cc; compr 11.1:1; 234kW (313bhp) @ 5400rpm; 39kW/L (52.2bhp/L); 463Nm (47.7mkp) @ 3750rpm.

ENGINE STRUCTURE
One chain-driven ohc per bank; aluminium alloy cylinder head and block; 7-bearing crankshaft; electronic fuel injection.

TRANSMISSION
Rear wheel drive; 4-speed GM 4L80E automatic; limited slip differential, 3.54.

CHASSIS DETAILS
Steel construction; front suspension, wishbones, telescopic dampers, coil springs; rear suspension, lower wishbones, semi-trailing arms, telescopic dampers; servo-assisted ventilated disc brakes; rack and pinion PAS; 86.5L (19 Imp gal) (22.8 US gal) fuel tank; 225/65 ZR 15 tyres, 7in rims.

DIMENSIONS
Wheelbase 287cm (113in), front track 150cm (59in), rear track 150cm (59in), ground clearance 12-17.5cm (4.7-6.9in), turning circle 12.4-12.9m (40.7-42.3ft), overall length 499cm (196.5in), overall width 179.5cm (70.7in), overall height 136-138cm (53.4-54.3in).

PERFORMANCE
Max speed 245kph (152.6mph), 34.5kph (21.49mph)@ 1000rpm; acceleration 0-97kph (62mph) 7-7.4sec; 8.5kg/kW (6.3kg/bhp); average fuel consumption 10.6-21.9L/100km (12.8-26.7mpg).

Jaguar XJ6 (X300) 3.2 1994-1997

The revised XJ6 which went on sale in October 1994 remained much the same as the old one mechanically, in a new body with traditional Jaguar hallmarks. Changes were devised to the front and back but the middle section comprising the doors and roof, the most expensive parts to re-tool, retained the familiar profile introduced with the XJ40 in September 1986.

The Jaguar grille was expanded, impertinently resembling the flared twin nostrils of a BMW, and a feature of the original XJ6 of 1968, curved humps over the four headlights, made a welcome return. The grille and bumper facings were painted to match the body colour, and there were new rear light mouldings following the sweeping curve of the bootlid, hollowed-out for the number plate.

The long rear overhang remained, and pre-production prototypes pictured on test in the Midlands, had disguises applied to the boot in an effort to keep some of the car's secrets until its official launch at the autumn motor shows. The interior had the customary wood and leather furnishings, with the instruments housed in a binnacle ahead of the driver. Prices for

BODY
Saloon; 4-doors; 5-seats; weight 1800kg (3968lb).

ENGINE
6-cylinders, in line; front; 91 x 83, 3239cc; compr 10:1; 161kW (216bhp) @ 5100rpm; 49.7kW/L (66bhp/L); 315Nm (32.5mkp) @ 4500rpm.

ENGINE STRUCTURE
AJ16 engine; 4-valves per cylinder in 46 deg V; 2 chain-driven ohc; aluminium alloy cylinder head and block; 7-bearing crankshaft; electronic fuel injection.

TRANSMISSION
Rear wheel drive; 5-speed synchro gearbox, 4-sp ZF auto; limited slip differential, final drive 3.77 (4.09 auto).

CHASSIS DETAILS
Steel construction; front suspension, transverse wishbones, coil springs, telescopic dampers; rear suspension, lower wishbone, semi-trailing arms, coil springs, anti-roll bars, telescopic dampers; servo-assisted ventilated disc brakes, ABS; rack and pinion PAS; 81L (17.8 Imp gal) (21.4 US gal) fuel tank; 225/60 or 225/55 ZR tyres, 7in rims.

DIMENSIONS
Wheelbase 287cm (113in); front track 150cm (59in), rear track 150cm (59in); ground clearance 17-11.5cm (4.5-6.6in); turning circle 12-12.8m (39.4-42ft); length 502.5cm (198in); width 180cm (70.9in); height 136-131cm (51.5-53.5in).

PERFORMANCE
Maximum speed 224kph (139.5mph); 43.3kph (27mph) @ 1000rpm; acceleration 0-96kph (62mph) 7.9-8.4sec; 11.1kg/kW (8kg/bhp); average fuel consumption 8-14.6/100km (19.3-35.3mpg).

the new range with a choice of 3.2 litre or 4.0 litre six cylinder AJ16 engines, were little changed, starting at around £27,000.

Jaguar was bracing itself for a fresh start. It needed to match Mercedes-Benz and BMW for quality and reliability and the new XJ saloons were the making of it. They looked superb, handled splendidly, they were quiet, sumptuously furnished, and serene. Had it not been a success the new X300 could have been the last Jaguar-engineered Jaguar, with successors conceived in Detroit with Ford parts, even though Ford was unlikely ever to surrender Jaguar's charisma intentionally. If like Lincoln, it became the Jaguar Division of Ford Motor Company, it could still be a commercial success, despite the loss of traditional Jaguar buyers to BMW or Mercedes-Benz. There would be plenty of new customers to take their place.

That was not Ford's plan, and there was scarcely a feature or a component on the new XJ that betrayed a Ford connection, partly because it was a development of a concept more than 25 years old. It was hard to believe the XJ6 spanned a quarter of the entire history of the motor car. What an inspired piece of work it was when new, and what a success it might have been throughout, if only it had always been put together properly.

Jaguar **XJ6** 4.0 1994-1997

The revised appearance of the X300 series of XJ6 was a thorough success, conceding little to fashion, echoing the original XJ with windswept fairings behind the four round headlights. The previous car's rectangular lights were not a success. The new car was slim and well proportioned, with a reassuring grandeur. Other manufacturers, for all their technological wit and quality, must have longed for such appeal.

Nobody in the world of production cars executed interiors as well as Jaguar, with customary leather in the top-range cars, and a new smoke-stained maple available instead of the traditional figured or burr walnut for the facia. Reclining in deep armchairs was a restful business with the engine refined and suppressed to Lexus levels of tranquillity. The smooth-changing automatic transmission wafted the car along, effective spring-damping, substantial weight, a long wheelbase, and a highly developed version of Jaguar's robust suspension kept the peace. Once again, it was a successful compromise between a serene ride and exquisite handling and roadholding, a combination which could elude all but the most competent engineers.

BODY
Saloon; 4-doors; 5-seats; weight 1800kg (3968lb).

ENGINE
6-cylinders, in line; front; 91 x 102, 3980cc; compr 10:1; 183kW (245bhp) @ 4800rpm; 46kW/L (61bhp/L); 392Nm (40mkp) @ 4000rpm.

ENGINE STRUCTURE
AJ16 engine; 4-valves per cylinder in 46 deg V; 2 chain-driven ohc; aluminium alloy cylinder head and block; 7-bearing crankshaft; electronic fuel injection.

TRANSMISSION
Rear wheel drive; 5-speed gearbox, 4-sp ZF 4HP 24E auto; traction control; limited slip differential, final drive 3.58:1.

CHASSIS DETAILS
Steel construction; front suspension, transverse wishbones, coil springs, telescopic dampers; rear suspension, lower wishbone, semi-trailing arms, coil springs, anti-roll bars, telescopic dampers; servo-assisted ventilated disc brakes, ABS; rack and pinion PAS; 81L (17.8 Imp gal) (21.4 US gal) fuel tank; 225/60 or 225/55 ZR tyres, 7in rims.

DIMENSIONS
Wheelbase 287cm (113in); front track 150cm (59in), rear track 150cm (59in); ground clearance 17-11.5cm (4.5-6.6in); turning circle 12-12.8m (39.4-42ft); length 502.5cm (198in); width 180cm (70.9in); height 136-131cm (51.5-53.5in).

PERFORMANCE
Maximum speed 230kph (143mph); 45.5kph (28.3mph) @ 1000rpm; acceleration 0-97kph (62mph) 7-7.4sec (auto 7.8-8.2sec); 9.8kg/kW (7.3kg/bhp); average fuel consumption 8.3-16.2L/100km (17.4-34mpg).

Right: XJ Sport 4.0

Jaguar XJR 4.0 supercharged (X300) 1994-1997

Following the investment by Ford of £200 million, the new range of Jaguars had some novel features, notably a supercharger on a new 4.0-litre model known as the XJR. Jaguar's cherished heritage was not compromised. The XJR was as exciting and dramatic as any Jaguar saloon had ever been even though it was not the first to carry the XJR title for a JaguarSport saloon. By the time of the X300's introduction, the JaguarSport title was discontinued.

The 1995 XJR, announced with a flourish amongst the other X300 codename cars in September 1994, was the first Jaguar with a supercharger. A Roots-type belt-driven American Eaton blower with a modest 10psi (0.7 kg-cm, 0.69bar) pressure was preferred to a turbocharger for its better throttle response. It was aimed at the BMW M5 and Mercedes-Benz E500 and although it could not match the BMW in top speed, it won on quietness and refinement as well as being a match in handling and roadholding. Springing was the sportiest of the five choices offered with the X300 and the high-gearing gave 30mph (48.28kph) per 1000rpm.

BODY
Saloon; 4-doors; 5-seats; weight 1875kg (4134lb).

ENGINE
6-cylinders, in line; front; 91 x 102, 3980cc; compr 8.5:1; 240kW (321bhp) @ 5000rpm; 60.3kW/L (80.7bhp/L); 512Nm (52.8mkp) @ 3050rpm.

ENGINE STRUCTURE
AJ6; 4-valves per cylinder; 2 chain-driven ohc; aluminium alloy cylinder head and block; 7-bearing crankshaft; Eaton M90 supercharger, maximum pressure 0.7 bar; intercooler.

TRANSMISSION
Rear wheel drive; 5-speed gearbox, 4-sp GM Hydramatic 4L80E auto; limited slip differential, traction control; final drive, 3.27:1.

CHASSIS DETAILS
Steel construction; front suspension, transverse wishbones, coil springs, telescopic dampers; rear suspension, lower wishbone, semi-trailing arms, coil springs, anti-roll bars, telescopic dampers; servo-assisted ventilated disc brakes, ABS; rack and pinion PAS; 81L (17.8 Imp gal) (21.4 US gal) fuel tank; 225/45 ZR 17 tyres, 8in rims.

DIMENSIONS
Wheelbase 287cm (113in), front track 150cm (59in), rear track 150cm (59in), ground clearance 10cm (3.9in), turning circle 12-12.8m (39.4-42ft), length 502.5cm (198in), width 180cm (70.9in), height 135-130cm (51-53in).

PERFORMANCE
Max speed 250kph (155.7mph); 48.4kph (30mph) @ 1000rpm; accel 0-97kph (62mph) 5.9-6.3sec; 7.8kg/kW (5.8kg/bhp); average fuel consumption 8.1-16.8L/100km (16.8-34.9mpg).

395

Jaguar XK8 1996

The creation of a successor to the E-type exercised minds at Jaguar for the best part of 30 years before the XK8 was finally given the go-ahead in 1992. There was a Pininfarina XJS in the 1970s, and F-type (codename Project 41) prototypes running when Ford bought Jaguar, but they were overweight and inappropriate for the 1990s. Studies were carried out at Ghia in Turin and Ford's own design office in Dearborn, but the one to succeed was a Jaguar design from Coventry (project X100), the work of a team led by Geoff Lawson and Keith Helfet. It was based round the Jaguar-designed 4-cam 32-valve 4.0-litre V8 AJ-V8 engine built at a new Ford plant at Bridgend in South Wales, with an XJS platform albeit modified, itself a descendent of the key car in Jaguar's history, the XJ6 of 1968.

By the time the XK8 appeared in October 1996, under the direction of styling manager Fergus Pollock, project director Bob Dover, and 250 Jaguar engineers, it was already assured of classic status. The XK8 had a design brief without parallel in the history of the motor industry. The market expected something conservative; not too trendy. It anticipated a car that would pay

BODY
Coupe/convertible; 2-drs; 2+2-seats; 1615kg (3560lb) coupe, 1705kg (3759lb) convertible .

ENGINE
8-cyl in 90 deg V; 86 x 86mm; 3996cc; compr 10.75:1; 216kW (289.7bhp)@ 6100rpm; 54kW/L (72.5bhp/L); 388Nm (40mkp) @ 4250rpm.

ENGINE STRUCTURE
AJ-V8; 4-valves per cylinder; 4 chain-driven camshafts, variable phasing; aluminium alloy cylinder head and block; 5-bearing crank; electronic engine management.

TRANSMISSION
5-speed electronic automatic; automatic traction and stability control; final drive ratio 3.06:1.

CHASSIS DETAILS
All-steel monocoque; front Computer Active Technology Suspension (CATS) opt, not USA; twin wishbone, steel coil springs, telescopic dampers; indep rear, double-wishbone, driveshafts upper links, coil springs, telescopic dampers; anti-roll bars front & rear; braking system electronically controlled variable ratio, speed proportional PAS, rack & pinion; 75L (16.5 Imp gal) (19.8 US gal) fuel tank; 245/50 ZR17 tyres, 8in rim.

DIMENSIONS
Wheelbase 259cm (102in); front track 150.5cm (59.3in), rear 150cm (59in); turning circle 11m (36ft); length 476cm (187.4in); width 183cm (72in); height 129.6cm (51in).

PERFORMANCE
Maximum speed 250kph (155mph); 52kph (32.4mph) @ 1000rpm; 0-96kph (60mph) 6.4sec, conv 6.7sec; 7.4kg/kW (5.6kg/bhp), conv 7.9kg/kW (5.9kg/bhp); av fuel cons (EEC combined) 12.3L/100km (22.9mpg), conv 12L/100km (23.3mpg).

homage to the C-type, D-type, and E-type without appearing too retrospective or obsequious, a car that would embody the essence of a Le Mans winner with the spirit of a grand tourer. The XK8 was preceded by the Aston Martin DB7 with a supercharged 6-cylinder AJ16-derived engine, and it had to appear longer yet distinctive. There was little cross-referencing or confusion. Above all the XK8 reflected traditional Jaguar values and had to reach the top end of the J D Power owner satisfaction surveys in the United States.

Changed days. Where once the chief requirements of a Jaguar engine had merely been to satisfy the customer on speed, power, appearance, economy, efficiency, and making the right noises, now it had to meet a whole raft of world-wide regulations on emission control, safety, reliability, crashworthiness, and environmental strictures. Yet it still had to satisfy the customers.

Jaguar's engineering director Clive Ennos convinced Ford that Jaguar had to have its own engine.

A modular derivative from one of Ford's own perfectly good engines would not do. Ford agreed. The Jaguar XJ-V8 with variable inlet cam timing, cylinder heads cast by Cosworth's unique process, Nikasil-coated aluminium bores, sump with built-in oil filter, and scarcely any conventional gaskets was the answer. The cooling system was arranged to keep the cylinder bores hot to reduce emissions, and the heads cool to prevent detonation.

Project engineer Martin Joyce related a long list of class-leading achievements: best power per litre; best peak torque per litre; best power per kg of engine weight; best power per unit volume of space occupied; lightest weight; lightest valvegear; stiffest structure, and fastest warm-up.

When it set sales records to become the fastest selling sports car in Jaguar history Nick Scheele, chairman and chief executive, a veteran who ran Ford in Mexico before taking charge at Jaguar in 1992 could reflect: "XK8 captured the attention of luxury sports car buyers round the world."

Jaguar XK8 1996 (3)

Right: Open-topped lineage. XK8 convertible with Jaguar Heritage cars behind *(left to right):* SS100 of 1938; Ian Appleyard's white XK120 NUB120 which he drove with his wife, the former Patricia Lyons, to triumph in the Alps; a 'series I' E-type; and a 1994 XJS Convertible.

Jaguar XJ8 3.2 and Sport 3.2 1997

The Jaguar tradition of straight-six cylinder engines that began in May 1931 ended in the summer of 1997, when the new Whitley-designed, Bridgend-made XJ-V8 was installed in the XJ saloon. The X300 platform, introduced in 1994, underwent material changes with the front of the frame stiffened and the B-post reinforced. The central bearing of the divided propellor shaft repositioned, but the body shape was left pretty much as it was. An XK8 front suspension with its revised kingpin angle, was added to reduce road noise and sharpen up the handling.

The new V8 also replaced the long-running V12 and was less expensive than it, although Jaguar's prices went up to reflect its status. On its UK introduction in September 1997, the 3.2's price of £34475 was £4000 more than the previous entry-level 6-cylinder 3.2, whose cloth upholstery and manual gearbox, Jaguar suspected, depressed the important residual values of the range. The 3.2-litre V8's bore was the same as the 4.0, and although it did without the variable timing inlet cam drive, gave a good account of itself with 17 per cent less power.

BODY
Saloon, 4-door; 5-seat; weight 1710kg (3770lb).

ENGINE
8-cylinders, in 90 degree V; front; 86 x 70mm; 3248cc; compr 10.5:1; 179kW (240bhp DIN) @ 6350rpm, 55.1kW/L (73.9bhp/L); 316Nm (32.6mkp) @ 4350rpm.

ENGINE STRUCTURE
AJ-V8; 4-valves per cylinder; Nikasil bores; quad chain driven camshafts; aluminium alloy cylinder heads and block; electronic ignition, sequential fuel injection, Denso engine management; engine weight 200kg (441lb)

TRANSMISSION
Rear wheel drive; 5-speed ZF automatic; ASC; traction control optional; final drive 3.27:1.

CHASSIS DETAILS
Steel monocoque structure; ifs unequal length wishbones, coil springs, telescopic dampers, anti-roll bar; irs double wishbones, coil springs, telescopic dampers, anti-roll bar on 3.2 Sport; ventilated disc brakes front and rear; Teves ABS; rack and pinion PAS; 81L (17.8 Imp gal) (21.4US gal) fuel tank; 8x16 alloy wheels; 225/55 ZR16 tyres.

DIMENSIONS
Wheelbase 287cm (113in); track 150cm (59.1in); turning circle 12.1m (39.7ft); length 502.4cm (198.7in); width 179.9cm (70.8in); height 131.4cm (51.7in).

PERFORMANCE
Maximum speed 225kph (140mph); acceleration 0-96kph (60mph) 8.1sec, 0-100kph (62mph) 8.5sec; 9.6kg/kW (7.1kg/bhp); fuel consumption 12.1L/100km (23.5mpg).

403

Jaguar XJ8 4.0 and Sovereign LWB 4.0 1997-

The principal car of the range, comprising three Jaguars and two Daimlers, was the normally aspirated 4.0-litre. The new aluminium V8 was smooth, quiet, and powerful, and corresponded perfectly with low road noise, long a key feature of Jaguars. Contemporary road tests praised the ride quality, describing the XJ8 as one of the best-handling large saloons in the world, if not the best ever. It was one of the few luxury saloons credited with the nimbleness of a small sports car.

The top Daimler Super V8 at £62775 was still something of a bargain against a Mercedes-Benz 5.0 V8 at £69,940 or £74,040 for the long wheelblase version. A BMW 750iL was £73,455, and Jaguar claimed that the cost of owning an XJ8 was reduced by servicing costs which were cut by one-third compared with its predecessor. Jaguar also benefitted from improved quality ratings in the JD Power surveys in the United States. Among the XJ8's clever details was automatic headlight switching, integrated hands-off telephone with a portable handset for use outside the car, and multiplex electronics to reduce the amount and complexity of wiring.

BODY
Saloon; 4-door; 5-seat; 1710kg (3770lb), lwb 1730 (3814lb).

ENGINE
8-cylinders, in 90 deg V; front; 86 x 86mm; 3996cc; compr 10.75:1; 216kW (290bhp DIN) @ 6100rpm; 54.1kW/L (72.5bhp/L); 393Nm (40.5mkp) @ 4250rpm.

ENGINE STRUCTURE
4-valves per cylinder; Nikasil bores; quad chain-driven camshafts; electronic and hydraulic variable phasing of inlet cams; aluminium alloy cylinder heads and block; electronic ignition, sequential fuel injection, Denso engine management; engine weight 200kg (441lb).

TRANSMISSION
Rear wheel drive; 5-speed ZF automatic; ASC; traction control; final drive 3.06:1.

CHASSIS DETAILS
Steel monocoque structure; ifs unequal length wishbones, coil springs, telescopic dampers, anti-roll bar; irs double wishbones, coil springs, telescopic dampers; ventilated disc brakes front and rear, Teves ABS; rack and pinion PAS; 81L (17.8 Imp gal) (21.4US gal) fuel tank; 8 x 17 alloy wheels (7 x 16 lwb); 235/50 ZR17 tyres (225/60 ZR16 lwb).

DIMENSIONS
Wheelbase 287cm (113in), 299.9cm (118in) lwb; turning circle 12.1m (39.6ft), lwb 12.4m (40.7ft); track 150cm (59.1in); length 502.4cm (198.7in), 514.9cm (202.7in) lwb; width 179.9cm (70.8in); height 131.4cm (51.7in), 133.3cm (52.5in) lwb.

PERFORMANCE
Maximum speed 240kph (150mph); acceleration 0-96kph (60mph) 6.9sec; 7.9kg/kW (5.9kg/bhp), 8kg/kW (6kg/bhp) lwb; average fuel consumption 11.9L/100km (23.7mpg).

Jaguar XJR s/c V8 1997

Computer Active Technology Suspension, CATS, fitted as standard on the supercharged XJ8 and carried over from the XK8, aimed to combine sports car handling with limousine comfort by electronic control of the dampers. Accelerometers on the engine bulkhead and in the boot automatically adjusted the damper settings to suit the current driving conditions. The ZF Servotronic steering, also inherited from the XK8, increased power assistance at low speeds, and gave more feedback for fast driving. Automatic Stability Control (ASC) reduced wheelspin by decreasing engine power, and traction control (TC) could apply a brake to an individual wheel to prevent over-speeding.

Yet the supercharged Jaguar was more than an electronic accomplishment. It was the most powerful Jaguar saloon ever, and as *Autocar* put it on its introduction, was the most technically advanced car ever to come out of Coventry. Yet it retained the traditional Jaguar features of Grace and Pace, even if it did earn some criticism for having less rear-seat legroom than some competitors. Unfettered by its electronic maximum speed control it was capable of 273kph (170mph).

BODY
Saloon, 4-door; 5-seat; weight 1775kg (3913lb).

ENGINE
8-cylinders, in 90 degree V; front; 86 x 86mm; 3996cc; compr 9.0:1; 276kW (370bhp DIN) @ 6150rpm; 69.1kW/L (92.6bhp/L); 525Nm (54.1mkp) @ 3600rpm.

ENGINE STRUCTURE
AJ V8; 4-valves per cylinder; Nikasil bores; quad chain driven camshafts; aluminium alloy cylinder heads and block; electronic ignition, sequential fuel injection, Denso engine management; Eaton M112 supercharger running at 2.0 x engine speed, driven by 8-rib poly V-belt; two intercoolers.

TRANSMISSION
Rear wheel drive; 5-speed DB automatic; ASC; traction control; final drive 3.06:1.

CHASSIS DETAILS
Steel monocoque structure; ifs unequal length wishbones, coil springs, telescopic dampers, anti-roll bar; irs double wishbones, coil springs, telescopic dampers, anti-roll bar; CATS; ventilated disc brakes front and rear; Teves ABS; rack and pinion PAS; 81L (17.8 Imp gal) (21.4US gal) fuel tank; 8 x 18 alloy wheels; 255/40 ZR18 tyres.

DIMENSIONS
Wheelbase 287cm (113in); track 150cm (59.1in); turning circle 12.1m (39.7ft); length 502.4cm (198.7in) 514.9cm; width 179.9cm (70.8in); height 131.4cm (51.7in).

PERFORMANCE
Max speed 250kph (155mph) limited; 0-96kph (60mph) 5.3sec, 0-100kph (62mph) 5.6sec; 6.4kg/kW (4.8kg/bhp); average fuel consumption 13.1L/100km (21.6mpg).

Jaguar XKR s/c V8 1998

Introduced at the Geneva motor show in the spring of 1998, a supercharged XK8 was a logical development which restored Jaguar to the ranks of the world's fastest sports cars. It was a response to rivals which had retained large V12 engines and showed substantial gains over the regular XK8 in middle-speed overtaking performance crucial to regular autobahn-users.

The XKR would have out-accelerated a Le Mans D-type, and been a match in top speed, except for its voluntary restraint to 250kph (155mph). The new car was almost indistiguishable externally from the XK8 save for bonnet-top louvres, a small bootlid spoiler, a different pattern of alloy wheels, and the addition of "supercharged" on the bonnet badge. All-round a sportier car than the XK8.

BODY
Coupe and Convertible; 2-door.

ENGINE
8-cylinders in 90 degree V; front; 86mm x 86mm; 3996cc; compr 9.0:1; 276kW (370bhp DIN) @ 6150rpm; 69.1kW/L (92.6bhp/L); 525Nm (54.1mkp) @ 3600rpm.

ENGINE STRUCTURE
AJ V8; 4-valves per cylinder; Nikasil bores; quad chain driven camshafts; aluminium alloy cylinder heads and block; electronic ignition, sequential fuel injection, Denso engine management; Eaton M112 supercharger running at 2.0 x engine speed, driven by 8-rib poly V-belt; two intercoolers.

TRANSMISSION
Rear wheel drive; 5-speed Daimler-Benz automatic; traction control; final drive 3.06:1.

CHASSIS DETAILS
Steel monocoque; ifs by unequal length wishbones, coil springs, telescopic dampers, anti-roll bar; irs double wishbones, coil springs, telesc dampers, anti-roll bar; CATS adaptive damping std; ventilated disc front and rear, Teves ABS; rack and pinion speed-related PAS; 75L (16.5 Imp gal) fuel tank; alloy wheels front 8 x 18 245/45ZR 18 tyres, rear 9x18 255/45 ZR 18 tyres.

DIMENSIONS
W/base 258.9cm (102in); track 150.4cm (59.2in); turning circle 11m (36.1ft); length 476cm (187.4in); width 201.5cm (79.3in); height 129.6cm (51in) coupe, 130.6cm (51.4in) conv.

PERFORMANCE
Coupe: max speed 250kph (155mph) [limited]; 0-96kph (60mph) 5.2sec; av fuel cons 12.6L/100km (22.5mpg).

Bibliography and Acknowledgements

This book is dedicated to the memory of the late David Boole, director of public relations, Jaguar Cars, 1982-1996.

ACKNOWLEDGEMENTS

The publishers thank Nick Scheele, chairman and chief executive, and Jaguar Cars Ltd for making this book possible. Our gratitude is also due to Autoglass for its encouragement and practical help in sponsoring the start-up costs. Thanks go to Jaguar staff, in particular the late David Boole, Jaguar's director of public relations, who approved plans for the book shortly before his untimely death at the age of 48 in January 1996. To his successor Joe Greenwell, and press relations managers Martin Broomer and Colin Cook, fell the task of providing the practical help and inspiration vital to the book's production. Our thanks are due to all the staff in the press relations department, and also to Paul Skilleter who with the benefit of his many years' experience with Jaguars read the finished manuscript. Thanks also go to Mike Cotton for his permission to republish material from Jaguar Quarterly on the XJR series of cars and their racing exploits. Our photographic research was based on the Jaguar Daimler Heritage archives, LAT Photographic, the Bovingdon Tank Museum, and the National Motor Museum at Beaulieu, with XJR help from Leslie Thurston. As with all Dove books, we thank David Bann, Andrew Barron, and Diane Lappage.

BIBLIOGRAPHY

Classic Car Profiles ed Anthony Harding, Profile Publications 1960s; **The Jaguar Tradition**, Michael Frostick, Dalton Watson 1973; **E-type, End of an Era**, Chris Harvey, Oxford Illus Press 1977; **Jaguar sports racing and works competition cars to 1953**, Andrew Whyte, Foulis 1982; **Jaguar V12 Race Cars**, Ian Bamsey and Joe Saward, Osprey 1986; **Jaguar sports racing and works competition cars from 1954**, Andrew Whyte, Foulis 1987; **Jaguar XJ40**, Andrew Whyte, Patrick Stephens 1987; **Jaguar Saloon Cars**, Paul Skilleter and Andrew Whyte, Foulis 1980-1988; **Jaguar Sports Cars**, Paul Skilleter, Foulis 1975-1988; **Jaguar XK Forty Years On**, Andrew Whyte, Aston Publications 1988; **Jaguar**, Philip Porter, Sidgwick & Jackson 1988; **Jaguar Rebirth of a Legend**, Ken Clayton, Century Hutchinson 1988; **Original Jaguar XK**, Philip Porter, Bay View Books 1988; **Original Jaguar E-type** Philip Porter, Bay View Books 1990; **Jaguar Mark II** Duncan Wherrett, Osprey 1990; **Jaguar Saloons**, Chris Harvey, Oxford Illus Press 1991; **Jaguar Catalogue Raisonné 1922-1992**, Vol 1 & 2 Ian Norris, Automobilia 1991; **Jaguar XK** Duncan Wherrett, Osprey Classics 1993; **Jaguar, the definitive history**, Andrew Whyte, Paul Skilleter and Michael Cotton, Patrick Stephens 1980-1994; **Jaguar Sports Racing Cars**, Philip Porter, Bay View Books 1995; **Jaguar**, Lord Montagu of Beaulieu, 1961-1997, Quiller 1997; **Jaguar**, Patrick Mennem, Crowood Press 1991. Among the sources used in research were the author's archive collections of the Swiss annual **Automobil Revue/ Revue Automobile** published by Hallwag, **Automobile Year** published by Editions J-R Piccard, **Autocourse** published by Hazleton, and also of **The Motor, The Autocar, Autosport, Motor Sport, Classic Car, Classic & Sportscar, The Automobile, Jaguar World, Automobile Quarterly**, and **Veteran & Vintage**, to all of whose proprietors motoring historians owe continuing thanks.

Philosophy Principles & Values

Being committed to giving the best service at the highest quality levels to all motorists in every market where the Autoglass family provide glass repair and replacement services.

The ability to remain focused on the main core of the business, and to deliver full value in all the services offered.

In a world where many pay little attention to the needs of the customer, the Autoglass family base all the service philosophies on delivering to the end user exactly what they require.

AUTOGLASS®

Autoglass Limited, 1 Priory Business Park, Cardington, Bedford MK44 3US

Index